Content-Area Reader

A World in Transition

The Fall of Rome to the Early Modern Era

Senior Consultant
Dr. Judith Irvin
Florida State University

HOLT, RINEHART AND WINSTON

A Harcourt Classroom Education Company

Austin · New York · Orlando · Atlanta · San Francisco · Boston · Dallas · Toronto · London

Staff Credits

EDITORIAL

Manager of Editorial Operations
Bill Wahlgren
Executive Editor
Patricia McCambridge
Project Editor
Victoria Moreland
Component Editors: Jane Archer Feinstein, Carolyn Logan, Victoria Moreland, Stephanie Wenger
Assistant Editor: Tracy DeMont
Writers: Terra Brockman, Colleen Hobbs, Lynn Hovland, Rose Sallberg Kam, Mara Rockliff, Elizabeth J. Smith
Copyediting: Michael Neibergall, *Copyediting Manager;* Mary Malone, *Copyediting Supervisor;* Christine Altgelt, Joel Bourgeois, Elizabeth Dickson, Emily Force, Julie A. Hill, Julia Thomas Hu, Jennifer Kirkland, Millicent Ondras, Dennis Scharnberg, *Copyeditors*
Project Administration: Marie Price, *Managing Editor;* Lori De La Garza, *Editorial Operations Coordinator;* Heather Cheyne, Mark Holland, Marcus Johnson, Jennifer Renteria, Janet Riley, Kelly Tankersley, *Project Administration;* Ruth Hooker, Joie Pickett, Margaret Sanchez, *Word Processing*
Editorial Permissions: Susan Lowrance, *Permissions Editor*

ART, DESIGN AND PHOTO

Book Design
Richard Metzger, *Design Director*
Graphic Services
Kristen Darby, *Manager*
Design Implementation
The Format Group, LLC
Image Acquisitions
Joe London, *Director;* Jeannie Taylor, Tim Taylor, *Photo Research Supervisors;* Rick Benavides, Terry Janecek, Cindy Verheyden, *Photo Researchers;* Sarah Hudgens, *Assistant Photo Researcher;* Michelle Rumpf, Elaine Tate, *Art Buyer Supervisors;* Gillian Brody, Joyce Gonzalez, *Art Buyers*
Design
Isabel Garza Design
Cover Design
Curtis Riker, *Director;* Sunday Patterson, *Designer*

PRODUCTION

Belinda Barbosa Lopez, *Senior Production Coordinator;* Beth Prevelige, *Prepress Manager;* Carol Trammel, *Production Supervisor*

MANUFACTURING/INVENTORY

Shirley Cantrell, *Supervisor of Inventory and Manufacturing;* Wilonda Ieans, *Manufacturing Coordinator;* Mark McDonald, *Inventory Planner*

Cover Photo Credits: (astrolabe by Gualtiero Arsenio, Museo della Sciencza, Florence, Italy), Scala/Art Resource, NY; (Abou Bakr Ibn Iousouf, Astrolabe, 1216 CE, Musee Paul Depuy, Toulouse, France), Giraudon/Art Resource, NY; (Castillos de las Herguijuelas, Caceres, Spain), Scala/Art Resource, NY; (Atlas Coelestis 1660), © Planet Art.

All art, unless otherwise noted, by ArtToday.com.

Contents

CHAPTER 6
Oceans of Exploration: From Europe to the Americas 179

CHAPTER 1

Empire on the Edge
The Fall of Rome   753 B.C.–A.D. 476

An Ancient Prophecy Comes to Pass

According to an ancient prophecy, the end of Rome was in the cards from the very beginning. Romulus, the city's founder, saw twelve eagles flying together. A legend said that the eagles predicted the city's future: Each bird represented a century that the Roman state would exist. Romans claimed that their city was founded in 753 B.C. Twelve centuries later, in the summer of A.D. 476, a group of German invaders removed the young Roman emperor from the throne. In a bizarre twist, the name of this last emperor was Romulus—the same name as Rome's founder. Rome had existed for 1,229 years, almost exactly the length of time predicted by the ancient prophecy of the twelve eagles.

INVESTIGATE: Rome was not always an empire ruled by an emperor. From the time of its founding, what other forms of government did Rome have?

Caesar Augustus

The first emperor of Rome may have begun his rise to power at age 12 when he delivered a memorable speech at the funeral of his grandmother Julia. The speech impressed an important politician who was attending the event: Julia's brother, Julius Caesar. When Julius Caesar was killed in 44 B.C., his will made provisions for adopting the young man, whose own father was dead. The young man went on to become the leader of Rome. He took on a new name, Caesar Augustus, which indicated his supreme importance as Rome's first emperor. Augustus lived up to his name. He ended a civil war that had raged in Rome for a hundred years, and he ruled during the Pax Romana (Roman peace), the longest period of prosperity and peace that Western Europe and the Middle East have ever known.

Robert Emmett Bright/Photo Researchers

▲ Statue of Augustus.

As you read about the Roman Empire, you will run across the word *barbarian* (bär•ber′ē•ən). Romans used this word to refer to the peoples from northern nations who eventually overthrew the empire. Barbarians are usually thought of as rude, savage, or uncivilized. The term "barbarian" began with the Greeks, who used it to refer to anyone who could not speak their language. Romans used the Latin word *balbus* to mean "stammering," or tongue-tied. Gradually, the word was applied to someone "not from around here."

Memorable Quote

"Catastrophe and ruin will fall one day on Rome . . . but order will come too . . . not all of our books shall perish and some few men will think and work and feel as we have done."

—Hadrian, emperor of Rome, A.D. 117–138

More Than Just Money

How could Roman rulers send messages from one end of their empire to another? They used a tiny piece of metal: money. Coins were designed with the head of the emperor on one side. Because coins were used by people everywhere, an emperor could be sure that everyone knew what he looked like. The emperor used the space on the reverse side of the coin to boast about his accomplishments. Because so much information was packed onto Roman coins, they continue to tell us stories.

Eating Like an Emperor

What would a Roman banquet have looked like? It could have included dishes made of sea urchins and camels' hooves! The ingredients may not sound appealing today, but cookbooks reveal that Roman food was sophisticated and strongly flavored. A salty fish sauce called *garum*, much like soy sauce, was a common part of meals. Romans showed off their wealth by offering unusual dishes to their guests. The emperor Caligula (kə•lig′yo͞o•lə) served flamingo tongue, and the wealthy Roman merchant Apicius prepared boiled ostrich. Not all Roman food was eaten at a banquet table, though. Busy Romans ate their snacks on the go, buying fast-food, such as dates, figs, cakes, and cheese, at shops that opened onto the street.

Adventures of an Empress

The daughter of an emperor, Galla Placidia ruled Rome during a difficult time of rebellion and invasion. She was in Rome when it was sacked by barbarian invaders, the Visigoths. Carried away as a captive, she married the king of the Visigoths in A.D. 414. After his death, she returned to Rome and married a general who later became a Roman emperor. When he died, Galla Placidia was named Augusta, or empress in the West, ruling for her six-year-old son. She held the crumbling empire together for twenty years, managing armies while keeping power-hungry generals from taking over.

A well-known proverb says, "All roads lead to Rome." The Roman Empire was crisscrossed by 48,500 miles of roads—a distance equal to twice the circumference of the earth! As you will see in the following excerpt, this vast network of highways was one of the keys to Rome's success.

from The Roads to the Spiceries

from *Roman Roads*

by VICTOR W. VON HAGEN

▲ Emperor Trajan.

Trajan, the greatest builder of roads Rome ever had, improved the existing roads all over Hither Asia.[1] He called over two legions:[2] the Legio III Cyrenaica guarded the north, the Legio VIII Hispania, drawn from his own Spain, guarded the south.

They kept the Pax Romana, or Roman Peace. They taught the people how to build roads and how to put up bridges. They erected guard stations and signal towers. Over the land came something the people had not known for centuries—security. With security came growth and freedom, trade and movement. Desert posts, forts, and checkpoints were put up to control the unruly tribesmen; swift Roman

You Need to Know...

Early Romans were content to eat a lot of porridge and plain roast pork. Later, as Rome's wealth increased, its rich citizens wanted the more exotic goods that traders could bring from afar. Many of these luxury items, such as spices, were found in the Middle East, but goods were often lost along trade routes because of robbers or bad roads. To help improve trade, the first Roman road in Turkey was built in 129 B.C. Emperor Trajan (trā'jən), who ruled from A.D. 98 to 117, expanded the Roman highway system to the farthest corners of the empire. Roman roads were an engineering marvel made of hard-packed gravel, concrete, or flagstones. Traces of them can still be seen today.

---

1. **Hither Asia:** Roman name for the Middle East, including the area now known as Turkey.
2. **legions:** divisions of the Roman army, each including 3,000 to 6,000 foot soldiers and 100 to 200 cavalry.

unruly (un·rōō'lē): difficult to manage; undisciplined.

justice was meted[3] out to those who broke the Pax Romana. In that atmosphere, the arts of peace, of which road building was one, flourished.

Romans on the March

Rome ruled the ancient world with its army, which was organized around the *legion*. A legion contained about 6,000 cavalry and infantry troops. Legions' numbers and nicknames reflected who created them and where the groups served. Legions' nicknames also could boast of soldiers' courage. Fighters could call attention to their skill and endurance with names such as VI *Ferrata fidelis constans*, which we today might call "iron-sides." Legions used two infantry weapons that packed quite a punch: a seven-foot javelin, or spear, for throwing and thrusting and a twenty-inch sword with a heavy blade for cutting and thrusting. Only the fiercest foe stood a chance against the mighty legions of ancient Rome.

hewn (hyo͞on): shaped with a tool such as an ax.

The great Via Traiana, ordered, built, and most of it personally financed by Trajan, ran the whole length of the desert land from Damascus to Aqaba, the port of the Red Sea route. It extended for four hundred miles, and to the north ran parallel to the river Jordan and the Dead Sea. Trajan appointed a well-known builder of roads, Claudius Severus, to be his legate and overseer[4] of the southern sections of the road. At the Wadi Musa, the road followed a deep canyon to the famous city of Petra. Petra belonged once to the Nabataean[5] kingdom. It is these people who began the famous rock city; its buildings, of the most beautiful classical style, were hewn out of the vari-colored limestone.

The Romans took over Petra in A.D. 106 to protect the caravans that went through these canyons. Whoever controlled Petra controlled the caravan route. Petra was redesigned on Roman lines; streets, fountains, theaters, all went up in the usual fashion. The ancient buildings of the Nabataeans they left alone.

Seventy Roman miles from Petra, the Via Traiana entered the port of Aqaba. There are no archaeological

---

3. **meted** (mēt′id): given out or distributed.
4. **legate and overseer:** A legate is an official ambassador, in this case a Roman province's governor or deputy. An overseer is a supervisor.
5. **Wadi Musa . . . Petra . . . Nabataean:** Petra, a city named for the Greek word for "rock," was a thriving trade center in the kingdom of Nabatea (nab′ə·tē′ə), an area located between Syria and Arabia. Wadi Musa, the Valley of Moses, runs through the ancient city.

remains here, only memory and bits of history. Aqaba provided the shortest route to the Middle East; caravans of ships sailed from Bombay into the Arabian Sea, avoiding the pirates if they could at the narrows of the Gulf of Aden. Then, with the trade winds, they sailed north on the Red Sea to the port of Aqaba. It was the roadhead for the desert caravans.

The Romans had a passion for pepper. It gave food a bounce. It was light and easily transportable. Loaded onto camels, it was brought four hundred miles over Trajan's Way, put on ships at the ports of Lebanon and then sent to Ostia, the port of Rome. The filling of the pepper barns beside the Tiber[6] was one of the primary functions of

---

6. **Tiber:** river in central Italy that flows through Rome to the Mediterranean Sea.

▲ Map of the Roman Empire at its height, A.D. 117. Trade thrived throughout the empire as a result of an improved system of roads. **? What trade goods were produced along trade routes in Syria and the Red Sea area?**

trade. So important was pepper that when the Goths[7] appeared before the gates of Rome in A.D. 408 they demanded three thousand pounds of pepper before they would treat[8] with the Romans.

Cinnamon, "the gift of kings," arrived at Aqaba curled up in long, pencil-shaped sticks. Cloves, called "little nails" because the head of a clove looked like a Roman nail, made its way from Ceylon. Nutmeg and its covering, mace, came from Malaya. Gingerroot, which grew in the wild parts of India, was easily packed and could withstand the many days of the long haul. These spices were best for trade; cheap at the source, they were dear at the market.

---

7. **Goths** (gäths): members of a Germanic people who invaded the Roman Empire beginning in the third century A.D.
8. **treat**: negotiate with; reach a settlement with.

SIDELIGHT

"In the 1960s, Peter Throckmorton excavated the wreck of a ship near the Italian coast that dated from the time of the Roman Empire. Throckmorton's research yielded much valuable and detailed information about shipbuilding in Roman times. It showed how the Roman shipbuilders used various types of wood, such as pine, cypress, and cedar. The research also yielded information about the shapes of the nails used in ship construction. Finally, Throckmorton showed how the bottoms of the ships were covered with large sheets of lead. This was done to protect the hull of the ship from damage by marine animals.

But perhaps the strangest and most interesting aspect of this wreck was the nature of its cargo. When the ship went down, it was carrying a load of coffins, obviously meant for the rich and important citizens of the Empire. The coffins had been carved out of marble, and they had been brought by sea all the way from Asia Minor in the east. We may sometimes think of these ancient ships as puny little wooden craft, and it is true that in comparison with our giant tankers, aircraft carriers, and ocean liners, the old wooden ships were small indeed. Still, they were not exactly rowboats. The marble coffins aboard this single wooden ship weighed more than 150 tons!"

—"A Cargo of Coffins" by Elisha Linder and Avner Raban
from *Introducing Underwater Archaeology*

Spices were light and easily transportable. Pliny, the great Roman naturalist, who was so curious about nature that he walked too near Vesuvius during its eruption and died of asphyxia,[9] said about the spice trade: "They sold at the market of Rome for a hundred times their original price."

"Bring us slaves and bring us ivory," was the demand of the rich in Rome. Both arrived at Aqaba. The whole ancient world, not alone Rome, dealt in slavery; conquered peoples, people who could not pay their debts, people who sold themselves into slavery, and others uprooted from their homes, all were brought into the slave markets.

And ivory—Romans had a passion for it. Judges sat on seats plaited[10] with ivory. The seats and the benches of the Roman Senate were of ivory. One Roman emperor had his horses eat from ivory mangers. Ivory was delicate in color with the feel of a water lily. It was never cold nor dead. It grew more beautiful with age. It was strong and elastic and could be easily and deeply cut. Roman jewelers loved to inlay[11] ivory with gold or turquoise.

Pearls came from the coasts of India, carried by traders and guarded by soldiers. Pearls relate themselves to flesh, and Roman women were proud when their skin gave the pearls <u>sheen</u> and sweetness. The best pearls came from Ceylon.

"I swear before the gods," said a returning trader, "that the bottom of the sea seems to be covered with them. There is no place in the world where more pearls are found."

And with pearls from India came diamonds. These were found in the gravel of river beds. That "invincible stone," they said of it because it could not be cut. The Romans called it by its Greek name *adamas*, meaning <u>invulnerable</u>. Kings who went to war placed them on their breastplates near to their hearts so that they would not be killed. The diamond was thought to be frozen water.

▲ Roman coin.

©Araldo de Luca/CORBIS

sheen (shēn): glistening appearance; shininess.

invulnerable (in·vul′nər·ə·bel): unable to be injured; not open to attack.

---

9. **Vesuvius . . . asphyxia:** Vesuvius (ve·sōō′vē·əs), a volcano located on the Bay of Naples in southern Italy, erupted in A.D. 79 and destroyed the city of Pompeii. Asphyxia (as·fik′sē·ə) is loss of consciousness caused by lack of oxygen, which occurs if someone inhales toxic gases.
10. **plaited** (plāt′id): woven or braided.
11. **inlay:** to set into a surface to create a design.

Lucius Trebonius Was Here

On March 25, 2 B.C., a Roman tourist carved *L. Trebonius Oricula hic fui* on a wall of the Egyptian Temple of Isis: "I, Lucius Trebonius Oricula, was here." This Roman tourist was taking advantage of the peaceful years of the Roman Empire to see the sights of Egypt. By using the well-built Roman roads and hopping on freight ships crossing the Mediterranean Sea, Roman travelers visited historic sites just as we do today. The Pyramids of Gîza, then as now, were a popular destination. Tourists also went to see where the Greeks fought the Trojan War and where Alexander the Great once lived. They could even buy souvenirs. In the city of Antioch, merchants sold many copies of a famous statue of Tyche, the city's goddess of fortune.

cultivated (kul′tə•vāt′id): grew or tended.

Emeralds came from India as well as from Egypt. And there were all the rainbow jewels destined for Rome: jade and jasper, agate and onyx, beryl and sapphire, "the most like heaven in fair weather and clear, most apt to fit the fingers of kings."

All these products of trade were luxury items. They were light and easily transportable; cheap at the source, and worth a fortune in Rome.

All these products of trade were luxury items. They were light and easily transportable; cheap at the source, and worth a fortune in Rome.

There were other trade items: linen and cotton, bananas and sugar cane. The banana, which is really a grass, was first developed in India. Only the traders knew of it and ate it. Bananas were bulky to ship, the passage to Rome too long to have them arrive eatable. Sugar cane was known to the Romans, but honey was the sweetener. Linens and cottons were, of course, known; mummies had been wrapped in linen, [which] could be woven almost as thin as silk.

The Indians <u>cultivated</u> cotton trees, and this cotton was known as "tree wool." In the Nile they grew a bush cotton, the long-staple cotton beloved by the weavers of cloth. They made gauzy[12] tissues of cotton of a thinness like a veil of mist, "there is a cloth a yard wide and twenty yards long that can be passed through a finger ring."

At the port of Aqaba, merchants had offices where the imports were received and duties[13] paid. The merchants waited to load the camel caravans until there was a large enough shipment—caravans numbered as many as five hundred camels. If the cargo was very precious, a company

---

12. **gauzy** (gô′zē): light; thin; easily seen through.
13. **duties:** taxes

of the Roman legion, commanded by a centurion,[14] was sent along to protect it. The camel made the caravan possible.

It is said that the first camel the Romans saw was in 46 B.C., when Julius Caesar,[15] at the Battle of Thapsus, in North Africa, captured twenty-seven of them as part of his war booty.[16] But as Romans had been in Hither Asia since 200 B.C., it seems certain that they knew of this strange beast before.

But they seem never to have been curious about it. It is never seen on the early monuments of Egypt, it did not come from Africa until late in history. Camels were used during the wars of the Persians and Greeks and "the reason," said a Greek, "of putting the camels face to face with the horses of the enemy is that horses fear camels and can endure neither the sight nor the smell of them."

---

14. **centurion** (sen·toor′ē·ən): officer who commanded a *centuria*, a military unit made up of 100 men.
15. **Julius Caesar** (jool′yəs sē′zər): Gaius Julius Caesar (c. 100–44 B.C.), Roman general, statesman, and dictator.
16. **booty:** goods taken from the enemy during war.

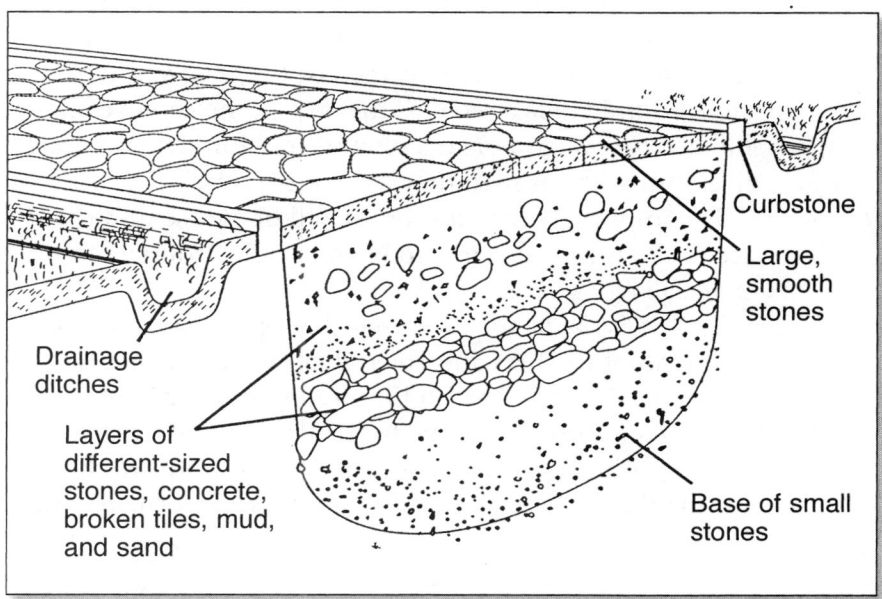

Curbstone

Large, smooth stones

Drainage ditches

Layers of different-sized stones, concrete, broken tiles, mud, and sand

Base of small stones

▲ Cross section of a Roman road.

▲ Relief sculpture showing Roman soldiers dressed for battle.

The camel came from Asia. There are two kinds: a two-humped camel, the Bactrian, which provides a natural saddle between the humps, and a single-humped camel, the dromedary. The name camel comes from the Arabic *jamal*. Wild camels are unknown. They live with man. Alive or dead, they contain in their bodies almost all that a desert traveler must have. Their milk is drunk, their dung[17] is used for firewood, their flesh can be eaten. The hair of the camel is soft and can be woven into cloth or into tough weavings for the Arabs' "black tents." They can carry a load of five hundred pounds twenty-five miles a day. They can live ten days without drinking water. Their nostrils have trap doors to keep out wind-blown sand. Their feet are like spongy foot pads and will not sink deeply into the sand. They can outrun a horse and can carry eight times more than a man can carry and four times that of a mule. Camels live in the desert where temperatures rise to 140 degrees, or they can survive in snowbound lands as cold as the arctic. The camel can be hitched to a wagon or to a plow. Cared for, they live long lives, but without man they cannot survive.

The important caravan routes had of course to be protected. This forced Rome to push back its frontiers to make all else secure.

East of Syria, farther east than Mesopotamia, was the vast land of the Persians, ruled then by the Parthians. Trajan pushed the Roman Empire into the lands of Parthia and brought Rome to the Persian Gulf. Trajan had set up his headquarters at ancient Antioch.[18] It was known as "the third city of the world" and was a favorite city of

17. **dung:** animal manure; excrement.
18. **Antioch** (an'tē·äk): ancient city that was a center for early Christianity; located in present-day Turkey.

the Roman emperors. Its climate was happy and it was an important center for trade.

The legions under Trajan fought to carry the empire to the greatest limits it had ever reached. And as soon as the campaign ended, public works began. "I will," said Trajan, "use the olive wood of my sword to make war breed peace." Trajan did it by building roads and thus creating trade.

✓ Reading Check

1. Under Trajan, what work did the Roman legions do in Hither Asia during Rome's time of peace?

2. How long was the road called the Via Traiana? What type of terrain did it pass through?

3. Why was Petra an important city? How did Petra change after the city was taken over by the Romans?

4. Why were spices such popular trade goods? What spices were transported to Rome to be sold?

5. Why were camels used in trade caravans?

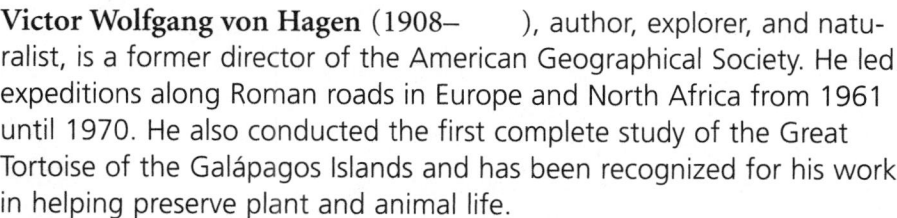

MEET THE *Writer*

Victor Wolfgang von Hagen (1908–   ), author, explorer, and naturalist, is a former director of the American Geographical Society. He led expeditions along Roman roads in Europe and North Africa from 1961 until 1970. He also conducted the first complete study of the Great Tortoise of the Galápagos Islands and has been recognized for his work in helping preserve plant and animal life.

Throughout history, building a wall was one solution when neighbors weren't quite getting along. It certainly was the solution of choice for the Romans in Britain in the second century A.D. The following selection describes why and how the Romans built the long, winding defensive structure that came to be known as Hadrian's Wall.

Hadrian's Wall

from *Walls: Defenses Throughout History*

by JAMES CROSS GIBLIN

The Roman soldier shivers as he gazes out from the top of Hadrian's Wall at the rolling lands of northern England. It is a chilly October morning in 135 A.D., and a ground fog obscures the view.

The soldier leans against the protective five-foot-high parapet[1] on the north side of the wall's flat top, and peers through the mist. Is that a band of roving barbarians out there? He looks more closely. No, it's just the shadow of a hill.

With a sigh of relief, the soldier turns away from the parapet and continues his patrol along the great stone wall. It rises fifteen feet above the surrounding countryside and stretches to a width of almost ten feet. If the soldier were to walk its entire length, he would cover a distance of more than seventy miles.

Hadrian's Wall is one of the best-known examples

You Need to Know...

The Roman emperor Hadrian (hā′drē•ən) ruled from A.D. 117 to 138, during the peak of Rome's wealth and power. A Roman biographer notes that the emperor "was the first to construct a wall, eighty [Roman] miles in length, which was to separate the barbarians from the Romans." Almost two thousand years after the construction of Hadrian's Wall, parts of it still stand as a reminder of the glories of Rome. Archaeological excavations at the site continue to unearth fascinating artifacts, including hearths, ovens, and even fragments of the game boards soldiers used to entertain themselves while guarding the northernmost Roman frontier.

---

1. **parapet** (par′ə•pet′): low wall or bank used to protect soldiers from an enemy's fire.

of a defensive wall meant to protect not just a town or city but an entire country. It bears the name of the Roman emperor Hadrian, who ordered its construction after he visited Rome's northern-most colony, England, in 122 A.D. The Roman army had subdued southern England, but wild tribes from the north were still raiding the border regions. Hadrian and his generals decided that a mighty wall was the only thing that would stop them.

© Archivo Iconografico, S.A./CORBIS

▲ Emperor Hadrian.

Wanting the wall to be as efficient as possible, Hadrian's engineers chose to build it at the narrowest point in northern England. There the country is only a little more than seventy miles wide from coast to coast. It is a landscape of rolling moors[2] and low hills, without the mountains that would have provided cover for hostile tribes and made building the wall more difficult.

Over ten thousand people took part in the construction of the wall. They included Roman soldiers, and men recruited from conquered English tribes. The laborers were organized into units of eighty and, judging by inscriptions[3] found on the wall, they probably worked in leapfrog fashion. As a unit completed one section, it would move past the neighboring unit and start in on the next section assigned to it.

The stones used to face the wall on both sides were generally wedge-shaped. Their surfaces measured eight or nine inches by ten or eleven inches, and the wedges were as much as twenty inches long. These stones had to be transported from quarries[4] seven or eight miles away. In hilly country,

Emperor and Tourist

The emperor Hadrian was always on the move. A historian observed that "hardly any emperor ever traveled with such speed over so much territory." Hadrian once climbed 10,000-foot Mount Aetna, in Sicily, just to view the sunrise from the mountaintop. His journeys were inspired, in part, by his keen intelligence and curiosity about the world. The energetic Hadrian visited Africa, Arabia, the Greek islands, and the Nile River, as well as Britain, Spain, and Gaul (present-day France and Belgium). His biographer wrote that the emperor went to "all parts of the world with bare head and often in severe storms and frosts."

subdued (sub•dood'): conquered.
recruited (ri•kroot'id): hired; enrolled.

---

2. **moors:** areas of open land covered with heather or peat vegetation.
3. **inscriptions** (in•skrip'shəns): markings.
4. **quarries** (kwôr'ēz): sites from which building stone is removed.

workers carried the stones on their backs; where the land was level enough, the stones were hauled in wagons.

The mortar used in the wall was much like today's concrete. It was made of lime[5] mixed with sand, gravel, and water, and was very tough. The interior of the wall was filled with rubble—a mixture of small rocks and pebbles, held together with mortar like the facing stones.

Approximately every four miles along the wall, laborers built a large fort. These forts covered four or five acres and contained barracks[6] for as many as a thousand soldiers or five hundred cavalrymen,[7] with stables for their horses. Stone walls five to eight feet thick enclosed the forts, and the northern wall was usually part of Hadrian's Wall itself. The forts had four gates, one in each wall, and outside the southern gate there was often a village of wooden dwellings, where the wives and children of the soldiers lived.

Besides the forts, structures called milecastles stood at intervals of a little less than a mile all along the wall. Each milecastle measured about sixty feet by fifty feet and was manned by patrols of forty or fifty soldiers. The northern wall of the milecastle was part of the main wall and contained a large, well-defended gate. There was another gate in the southern wall.

Between each milecastle, at equal distances, rose two watchtowers. These towers were small, two-story stone structures that were built directly into the wall itself. Four soldiers were usually assigned to each tower. Two stood guard on the top story, watching

intervals (in′tər·vəlz): spaces between objects or points.

Holding Up the Wall

Hadrian's Wall was made possible by a very basic, very important building material—concrete, or as Romans called it, *caementicum*. For ages, builders had used mud and mortar for construction. The Romans improved on this formula by adding the mineral *pozzolana*, a volcanic earth. This mineral, when added to concrete, would harden when it came in contact with water. Roman concrete was fire-resistant and waterproof. It was also the first concrete strong enough to allow arches and domes that could stand alone, without pillars for support. As Hadrian's Wall shows, the Roman formula for concrete can withstand the test of time, too.

5. **lime:** white substance produced by heating materials that contain calcium carbonate, such as limestone and shells.
6. **barracks** (bar′əks): housing for soldiers.
7. **cavalrymen** (kav′əl·rē·mən): troops mounted on horses.

the surrounding landscape through peepholes, while on the floor below, the other two rested, ate, or played dice.

If any point along the wall was attacked by a hostile tribe, signals were sent from watchtower to watchtower, from milecastle to milecastle. Soldiers from nearby towers and milecastles could race along the top of the wall to the aid of their neighbors. If additional help was needed, soldiers and cavalry from the nearest fort sped to the endangered <u>sector</u> by means of the broad stone road that ran directly south of the wall.

If any point along the wall was attacked by a hostile tribe, signals were sent from watchtower to watchtower.

Some historians have said that lead pipes or speaking tubes were built into the wall between the watchtowers. Through these pipes soldiers could sound the alarm if they saw an enemy coming. It's a clever idea, but no evidence of such tubes has been found. Besides, they would hardly have been needed since the watchtowers were close enough for a trumpet blast to be heard from one to another.

The defenses of Hadrian's Wall didn't end with the forts, milecastles, and watchtowers. Leaving nothing to chance, the Roman builders also dug a V-shaped ditch, twenty-seven feet wide by nine feet deep, on the north side of the wall. Beyond the ditch they piled up the earth they had excavated and made a second wall.

And that wasn't all. To the south of the wall, on the other side of the stone road, the Romans dug an even deeper ditch and heaped the earth and rubble from it in huge mounds along both banks.

Many people have wondered why, if their enemies were to the north, the Romans felt it necessary to build such

massive fortifications[8] on the south side, where supposedly friendly tribes lived. Perhaps it was because the Romans feared the southern tribes would join forces with their kinsmen if the tribes from the north succeeded in breaking through the wall. Or perhaps the Romans were simply following through on something one of their generals, Agricola, is reported to have said: "It has long been my opinion that the back of a general or his army is never safe."

Hadrian's Wall and all its defenses took more than six years to build and cost the equivalent of hundreds of millions of dollars in today's money. About fifteen thousand soldiers were required to garrison[9] the forts, milecastles, and watchtowers along the wall. Many of them came not from Rome, but from other parts of its empire. There were infantrymen[10] from Greece, archers from Syria, and cavalrymen from northern France.

Occasionally a raiding party from the north would seize a watchtower or milecastle, burn its wooden furnishings, and destroy as much of the stonework as they could. But the raiders were invariably repulsed[11] and the damage repaired. During the more than 250 years that Hadrian's Wall was actively defended, there is no evidence that any large portion of it was ever captured or held by an enemy.

The wall's collapse came about in a different way. During the last years of the fourth century A.D., the tribes to the north of the wall formed an <u>alliance</u> with the Scots

SIDELIGHT

"It is impossible for a man to live there for half an hour, but vipers and many snakes and all other kinds of wild beasts live there, strangest of all, the natives say that if a man crosses the wall he immediately dies, unable to stand the poisonous air. Wild beasts that go there die too!"

—description of northern Britain written in the sixth century A.D. by the Roman historian Procopius,
from *The Roman Empire* by Marilyn Whittock

alliance (ə·lī′əns): association or union created for a common purpose.

---

8. **fortifications** (fort′ə·fi·kā′shənz): defensive structure.
9. **garrison** (gar′ə·sən): to defend a position by stationing troops there.
10. **infantrymen** (in′fən·trē·mən): soldiers trained and equipped to fight on foot.
11. **repulsed** (ri·pulsd′): driven or beaten back.

in the west and the Saxons[12] in the east. The wall's defenders might have been able to repel[13] the combined forces of their enemies if the garrisons had been maintained at full strength. But many Roman soldiers had been transferred from Britain to fight more dangerous foes, like the Goths and the Persians,[14] in the eastern part of the empire.

The remaining soldiers walled up the gateways in many of the forts and milecastles so that the wall would be easier to defend. When their numbers were reduced even further, the soldiers knew they could no longer hold the wall. Eventually, the soldiers withdrew to the south of England. By 400 A.D. Hadrian's Wall was abandoned.

In the centuries that followed, the wall never again served as a fortification. But stones from it were put to many other uses by the English people who lived nearby. Some of the stones became the foundation and walls of churches; others were used in the construction of barns and houses; still others were cut into paving blocks for streets and roads.

▲ Hadrian's Wall as it appears today. **❓ What was the landscape like in the part of northern England where Hadrian's Wall was built?**

In less populated areas, though, many sections of the wall remained much as they were in Roman times. Today a visitor can walk along these sections and look out at the rolling lands to the north, just as Roman sentries did almost sixteen hundred years ago.

---

12. **Saxons:** Germanic people who conducted raids along the North Sea.
13. **repel** (ri•pel′): to hold off or force back.
14. **Goths . . . Persians:** Goths (gäths) were members of a Germanic tribe of people that originally came from southern Scandinavia. Persians (pur′zhənz) were people belonging to the kingdom of Iran in southwestern Asia.

✓ Reading Check

1. Where is Hadrian's Wall located? Why did the Romans build it in that spot?

2. What materials were used to make Hadrian's Wall?

3. What defensive features did soldiers build along the wall? What purposes did these features serve?

4. How many soldiers were stationed at the wall? Where did they come from?

5. How did Hadrian's Wall finally collapse?

MEET THE *Writer*

James Cross Giblin (1933–   ) edited children's books for many years before he began writing them himself. He has written about chimney sweeps, chairs, the Rosetta stone, the invention of eating utensils, and other interesting subjects. Many of his books have received awards. *Walls: Defenses Throughout History* received the Golden Kite Award from the Society of Children's Book Writers in 1984.

In the first century A.D., a new religion burst onto the scene and began to attract followers. Some Roman people began to question their old religious beliefs. Read on to find out how the message of Christianity survived through times of trouble—and how it became a major force for change in the Roman Empire.

A Persecuted Faith Becomes a World Religion

from *Calliope*

by S. E. TOTH

In A.D. 64, a raging fire destroyed much of Rome. The Roman emperor Nero blamed the Christians for the disaster, and ordered the first mass persecution of the followers of Jesus Christ as punishment. Nero's edicts (decrees) against Christianity gave license to future Roman emperors to inflict new persecutions on this religious sect[1] whose members refused to worship Roman gods.

In the two centuries that followed Nero's reign, there were nine more persecutions. Then, in A.D. 303, in an effort to restore the prestige of the crumbling empire and a belief in the ancient Roman gods, the Roman emperor Diocletian

persecution (pɥr′sə•kyo͞o′shən): repeated acts of torment or cruelty; harassment.

> ## You Need to Know...
> Like most ancient peoples, the Romans worshiped many different gods. The Roman Empire embraced the religions of the countries it governed, freely borrowing from many beliefs. For example, many Greek gods and goddesses were adopted almost unchanged into the Roman religion. After the death of Rome's first emperor, Augustus, emperors themselves began to be worshiped as gods. Christianity was the only religion in the empire that was banned by the Roman government. Christians believed that Rome's state religion was false, and so they refused to conduct Roman religious rituals, such as burning incense before the emperor's statue.

---

1. **sect** (sekt): religious body or faction, especially one separated from a larger group.

Underground Cities of the Dead

When Christian persecution ended, the catacombs became holy shrines, popular sites for religious pilgrims. Saint Jerome (A.D. 347–420) recalled that he visited the tunnels regularly as a child. "My friends and I used to visit the tombs of the apostles and martyrs on Sundays," he wrote. In the utter darkness of the tombs, Jerome observed that "the prophetic saying, 'We descend live into the inferno,' seemed to be fulfilled."

Underneath the city of Rome is a network of catacombs that stretches for about 600 miles. Some catacombs were built four or five levels deep, connected by winding passages with narrow, steep steps. Modern visitors to the catacombs have described the air as sweet and warm and the atmosphere as not at all unpleasant.

launched the tenth persecution. In this bloodiest of all persecutions, innumerable Christians were tortured and killed or thrown into arenas with bulls, leopards, or bears. These men, women, girls, and boys came from all social groups, although most were poor.

In such times of danger, the early Christians gathered in multilevel underground quarries called catacombs, which served as burial sites, shrines to martyrs,[2] places to hide, and rooms for religious services. Along the narrow hallways were niches (small carved-out rectangular areas) where bodies were put to rest. Groups of niches often formed a place for worship. Many of the walls and ceilings were covered with fresco[3] decorations. Rome's San Sebastiano catacombs may have once housed the bodies of saints Peter and Paul. The neighboring San Callistro catacombs contain more than twelve miles of underground paths. Today, visitors are welcome to enter these catacombs, but only if accompanied by a guide. Historians have learned much about early Christian life by studying and excavating catacombs in Italy, North Africa, and Asia Minor (present-day Turkey).

On the anniversary of a martyr's death, Christians celebrated communion[4] at the burial site. When the threat of persecution was not great, many Christians chose to pray together in private houses or in specially built community houses. They often relocated the

▲ The head of an enormous statue of Emperor Constantine.

2. **martyrs** (märt′ərz): people who suffer for their beliefs.
3. **fresco** (fres′kō): watercolor painting created on wet plaster.
4. **communion** (kə•myо̄о̄′yən): special religious service, usually including eating bread and drinking wine, according to well-defined rituals.

▲ This inscription on the tomb of Severa in the Catacombs of Saint Priscilla in Rome shows the three wise men bearing gifts to the infant Jesus. **⁈ What can we learn about the early Christians by studying the Roman catacombs?**

bodies of the martyrs or portions of them under the altars in these communal places of worship.

In A.D. 306, the Roman army in Gaul (present-day France) urged their general, Constantine, to assume the title of Roman emperor. Constantine refused the honor, but did agree to rule Gaul and Britain. To extend his control over the whole Roman empire, Constantine then waged wars against other Roman rulers, each of whom controlled a portion of the coveted[5] empire.

Six years later, as he prepared to battle his arch rival, Maxentius, just north of Rome at the Milvian Bridge, Constantine believed he saw an unusual sign in the sky and heard the words, "In this sign thou shalt conquer." That night, before the battle, he had made a *labarum* (an imperial military standard) bearing this heavenly sign: ☧. The sign depicts the first two letters of the name Christ in Greek: X (equivalent to "ch") and P (equivalent to "r"). The next morning, Constantine ordered his troops to place the same letters on their shields.

With his army marching behind the newly fashioned labarum, Constantine defeated his enemy at the Milvian Bridge, and gained control of Italy, Spain, and North Africa. Constantine was now proclaimed the emperor of the Western Roman Empire. Crediting the Christian God for this victory, he freed the Christians, as a way of saying

---

5. **coveted** (kuv'it·id): envied or greatly desired.

tolerated (täl'ər•rāt'id): permitted or respected; endured.

rigor (rig'ər): strictness or precision.

fervor (fʉr'vər): intense emotion; passion.

Constantine. ▶

From Roman Empress to Christian Saint

The emperor Constantine influenced his own mother, Empress Helena, to become a Christian. Helena had humble beginnings working as a servant in a tavern. Her fortunes changed, however, when she married a Roman general who became emperor. When she was in her eighties, her son sent her to the Holy Land to search for Christ's tomb. In Jerusalem she ordered a pagan temple torn down, and in the rubble she found what she believed to be the tomb and parts of the cross on which Christ died. After her death around A.D. 328, Helena was made a saint in the Christian church.

thanks, by issuing the Edict of Milan jointly with Licinius, ruler of the Eastern Roman Empire. By this edict,[6] Christianity was no longer a persecuted religion. Property that had been taken from Christians was to be returned. The edict also stated that persecutions of any religious sects were not to be tolerated.

Nine years later, Constantine attacked and defeated Licinius, finally uniting the Roman Empire. As at the Milvian Bridge, the army had advanced behind Constantine's newly designed labarum.

As emperor, Constantine was still officially the high priest of paganism,[7] and he viewed the Roman supreme god and the Christian God as peers, or equals, and served both. Yet, although he accepted instruction in Christianity, Constantine for some unknown reason put off his own baptism until hours before he died.

As the standards of Christian membership lost rigor and definition, a large number of Christians flocked to the monastic[8] life and a few became hermits. These individuals felt they could channel their religious fervor and zeal into prayer, penance, and manual work.

As Christianity matured, more interpretations of the teachings of Jesus Christ evolved, and some led to stormy heresies[9] and infighting. Monks marched against monks, and people divided into menacing crowds. Soldiers came out to establish order. To assure peace in his empire, Constantine attempted to stop the stream of heresies by establishing a set of dogma[10] and ritual. When Arius, a priest in Alexandria, Egypt, denied the divinity of Jesus Christ, and won much support, including that of

6. **edict** (ē'dikt'): official public decree from an authority.
7. **paganism** (pā'gən•iz'əm): word used to describe some types of religion that existed before Christianity, such as the worship of nature or of numerous gods.
8. **monastic** (mə•nas'tik): relating to conditions in a monastery; secluded life of monks or nuns.
9. **heresies** (her'ə•sēz): beliefs that contradict official views or doctrines, especially established religious doctrines.
10. **dogma** (dôg'mə): established belief or opinion.

Constantine's sister, the emperor worried that Arianism might become a threat to peace. In A.D. 325, he called the first General Council of Nicaea. At this meeting, the first ecumenical[11] "world council," Arius was condemned, and the Council members crafted the Nicene Creed (prayer) to proclaim the divinity of Jesus. (Through the centuries, the Nicene Creed has undergone several changes, but it is the only prayer currently accepted by the Roman Catholic, Eastern Orthodox, Anglican, and major Protestant churches.)

Constantine then made the most radical change of his rule—he moved the capital of the Roman empire from Rome to Byzantium (present-day Istanbul). He changed the name of this ancient city at the commercial crossroads of East and West to Constantinople, "the city of Constantine." There were many reasons for his decision. He thought the move would weaken the power of Rome's ruling families. Also, he wanted to move the center of government away from the many pagan sacrifices and rituals being observed in Rome. But, according to Constantine himself, the main reason for the move was because the Christian God had commanded it.

As the number of Christians multiplied, worship began to take place in <u>ornate</u> churches built by Constantine in several cities, including his palace church, *Magale Ekklesia* (Greek for "great church"), in Constantinople. It was built

© *Craig Lovell/CORBIS*

▲ This famous mosaic of Jesus in the Hagia Sophia is thought to date from the twelfth century.

ornate (ôr·nāt′): elaborately decorated.

---

11. ecumenical (ek′yo͞o·men′i·kəl): universal, especially in relation to the Christian church.

on the highest point in the city, a point where a pagan temple dedicated to the sun god Apollo is thought to have once stood. The Magale Ekklesia was richly decorated with over four hundred statues. Damaged by an earthquake and then destroyed by a fire in A.D. 404, it was rebuilt by the Roman emperor Theodosius I and given the new name of *Hagia Sophia*, Greek for "holy wisdom." After this church burned to the ground, in A.D. 532, the Roman emperor Justinian rebuilt it to its present-day magnificence. Until 1453, when Constantinople fell to the Ottoman Turks,[12] the Hagia Sophia was the center of the Christian Church in the East, known today as the Eastern Orthodox Church.

---

12. **Ottoman Turks** (ät′ə·mən tʉrks): people belonging to Turkish tribes that created the Ottoman Empire (c. 1300–1918).

© Peter Wilson/CORBIS

▲ The Hagia Sophia in present-day Istanbul, Turkey, which was formerly the city of Constantinople.

The local historian Procopius described it as: "[soaring] to a height to match the sky, and, like a ship riding at anchor, higher than the other buildings, [to look] down upon the remainder of the city."

Incense, luxurious attire for priests, processions, choirs, and imperial rituals gradually crept into the Christian Church. In artworks, Jesus went from being depicted as a poor, barefoot carpenter to the son of God sitting on a throne like a Roman emperor. Christianity was becoming rich, powerful, and respected.

✓ Reading Check

1. What reason did Emperor Nero use to begin persecuting Christians?

2. Where did persecuted Christians hide and hold religious services?

3. What sign did Constantine believe he saw in the sky before an important battle? How did he react to this vision?

4. Why did Constantine call the first General Council of Nicaea?

5. Why did Constantine move the capital of the empire from Rome to Byzantium?

How, in less than two hundred years, could one of history's mightiest empires collapse into ruin? For twelve centuries since its founding, Rome had grown to be the envy of the world. Read on to discover how a complex chain of events led to the end of "the glory that was Rome."

The Fall and the Legacy

from *Ancient Rome*

by CHRISTOPHER FAGG

rivals (rī′vəlz): competitors.

treacherous (trech′ər•əs): disloyal; not trustworthy; unfaithful.

Diocletian knew that the empire was too big to be governed by one man. By dividing it he hoped to do two things. Firstly, he wanted to make sure that the frontiers were well defended. But he also wanted to make certain of a smooth handover of power from one emperor to another. He knew that, in the past, armed struggles between rivals for the throne had badly weakened the empire. So Diocletian, as emperor (Augustus) of the east, appointed a second-in-command—a Caesar—who would take over after 20 years.

This system was only partly successful. Without it, the empire would certainly have fallen much sooner. But, time and again, rivalries between emperors flared up into civil war.

The strongest ruler of the 4th century was Constantine the Great, the first Christian emperor. He became Augustus of the west in A.D. 307, and tried hard to make Diocletian's system work. But his co-rulers proved treacherous and Constantine, having defeated them, ruled alone from 324 to his death in 337.

You Need to Know...

From the second century A.D., Rome was an empire in crisis. For one thing, the empire was beginning to have trouble defending itself against barbarian invaders. The Roman population was declining, in part because of plagues, high taxes, and poor harvests. Rome's rich citizens refused to allow the men working on their estates to join the army. Because there was a shortage of soldiers, Roman armies hired men from the same barbarian tribes that were threatening the empire, such as the Goths. More and more rich Roman lands were being lost. In A.D. 284, the emperor Diocletian (Dī′ə•klē•shən) had an empire on his hands that was beginning to fall apart.

Rome was no longer the center of the empire. Instead, Constantine built a great new Christian capital for the empire, Constantinople, on the site of the ancient city of Byzantium.[1] The state took complete control of people's lives. The emperor's subjects were tied to their occupations by law. Taxes became heavier and heavier in order to pay for the much larger army needed to defend the empire.

All the while the frontiers were under constant attack. In the west barbarians raided along the coasts and attacked the Rhine–Danube line.[2] The Sassanids, a warlike Persian people, menaced the eastern provinces. The Visigoths and Vandals, driven westward by other tribes (the Huns)

1. **Byzantium** (bi·zan′shē·əm): ancient city founded about 600 B.C. on the present site of Istanbul, Turkey.
2. **Rhine-Danube line:** boundary of the Roman Empire, marked on the east by the Rhine River, and on the north by the Danube River.

▲ The Huns, shown here attacking another barbarian tribe, were experts at fighting on horseback.

forced the Romans to accept them into the empire. They were allowed to settle along the Danube in return for defending the frontier.

After the death of Constantine, strong emperors like Julian, Valentinian, and Theodosius made brave attempts to roll back the barbarian attacks. In the east these efforts were successful. But in the west there was a run of young, weak emperors who could not hold on to what the strong emperors had won.

In 395, Alaric, a Visigoth who had once been a Roman commander, <u>seized</u> the provinces along the Danube. Ten years later, he invaded Italy and finally, in 410, captured Rome. For six days his army sacked and burned the city. After two years the Visigoths left Italy for Gaul.[3] In Ravenna,[4] western emperors continued to rule their shrinking empire for another 64 years. In 476 a new wave of invaders, the Ostrogoths, swept into Italy and <u>deposed</u> the last western emperor, Romulus Augustulus. They

seized (sēzd): took by force.

deposed (dē·pōzd′): removed from power.

---

3. **Gaul** (gôl): early name for present-day France and Belgium.
4. **Ravenna** (rə·ven′ə): city in northern Italy; important Roman naval center.

SIDELIGHT

"The first impression we receive of the barbarians is one of incredible energy. As described by the classical Roman historians (who more often than not were actually Greek), the various tribes of Celts and Goths that streamed out of the north were creatures of boundless, unfocused chaos. They appeared suddenly out of nowhere. They were noisy. They did not fight the way armies were supposed to fight. . . . They had all those horses. They were blonde. Some of them even fought naked. And they were big. The barbarian's size is mentioned so often, it is hard not to suspect that the Romans were really quite short and perhaps self-conscious about it."

—from "'They Came Like Locusts'" in *Chronicles of the Barbarians* by David Willis McCullough

▲ Relief sculpture showing a Roman soldier and an attacking barbarian.
🔢 How did barbarian invasions change the Roman Empire?

proclaimed their leader, Odoacer, as king; the young Romulus was given a pension[5] and sent to live with his family in Campania. The western empire was finally at an end.

The legacy

About the time of the sack of Rome, the Vandals, Suevi, and Alani broke through the middle Rhine and scoured[6] Gaul before settling in Spain and Africa. In Britain Angles, Saxons, and Jutes landed on the east coast and drove the Romanized Britons before them. The Britons took refuge in the far west, in Cornwall and Wales. Some people believe that the legends of King Arthur and his knights remember some British leader of the time.

Mainland Europe became a patchwork of Germanic kingdoms—some independent, some still recognizing the

---

5. **pension** (pen'shən): regular payment sometimes given as a reward or to support a person who has retired from service.
6. **scoured** (skourd): passed quickly through, as in a search or pursuit.

Roman law is one of the great legacies Rome left to the modern world. The Roman lawyer Cicero believed that we "obey the law to the end that we may be free." In A.D. 528, the emperor Justinian began the process of organizing the complicated Roman law codes. He appointed a panel of legal scholars who, after six years' work, produced the Body of Civil Law. Justinian's Code, as it was called, set out the purpose of these laws as "to live honestly, not to injure another, and to give to each one that which belongs to him." Today, Justinian's Code is the basis of the legal system in many European countries.

convert (kən·vʉrt'): to change; transform.

authority of the eastern emperor. But although Roman power was gone, Roman influence was strong. The barbarian kings took to town life, adopted what remained of Roman law and government and even issued coins with the heads of long-dead emperors.

Christianity was one of the strongest reminders of Roman civilization. Missionaries like St. Augustine traveled across Europe to convert barbarians to Christianity. Rome had lost its ability to rule, but Christian barbarians still looked to the "eternal city" as the center of the world.

In the east, Roman power lasted for much longer. From Constantinople, the eastern emperor controlled Moesia, Greece, Macedonia, Thrace, and the provinces of Asia down to Egypt. The riches of the east paid for the troops which kept the Persians and barbarians at bay. Strong emperors, like the great Justinian, kept alive the ideas of Roman government and law. It was not until 673 that the Saracens, followers of the prophet[7] Muhammad, overran the east and laid siege to Constantinople. Although the city survived, its empire was gone for good.

---

7. **prophet** (präf'it): religious leader or teacher who claims to be divinely inspired.

✓ Reading Check

1. Why did Emperor Diocletian divide the Roman Empire into two parts?

2. After Constantine became emperor of the western empire, what happened to Diocletian's system of co-rulers?

3. What changes and developments took place in the Roman Empire during the reign of Constantine? What happened after his death?

4. What important event occurred in A.D. 476?

5. After the fall of the Roman Empire, what aspects of Roman power and influence lived on?

Cross-Curricular ACTIVITIES

■ GEOGRAPHY/SPEECH

Can You Get There from Here? If you traveled during Roman times, what roads would you use to get from one end of the empire to another? What cities would you pass through, and what sights might you see? Alone or with a partner or small group, investigate the Romans' extensive network of roads and plot a trip between two cities. Use books or Web sites to find out more about traveling conditions, terrain, and people and towns along your route. Present your classmates with a map and a description of your travels.

■ HISTORY/HEALTH

Eating in the Empire Some foods found on a Roman banquet table would seem appealing to us today; we might find other dishes very unusual. With a partner, research a typical Roman meal, noting where different types of ingredients might have been grown or hunted. Using the Internet or other research tools, you might even find recipes from Roman cookbooks. Compare the Roman meal to modern guidelines for healthy, balanced diets. Do you think the Roman diet was a healthy one? Discuss your findings with your classmates. If possible, prepare a Roman dish to share with your class.

■ LANGUAGE ARTS/HISTORY

Dear Diary People living during the time of the fall of the Roman Empire witnessed enormous changes and unrest. Imagine that you are living during this period, and write a series of diary entries that describe what you see going on around you. You could take the perspective of a Roman soldier, a priest in a pagan temple, or a Visigoth living on the edge of the empire. What changes are occurring? How do these changes affect your everyday life?

■ LANGUAGE ARTS/DRAMA

Positions Available Thousands of soldiers were needed to guard Hadrian's Wall. Imagine that you're a Roman army commander looking to hire new recruits. Write a job description that tells what duties the soldiers would have to perform, what skills would be required, and what types of situations they might encounter. You might also want to indicate a salary and any special benefits. Then, with a partner, conduct a mock interview between a recruiter and a potential defender of Hadrian's Wall.

■ ART/ARCHITECTURE

Same Empire, Different City Constantine moved the empire's capital from Rome to Constantinople, creating a whole new list of tourist destinations. Create a travel brochure that describes popular sites found in the new capital. Your brochure should describe the city's important buildings and works of art. Since Constantine emphasized the new Christian religion, be sure to pay special attention to the art and architecture found at religious sites. Illustrate your brochure, and present it to your classmates, taking them on a spin through the city.

READ ON: FOR INDEPENDENT READING

■ NONFICTION

Land Beyond the River: Europe in the Age of Migration by Richard B. Lyttle
(Atheneum, 1986). Meet the Huns, Vandals, and Goths—the wandering tribal peoples that helped bring down the mighty Roman Empire. Numerous maps and illustrations help you follow the travels of these "barbarian" people who changed the map of Europe.

Outrageous Women of Ancient Times by
Vicki León (John Wiley, 1997). What did Hortensia of Rome, Locusta of Gaul, and Mary Prophetissa of Alexandria have in common? Attitude! Here are the stories of 21 smart, original women of ancient times. The tales of these artists, warriors, and empresses provide an "outrageous" perspective on history.

City: A Story of Roman Planning and Construction by David Macaulay (1974). Roman
cities had a unique feature: They were *organized!* Award-winning author and illustrator David Macaulay uses his brilliant drawings to show us the way things work; in this book his imaginary city called Verbonia reveals the genius of Roman urban planners. An ALA Notable book.

Oxford First Ancient History by Roy Burrell
(Oxford University Press, 1997). Fictional eyewitness accounts of everyday life in a number of ancient civilizations add to this fact-filled, highly illustrated book. In the extensive section on the Roman world, for example, an elderly citizen explains how times have changed from Nero's reign to Hadrian's.

■ FICTION

The Bronze Bow by Elizabeth George Speare
(Houghton Mifflin, 1997) is a classic story about Christianity's beginnings in the Roman Empire. This Newbery Award–winning book tells the tale of a bitter young Jewish rebel who, with his outlaw band, works to drive the Roman legions out of Galilee— until he learns the lessons of a prophet named Jesus.

The Lantern Bearers by Rosemary Sutcliff
(Peter Smith,1994). When the Roman legions leave Britain in A.D. 450, the young soldier Aquila struggles to keep the fires of civilization burning. This ALA Notable book is a fast-paced historical adventure; for more on the Roman occupation of Britain, see Sutcliff's **The Eagle of the Ninth**.

The Ides of March by Thornton Wilder
(Buccaneer Books, 1997). Discover what important events Mark Antony, Cleopatra, Catullus, and Julius Caesar might have written about in letters to their friends—just before the most famous murder in ancient Rome. History and philosophy merge with the drama of the times in this account by a Pulitzer Prize–winning novelist and playwright.

Illustrated Book of Myths by Neil Philip (DK
Publishing, 1995). If you are curious about Roman mythology as it compares to other world myths, then this is the book for you. Arranged thematically, the book retells myths, using colorful illustrations and photographs. An appendix and pronunciation key help you keep track of who's who in mythology.

CHAPTER 2

Lasting Legacies
From the Islamic World to Africa
A.D. 600–1600

"The Hot Month" of Ramadan

The ninth month of the Muslim calendar is called Ramadan (ram´ə·dän´) in Arabic, literally "the hot month." Observing Ramadan is one of the five principles of the Islamic faith. During this month in A.D. 610, the prophet Mohammed first received his holy revelations. During Ramadan, Muslims fast for thirty days. At sunrise, when there is enough light to tell a white thread from a black thread, believers stop eating or drinking. They eat only after sundown. Fasting is intended to remind Muslims of those who suffer from hunger and poverty. After this experience of hunger, Muslims can look forward to a festival that celebrates the end of Ramadan with a day of feasting.

© Bettmann/CORBIS

▲ The family meal takes place after sunset during Ramadan.

Back to the Salt Mines

Salt was literally worth its weight in gold during the Middle Ages. In the African kingdom of Ghana, salt was traded for gold. Most of the salt came from the mines of Taghaza, a desert village where the buildings were actually made of salt slabs. Despite the wealth brought by the sale of salt, Taghaza was inhabited by slaves, who worked in the mines. No one else wanted to live in a place where food could not grow, and salt ruined even the water. The slaves had to depend on traders for fresh food and water. When traders were delayed, many slaves died of starvation or thirst.

© Bernard and Catherine Desjeux/CORBIS

▲ Modern-day workers in a salt mine.

Memorable Quote

"No people in the early Middle Ages contributed to human progress so much as did the Arabs. . . ."

—Philip K. Hitti,
The Arabs: A Short History

INVESTIGATE: Why was salt so valuable during the Middle Ages? How is salt formed and mined?

Some of the Islamic names you will run across in this chapter may have slightly different spellings. For example, the name of the founder of the Islamic faith, Mohammed (mō•ham′id), is also spelled "Muhammad." The name for a follower of Islam can be spelled either "Muslim" (muz′ləm) or "Moslem." The Islamic holy book, the Koran (kə•ran′), can also be spelled "Quran" or "Qur'an." Another important name you'll see is Allah (al′ə), the Islamic name for God.

▲ A griot entertains her audience.

Calligraphy: Teaching by the Pen

Calligraphy is the art of beautiful handwriting. It is used to inscribe

passages from the Koran and the words of Mohammed on the walls of homes, tombs, mosques—and even on furniture. In the eleventh century, calligraphers began using the letters of the passages as ornaments, adding geometric elements. Calligraphers were considered great artists, and, when they died, they were often buried with their cherished pens.

Girl Power in Medieval Africa

Women in the African kingdoms enjoyed great influence and freedom. Unlike women in Muslim countries, they were allowed to appear in public and to choose their husbands. Although women were not allowed to rule, power was passed down through women's families. One exception to the "no girls rule" was Queen Amina, who ruled the city-state of Zaria in the late 1500s. She is honored today on Amina Day, a holiday celebrated by schoolgirls in modern Nigeria.

Living Libraries

A griot (grē′ō) is a respected storyteller from West Africa. The history and literature of West African peoples have been passed from one generation to the next by griots. (This process of "handing down" is called the oral tradition.) With their well-trained memories, griots can recite long family histories of births, deaths, and marriages, and long epics such as *Sundiata* and the *Dausi*. In a sense, griots are "living libraries," carrying the African oral literary tradition inside them. As one African explained, "Other people use writing to record the past, but they no longer *feel* the past because writing does not have the warmth of the human voice."

Imagine swaying along for thousands of miles on the back of a camel, with nothing but scorching sun and hot desert sand between you and your destination. During the Middle Ages, few people undertook such a journey alone. Read on to find out how travelers in the Arab territories banded together to get from one place to another.

NONFICTION BOOK

HISTORY ●

GEOGRAPHY ●

from Travel Through the Empire

from *The Arabs in the Golden Age*

by MOKHTAR MOKTEFI

The ancient Arab world contained many large expanses of sand and rock—the Sahara in North Africa, the deserts of the Arabian Peninsula, and those of Asia to the northeast. Such <u>terrain</u> meant that every traveler making an overland journey had to cross a wide expanse of desert. Nobody who embarked on such a dangerous adventure ever did so without risking death by thirst, exposure, or exhaustion. This explains why all voyages were made in groups, or caravans.

The Bedouins were excellent guides and herdsmen. They knew how to <u>navigate</u> across the flat, infertile steppes[1] without any navigational instruments whatsoever. Their vast knowledge encompassed not only animals but stones,

> ## You Need to Know...
> For the people of Arabia, with its miles of sand and small amount of water, a settled way of life based on farming was not possible. They soon found that their future depended on their location at the heart of trade routes to Asia. Merchants and tradespeople began to transport goods across vast distances with the help of the nomadic Bedouin people. The lifestyle of the Bedouins was one of constant movement. They lived in tents and herded their camels, sheep, and goats between various water holes and pastures according to the season. The Bedouins found a new outlet for their desert knowledge by leading caravans of travelers across barren stretches of the Arabian Peninsula.

terrain (tə·rān′): natural features of land.

navigate (nav′ə·gāt′): to plot a course across or through; find the correct direction.

---

1. steppes (steps): grassy plains.

winds, and plants. Merchants transporting goods and travelers of all kinds found that Bedouins were indispensable guides and caravaneers.

THE CARAVAN

Several dozen camels usually made up a caravan, but sometimes hundreds of them traveled together. Once in a rare while, caravans with five or six thousand camels passed by! When caravans grew to be this large, it appeared as if the whole world were in motion. The caravan's collective movements, such as departures, rest stops, and the setting up and taking down of tents, were announced by drum rolls. Overland journeys usually lasted several months. Since each camel could carry a load weighing over 220 pounds (100 kilos), caravans were able to transport as much cargo as would fit into a very large ship. Wealthy merchants, important people, and women rode in palanquins, enclosed couches with shafts that rested on the camels' backs.

SIDELIGHT

"There he was: an ancient Arabian traveling across the desert with no one for company but a camel with yellow teeth, bad breath, and a bad temper.

At least the fellow had food along. He had poured some milk into a pouch made from a sheep's stomach. During his journey, he opened the pouch and discovered the milk had separated and formed thick masses, which we call curd, and a watery fluid, which we call whey. The Arabian traveler had accidentally invented cheese.

Two elements transformed the milk into cheese: First, the sun warmed the bag of milk during the journey. Second, the sheep-stomach bag contained dried digestive juices. The digestive juices included "rennet," which is necessary to make cheese even today.

The Arabian traveler told his friends about his discovery and for four thousand years people have continued making cheese. Cheese quickly became important all over the world. Milk spoiled quickly, but by making cheese, people could preserve the milk's nutrition for long periods of time."

—from *Mistakes That Worked* by Charlotte Foltz Jones

Traveling in caravans was not always safe. At certain points throughout history it was risky to travel by caravan in some regions of the Arab world. Wars and local revolts disturbed the long-distance trade that caravans made possible. In the ninth century, for example, serious trouble in China interrupted the overland trade of silk. On the other hand, the crusades, which began in the eleventh century, greatly contributed to the exchange of goods between merchants in French and Arab territories.

Caravans always traveled with escorts hired to protect against attacks by bandits or wild beasts. In some cases, journeys through unfriendly territory had to be arranged ahead of time with the heads of local tribes who would grant safe-conduct passes to the <u>convoy</u> or have it accompanied by designated tribe members.

Chris Beetles, Ltd., London, UK/Bridgeman Art Library, New York/London

▲ Arab travelers in a camel caravan. ❓ **Why were camels used for desert travel?**

convoy (kän′voi′): group traveling together for convenience or safety; caravan.

TRAVELING FAR

"Go far and wide in search of your subsistence.[2] If you do not find great wealth, you will have nourished your mind and your spirit." The Arab author of the *Book of Countries* shared this wisdom with his compatriots in the year 896.

In the tenth century, the *dar al Islam,* as Arab territory was called, extended from the borders of China to Spain, from the coast of the Caspian Sea in Russia all the way to southeastern France and central Africa. People, products, and ideas circulated back and forth within this vast region. Each year tens of thousands of people came to Mecca.[3] Arabs were always traveling the roads, rivers, and seas of their known world. But they never ventured beyond its borders into South Africa or into northern or eastern Europe.

---

2. subsistence (səb·sis′təns): means of support.
3. Mecca (Mek′ə): city in Saudi Arabia; the birthplace of Mohammed.

A Horse for All Seasons

The camel isn't the only animal made to last in the desert. The Arabs developed a breed of strong, fairly small horses that could also withstand the harsh, dry climate. The Arabian horse, known for its speed and stamina, was developed as early as the seventh century. One notable characteristic is its short back. While most horses have twenty-four vertebrae, the Arabian horse has only twenty-three, making for greater strength.

Merchants Buying and Selling

Merchants traded many luxury products—silk, porcelain, pearls, precious stones, coral, ivory, furs, and perfume. They also bought and sold wood, iron, pewter,[4] mercury, gold, and silver. Some merchants purchased their goods with sacks full of gold and silver coins. Others used more modern forms of payment such as letters of credit and *chakk*, or checks.

Travel by Boat

How would Arab merchants ever have been able to travel to the farthest outreaches of the empire without boats? Arabs traveled frequently to Asia to trade at the ports of Vietnam and Ceylon. Some who had come to know the Orient even chose to set up shop and live in the Cantonese province of China. Large Chinese junks[5] laden with goods came to trade at the ports of the Persian Gulf.[6]

Arab navigators knew how to use the monsoon[7] winds to their advantage. On their return trip from India, they sailed with the wind lashing behind them directly toward Arabia or East Africa. Passengers and goods also traveled frequently down navigable rivers, and Arab sailors were not afraid to hoist their sails out in the great expanse of the Mediterranean Sea.

Ports, beacons, and lighthouses stretched along the coasts of the Arab world. However, despite all this protection, Indian pirates riding in swift rowboats sometimes managed to attack the Arabs' slow, heavy sailboats.

Other Arab ships equipped with large sails could transport over a thousand passengers. These large ships contained as many as a hundred sleeping compartments and were equipped with shops for snacks and refreshments, a laundry, and even a hair salon.

---

4. **pewter** (pyoo͞t′ər): metal alloy consisting mostly of tin, as well as small percentages of copper, lead, and other metals.
5. **junks** (juŋks): flat-bottomed ships with high central masts and deep rudders.
6. **Persian Gulf:** also called the Arabian Gulf; arm of the Arabian Sea between Iran and the Arabian Peninsula.
7. **monsoon** (män•soo͞n′): wind that blows from different directions according to the season, bringing heavy rains off the Indian Ocean from April to October.

Caravansaries

Caravansaries,[8] or inns designed to accommodate caravans, welcomed travelers and their goods all over the Arab world. Sometimes caravansaries were large buildings whose single entrance opened onto a courtyard with a drinking trough and a fountain. Offices, guard posts, stables, and shops were located around the courtyard on the first floor. Communal sleeping rooms were located on the first floor. Large caravansaries served as wholesale markets where retailers and shop owners came to purchase their wares.

© Keren Su/CORBIS

communal (kə•myōōn′əl): shared by all; belonging to the community.

Often there was a mosque[9] in these large complexes, and attached to the mosque was a *hamman*, or bathhouse. Public baths were popular among Muslims for ceremonial ablutions[10] and health reasons as well as for fun. Steam rose from a jet of hot water that was piped up into a basin in the central, domed room of the hamman. In the cooler, outer rooms, people relaxed with drinks and chatter.

---

 8. **caravansaries** (kar′ə•van′sə•rēz).
 9. **mosque** (mäsk): Muslim house of worship.
10. **ablutions** (ab•lōō′shənz): washing the body.

> ✓ **Reading Check**

1. Why were the Bedouins such excellent guides?

2. What arrangements did people in caravans make to protect themselves from attack?

3. What forms of payment could Arab merchants use for their purchases?

4. Where did Arab merchants travel by boat to trade their goods? What was one of the dangers they faced?

5. What services were provided at caravansaries?

The Islamic love of learning and art found a rich field for growth in the sunshine and mild climate of Cordoba, Spain. The following article describes this glorious center of Islamic culture that drew artists, tradespeople, and royalty from all over western Europe.

Cordoba—Jewel of the World

from *Calliope*

by DIANA CHILDRESS

Mezquita (Great Mosque) Cordoba, Spain/Index/Bridgeman Art Library

▲ Interior of the Great Mosque of Cordoba.

"**D**o not talk of the court of Baghdad and its glittering magnificence; do not praise Persia and China and their manifold[1] advantages; for there is no spot on earth like Cordoba."

The author of this passage was not just trying to make his hometown sound good, for at this time approximately one thousand years ago, his city of Cordoba was the capital of Islamic Spain and ranked among the major cities of the world.

Arab emirs[2] had chosen Cordoba as their capital early in the eighth century A.D. Already a metropolis centuries before, Cordoba and its surroundings offered many advantages for urban growth: a central location, a navigable river, mountains rich in minerals, and broad farmlands.

Under Islamic rule, the city soon grew large enough to need a larger mosque to accommodate the many Muslim

You Need to Know...

The part of modern-day Spain that is bounded by the Mediterranean Sea and the Atlantic Ocean has a long and exciting history. Colonized around the ninth century B.C., it was conquered by the Romans and flourished under Roman rule. Germanic tribes called Vandals and Visigoths later invaded. They were ruling this region when the Arabs arrived from Africa in A.D. 711. The Arabs called the area Al-Andalus, which probably meant "country of the Vandals." Today, southern Spain, where Cordoba is located, is called Andalusia.

metropolis (mə·träp′ə·lis): large center of population.

1. **manifold** (man′ə·fōld): of many parts.
2. **emirs** (e·mirz′): rulers, princes, or commanders.

worshippers. In 785, the emir of al-Andalus, Abd al-Rahman I, began building the Great Mosque for which Cordoba is still famous today.

Recycling columns from ancient ruins in the area, the architect built a magnificent grove of multi-hued pillars of marble and jasper. Two tiers of arches, one horseshoe-shaped, the other a half circle, added height to the columns. The red and white stones of the arches reached up and out like rays of the sun.

During the next two centuries, as the Muslim community grew, the Great Mosque was expanded several times. The forest of columns and arches spread, made more beautiful by new styles of ornamentation. In the tenth century, Cordoba's caliph (ruler) brought a craftsman from Constantinople (modern-day Istanbul) to teach local artisans how to decorate the *mihrab* ("prayer niche") with glittering gold, blue, and red mosaics.

By 988, the Great Mosque was enormous. Its vast roof rested on twelve hundred and ninety-three pillars. A staff of three hundred kept ten thousand oil lamps lighted in its dim interior.

Around the mosque, Cordoba prospered. Wide paved streets, lighted at night with torches, led from the seven city gates into the central marketplace. Pack animals brought grain, wheat, olive oil, dried fruits, silk, iron, silver, lead, and mercury from the surrounding countryside.

Narrower alleyways twisted off to the workshops of weavers, tailors, cobblers, jewelers, saddle-makers, and bookbinders. Toward the outskirts of town, grain mills, tanneries, glassworks, and pottery factories hummed with activity.

Tooled leather goods, silk fabrics, and other Cordoban wares traveled by boat down river to the Atlantic Ocean or by donkey and mule trains to the Mediterranean seaport

Bridgeman Art Library, New York/London

▲ Decoration above a doorway on an extension added to the Great Mosque in 961–966. **?** **Why was it necessary to expand the Great Mosque after it was first built?**

artisans (ärt′ə•zenz): workers skilled in a particular trade or art.

mosaics (mō•zā′iks): images or patterns made from small pieces of colored stone, tile, or glass set in mortar.

(top) *The Granger Collection, New York;* (center) *Instituto Municipal de Historia, Barcelona/Bridgeman Art Library, New York/London;* (bottom) © *Archivo Iconografico, S.A./CORBIS*

▲ Islamic coins called *dinars*.

The Art of the Arabesque

In many holy books, pictures of characters and events illustrate religious stories. Islamic art, however, is known for its absence of human figures. Muslims believe that a person who draws a living being is trying to be like God, the original creator of all life. Instead, Islamic art developed an abstract decoration that Europeans called the arabesque. This style uses a winding, twining geometric pattern that can continue in any direction. Arabesques could be used in many ways. They decorate copies of the Koran, as well as Islamic buildings such as the Great Mosque of Cordoba.

textiles (teks′tilz): woven fabrics.

conservative (kən·sur′və·tiv): wanting to keep things as they have been; against change; traditional.

of Almeria. Ships transported Andalusian products across the sea to North Africa, Europe, and the Middle East.

In exchange came gold and ivory from Africa, slaves from eastern Europe, and spices, dyes, rare woods, and fine cotton textiles from the East. To facilitate[3] trade, Cordoba's rulers minted silver *dirhems* and gold *dinars*. A market inspector supervised prices and controlled quality, and each artisan group chose a representative to settle disputes. Traveling merchants rested at caravanserais, or inns, which also provided warehouse space and stables.

The rulers spent their riches copying the luxurious lives of their rivals, the caliphs in Baghdad. They built elegant country palaces with extensive gardens where fruit trees, jasmine, and roses perfumed the air. In the ninth century, Abd al-Rahman II kept a splendid court, overseen by the musician Ziryab, who brought all the latest fashions in music, clothing, table manners, and hairstyles from Baghdad. Abd al-Rahman II also collected books, developing a valuable library of science and literature.

During the tenth century, Cordoba was the cultural center of Islam. Scholars from Europe, Africa, and Asia flocked to the courts of the Ottoman caliphs. Philosophy, astronomy, mathematics, alchemy (an early form of chemistry), geography, and history flourished. Christian kings and wealthy people from all over western Europe came to the capital for medical treatment, for Cordoban physicians excelled in their knowledge of herbs, drugs, and surgery.

Women also took part in the cultural and intellectual life of tenth-century al-Andalus as singers, writers, librarians, booksellers, and copyists. Even the poor could learn to read in free schools paid for by the caliph.

After Islamic Spain broke up into many small kingdoms in the eleventh century, Cordoba remained a major center of learning, home to, among others, the famed geographer al-Idrisi and the philosopher Ibn Rushd. But the days of glory were over. Conservative religious leaders discouraged scientific and philosophical exploration. Soon warfare and political instability took their toll.

3. facilitate (fə·sil′ə·tāt′): make easier; help.

"Weep for the splendor of Cordoba," wrote an eleventh-century poet, *"for disaster has overtaken her. . . . She was at the height of her beauty; life was gracious and sweet until all was overthrown."*

The learning of Islamic Spain, however, continued. Books from the caliphs' libraries preserved Greek philosophy and science in Arabic translation, which Christian scholars discovered as the Crusades and the Christian reconquest of Spain brought Europeans into closer contact with the Muslim world. Islamic technology and experimental science stimulated Renaissance thinkers to new theories and scientific advances. Muslim maps helped European explorers to discover "new" lands. Thus the cultural wealth of Cordoba forged a valuable link between earlier civilizations and what was to become "European" or "Western" civilization.

Giraudon/Art Resource, NY

▲ This ivory box from Cordoba was carved during the city's golden age in the tenth century.

✔ Reading Check

1. Why was Cordoba a good location for a capital city?

2. Where did the architect obtain the columns used to build the Great Mosque?

3. What new style of decoration was used in the Great Mosque? How did craftspeople learn this new technique?

4. What conditions encouraged trade in Cordoba?

5. How was the learning of Islamic Spain passed on to Christian scholars?

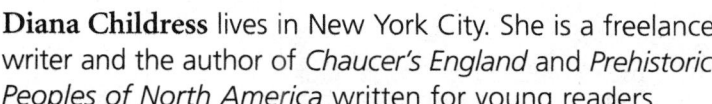

MEET THE *Writer*

Diana Childress lives in New York City. She is a freelance writer and the author of *Chaucer's England* and *Prehistoric Peoples of North America* written for young readers.

If an Islamic scholar could travel through time from the Middle Ages, he would probably be quite comfortable working problems from today's algebra textbooks! Read on to discover how the kinds of mathematics we use today were developed and refined by the early Islamic math whizzes.

from **The Magic of Mathematics**

from *Science in Early Islamic Culture*

by GEORGE BESHORE

A Major Mathematician

Although Severus Sebokht[1] wrote about the Indian numbers in the seventh century A.D., it took another two hundred years for this system to be accepted by the Islamic world. When the numerals from India became popular in the Moslem world during the ninth century, they were being enthusiastically praised by one of the greatest Moslem mathematicians. This was a person named Al-Khwarizmi (780–850), who was a giant of Islamic mathematics. His Latin name, Algorithmi,[2] is today associated with any system of arithmetic based on the use of decimals.

You Need to Know...

The great leader of Islam, Mohammed, taught that "He who travels in search of knowledge travels along Allah's path to paradise." Following Mohammed's teachings, Islamic scholars collected scientific information from conquered lands. They learned medicine and mathematics from Greece and Egypt, astronomy from Persia and India, and engineering from Egypt. They also discovered unusual-looking numerals that had been borrowed from India and would come to be known as Arabic numerals. These nine symbols were much simpler to use than the Roman numbering system, and they helped Islamic mathematicians make great advances in their search for knowledge.

decimals (des'ə·məlz): fractions with unwritten denominators of ten, which is indicated by a decimal point before the numbers.

---

1. **Severus Sebokht:** Christian bishop of seventh-century Syria.
2. **Algorithmi:** the origin of the word *algorithm* (al'gə·rith'əm). Algorithms are used in writing computer programs.

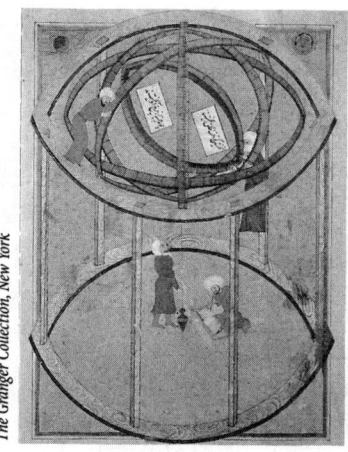

▲ The armillary sphere was a device that gave astronomers the position of an object in numerals. This illustration from a medieval manuscript shows a giant sphere with Moslem astronomers at work.

Al-Khwarizmi was born in an area called Khwarizm that lay east of the Caspian Sea. He used his place of birth in his name as was the custom at that time in the Islamic world. In Baghdad, an important center of Islamic learning, Al-Khwarizmi wrote glowing accounts of the numbers from India and encouraged their use in all <u>calculations</u>. His books include one titled *Al-Khwarizmi on the Numerals of the Indians* that did much to extend the use of these symbols throughout the Western world.

Al-Khwarizmi developed algebra as it is known today, refining the process from older forms used by the Greeks and Egyptians. He also introduced the name into the language, writing about *al-jabr*. This is an Arabic word that means "restitution."[3] In algebra a mathematician substitutes symbols, such as *x*, *y*, or *z*, for numbers in order to solve certain types of problems.

Algebra is a process used when some information is known about a problem and other things are not. The letters are used for the unknown parts, which are set up in relationship to the things that are known. Such relationships, called equations, are then solved to supply the unknown information.

calculations (kal′kyoo·lā′shənz): acts or processes of figuring or computing, usually with numbers, as in addition or subtraction.

▲ An astrolabe, similar to this, and a compass were the main instruments used by Islamic navigators to guide ships. An astrolabe uses the sun to determine a ship's position.

Trigonometry

Moslem mathematicians also improved upon older methods used when working with angles and triangles. The branch of mathematics dealing with angles and triangles,

---

3. restitution (res′tə·too′shən): act of giving back something that has been taken away.

▲ Islamic scholars were given the task of measuring the earth. **❷ Why were their attempts unsuccessful?**

ratios (rā'shōz): comparisons of two numbers by division; for example, a ratio of one to two is one divided by two, or one half.

compute (kəm·pyo͞ot'): to use arithmetic to find a number or amount; to work out an answer to a math problem.

called trigonometry, is extremely important to surveyors[4] and astronomers in their measurements of the space between objects on earth or in the skies.

Al-Khwarizmi did some of this work, but the major contributions came from another scholar, Al-Battani (850–929). Born the same year that Al-Khwarizmi died, Al-Battani became famous as one of the leading astronomers and mathematicians of Islam. He constructed tables giving the ratios between the sides of any right triangle (one containing an angle of 90 degrees). When two angles and the side between them are known, the remaining angle and the unknown sides of a right triangle can be found. This is also true if two sides and the angle between them are known.

Surveyors use trigonometry to figure out how far it is across a river or a swamp where an actual measurement is impossible. They do this by sighting an object (such as a tree or rock) on the other side. Then they turn at a right angle and measure a distance along their side of the river or swamp. Finally, they take a second sighting of the object and measure the second angle. This gives them the two angles of the triangle they have created plus the length of the one side they have measured. Using trigonometry tables first calculated by Al-Battani and other Islamic mathematicians, modern surveyors can compute the unknown side of the triangle. This tells them how far it is across the river or swamp to the object they sighted on the other side.

Mission: Measure the Earth

The size and shape of the earth had fascinated scientists since ancient times. Although most ordinary people thought the earth was flat, careful observers noticed things that led them to believe the earth was round. For example,

4. **surveyors** (sər·vā'ərz): people who map the location or boundaries of a section of land.

some looked at the earth's shadow on the moon during an eclipse[5] and saw that it was curved. Others noticed that they could see a ship's sails as it approached port before the hull[6] appeared, indicating that the ship was sailing on a curved sea.

In the third century B.C. a Greek mathematician named Eratosthenes measured the angle of the sun from two different places along the Nile River. From these observations he concluded that the earth was round. He then calculated the distance around the earth (the circumference) at about 24,600 miles (39,400 km)—extremely close to the 24,900 miles (39,800 km) that scientists accept today.

Over a century later, around 100 B.C., another Greek astronomer, named Posidonius of Apamea, repeated Eratosthenes' work. Even though he used the same method, Posidonius reached a different conclusion. He thought the earth was only about 18,000 miles (29,000 km) in circumference.

This smaller figure was used by a Greek astronomer and geographer named Ptolemy, who lived in Alexandria[7] in the second century A.D. Ptolemy went on to develop many maps using the 18,000-mile figure, so it became much better known than the more accurate figure calculated by Eratosthenes.

Accounts of these attempts to measure the earth were collected by Islamic scholars, who sought out all of the old scientific manuscripts they could find. These were taken to Baghdad, where in 830 a Moslem ruler named Al-Ma'mun built a huge center of learning called the House of Wisdom. Soon after he founded this center, Al-Ma'mun assigned the scholars there a major mission: they were to measure the size of the earth.

Following the <u>procedures</u> of Posidonius and Eratosthenes, the mathematicians at Baghdad measured the distance between two cities and found the angle of the sun

Poet and Astronomer

Today we know him for his poetry, especially the famous lines: "A Jug of Wine, a Loaf of Bread—and Thou/Beside me singing in the Wilderness." In his lifetime, though, Omar Khayyám was best known as a scientist. Born in what is now Iran around 1048, he became an important astronomer and mathematician. By royal request, Khayyám set up and directed an observatory for many years. He watched the stars and calculated the length of a year with amazing accuracy. His understanding that a year was more than 365 days long changed the calendar of the time.

procedures (prō·sē'jerz): usual methods or series of steps.

---

5. **eclipse** (i·klips'): a blocking from view of one celestial body by another, such as when the moon comes between the sun and the earth.
6. **hull:** main body of a ship, the lower part of which is usually in the water.
7. **Alexandria:** Mediterranean port city and cultural center in northern Egypt, founded by Alexander the Great.

from each of them. The Moslem scientists used correct procedures, but their actual measurements were flawed. As a result, they arrived at a figure of 20,400 miles (32,600 km) for the distance around the globe. This seemed to confirm the figure used by Ptolemy, so this mistaken belief that the world was only about 20,000 miles (32,000 km) in circumference was passed on to future generations.

Moslem scientists continued to search through the ancient manuscripts coming into Baghdad from the many countries that the Moslems conquered. From these they learned more and more about older scientific views of the world in which they lived.

✓ Reading Check

1. What types of mathematical problems can be solved using algebra?

2. Why is trigonometry important to surveyors and astronomers? How do they use this type of mathematics in their work?

3. What important information did Eratosthenes and Posidonius discover? Whose calculations were more accurate?

4. Why were more people familiar with Posidonius's calculation of the earth's circumference than with Eratosthenes'?

5. Why did Islamic scholars carefully collect ancient manuscripts that described attempts to measure the size of the earth?

MEET THE *Writer*

George Beshore, a world traveler and photographer, has been explaining science and technology for over thirty years in newspaper and magazine articles, books, and movie scripts.

Like Jews and Christians, Muslims—the followers of Islam—believe in one God and respect traditions that date from the time of the Hebrew Bible. Read on to discover how the Islamic religion got its start.

The Coming of Islam

from *The Royal Kingdoms of Ghana, Mali, and Songhay: Life in Medieval Africa*

by PATRICIA and FREDRICK McKISSACK

La ilaha illa Allah; Muhammad rasul Allah.
There is no God but Allah and Muhammad is his prophet.

revelation (rev'ə•lā'shən): a revealing or understanding of something not known before.

In A.D. 610–11, a man named Muhammad had a revelation that led to the formation of one of the world's great religions: *Islam*, which means "submission."

He went to Mecca, where he spread the message of God and wrote the Koran as it was revealed to him. Unlike the Christian Bible or the Jewish Torah, which were written by different people during various historical periods, the Koran—the sacred scriptures of Islam—was written by Muhammad during the twenty-two years of his prophethood.[1]

During his life Muhammad taught that Allah was the one and only God of all the universe; all believers—known as *Muslims—*

> ## You Need to Know...
> In the sandy hills surrounding the city of Mecca, a successful merchant named Muhammad often escaped to a nearby cave to sit and think. There, he said, he received a message from the angel Gabriel: "There is no God but Allah, and Muhammad is his prophet." Muhammad continued to receive such messages throughout his life, and he eventually gained many followers. His followers were called Muslims, meaning "those who have surrendered" to God's will.
>
> Perhaps Muhammad's most influential teaching was his urgent message to his followers to spread the Islamic religion. In the eighth and ninth centuries, Islam reached North Africa and Europe, bringing with it new trade, new knowledge, and new beliefs.

sacred (sā'krid): holy; from or belonging to a god or religion.

---

1. prophethood (präf'it•hood): the state or situation of being a person who speaks for God.

destiny (des′tə·nē): fate; events that are certain to occur.

obligations (äb′li·gā′shənz): duties.

testify (tes′tə·fī′): to declare; bear witness.

were equal before God, and the rich had to share their wealth with the poor, for on the final judgment day, all people would be judged equally before God. Human destiny was in God's hands and everything was predetermined[2] by Allah. Neither men nor women could escape their fates.

Those teachings have been expressed in the five "pillars," or obligations, of Islam—prayer; the giving of alms;[3] fasting during the holy month of Ramadan; pilgrimage to Mecca, the holy city of the Muslims; and the most important one, faith. Any person choosing to be a Muslim has only to repeat these words in front of another Muslim: "I testify that there is no god but Allah, and Muhammad

---

2. **predetermined** (prē′dē·tʉr′mənd): decided in advance; decreed.
3. **alms** (ämz): charity; money or food given to poor people.

SIDELIGHT

Muslims believe that Muhammad directly received God's word, then recited the messages, which were compiled into the 114 chapters of the Koran. Muslims believe that the Koran—which means "recitation"—cannot be translated without losing some of its meaning. Thus, it is the book most read in its original language. Here is the opening chapter, or Surah, called "The Exordium."

IN THE NAME OF ALLAH
THE COMPASSIONATE
THE MERCIFUL
Praise be to Allah, Lord of the Creation,
The Compassionate, the Merciful,
King of Judgment-day!
You alone we worship, and to You alone
we pray for help.
Guide us to the straight path
The path of those whom You have favored,
Not of those who have incurred Your wrath,
Nor of those who have gone astray."

— from The Koran,
translated by N. J. Dawood

The Granger Collection, New York

▲ This medieval Islamic illustration shows Muhammad meeting the angel Gabriel.

is his prophet." Recited in Arabic, this phrase is called the *shahada* and it sounds like a song, so much so that in times of joy or sadness it is very often chanted by believers.

The Muslims have always believed it is their duty to take Islam into every part of the world. The new religion grew quickly though *jihads* (holy wars), trade, and cultural exchange. North Africa—Algeria, Tunisia, and Morocco—was taken by Arabian conquests between 639 and 708. For centuries North Africa had been the battlefield of conflicting ideas. Now North Africa was a political, economic, and military stronghold, unifying, for the first time, people who had long been divided. Eventually Arabic would be the common language of ninety million people, and Islam would be practiced in such varied places as Spain, Persia, Turkey, Egypt, East and West Africa, and India.

Interest in the Western Sudan grew when the sultans of Arabia heard traders' stories about the gold-rich country south of the Sahara. The Arabs wanted very much to add West Africa's wealth to the ever-expanding Arab-Islamic empire, as well as to add believers to the Islamic world. But to launch a jihad against Ghana[4] would not have been practical. Ghana was too far away and protected by an enormous desert.

Over time, though, Islam reached Ghana anyway. This happened in the same way as missionaries, fur trappers, and traders spread across the American west, bringing a new religion and a new economy with them.

Islam has no organized priesthood, but educated religious teachers and professionals were and are important and powerful people. As a group they are called the *ulama* (the learned), and their opinions still play a large role in places where Islam is practiced.

The first contact Ghana had with Islam was through merchants and travelers. The ulama, in turn, introduced the Soninke[5] to Arabic, their first written language.

---

4. **Ghana** (gä′nə): medieval kingdom in West Africa.
5. **Soninke** (sän′iŋ‧kā): group of people located in Senegal who founded the ancient kingdom of Ghana.

Sacred Stone

At the center of a faithful Muslim's pilgrimage to Mecca is a towering black monument shaped like a cube. This is the Ka'aba, which houses the Black Stone—one of the most sacred treasures of the Islamic faith. The Black Stone is said to have fallen from heaven. Some scientists believe the stone is probably a meteorite. For thousands of years, Arabs visited the Ka'aba to worship statues of gods housed there and kiss the black stone from heaven. Today, Muslims all over the world face in the direction of the Ka'aba to recite their daily prayers.

Although they came to win converts,[6] these scholars also wrote profusely[7] about their experiences. It is from these early writings that we get a glimmer of what old Ghana was like.

Islam reached old Ghana. But the Ghanaian king and a majority of his subjects remained loyal to their traditional African religions. This disturbed the more devout Muslims, who would later use religion as a reason to attack the kingdom. But for a time, the Ghanaian kings allowed Muslims—and any other group—to work, teach, and build their institutions within their empire.

---

6. **converts:** people who have joined a religion instead of growing up in that religion.
7. **profusely** (prō·fyōōs'lē): generously; abundantly.

Reading Check

1. How is the Koran different from the Bible or the Torah?

2. List the five "pillars" of Islam. Which one is considered most important?

3. How did the new Islamic religion spread throughout the world?

4. How did Islam reach West Africa? What protected Ghana from an Islamic holy war?

5. What writings provide a record of life in old Ghana?

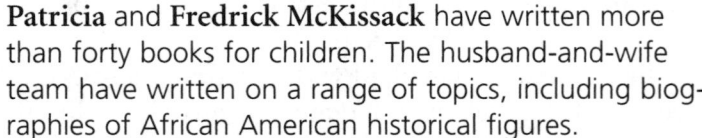

MEET THE *Writers*

Patricia and **Fredrick McKissack** have written more than forty books for children. The husband-and-wife team have written on a range of topics, including biographies of African American historical figures.

Today, when presidents or royalty decide to make a visit, they usually travel in style, take a lot of people with them, and attract big crowds. Still, it would be hard to match the dazzling display of wealth in the year 1324 when a certain African ruler traveled abroad to fulfill a religious duty. Read on to relive the incredible journey of Mansa Musa!

from Mali: Empire of the Mandingoes

from *A Glorious Age in Africa: The Story of Three Great African Empires*

by DANIEL CHU and ELLIOTT SKINNER

Unlike the pagan[1] empire of Ghana, the new empire of Mali was founded on the Moslem faith. After Sundiata, the rulers of the empire took the proud title of Mansa, which means emperor or sultan.

Sundiata had several sons (the exact number is not known), and one of them named Wali succeeded him to the throne. Mansa Wali was known as "the Red King" because his skin was said to have had a copperish tone to it. He was not as spectacular as his father, but he took his job seriously and worked conscientiously[2] to expand the Malian Empire both eastward and westward.

You Need to Know...

For three hundred years, from about 1200 to 1500, Mali was the second-largest empire in the world and one of the wealthiest. Sundiata, the leader of the Mandingo people, built the empire of Mali from the ruins of the empire of Ghana. At its height, Mali equaled the size of Western Europe. An Egyptian who lived in Mali described it as "four months of travel long and four months wide." The empire bordered deserts, jungles, and ocean. The riches provided by Mali's gold, salt, and copper made its rulers the richest men in the world and famous far beyond Africa.

---

1. **pagan** (pā'gən): person not following any of the world's major religions.
2. **conscientiously** (kän'shē·en'shəs·lē): doing something carefully and honestly.

▲ This Malian headdress was
worn for special ceremonies.
**❓ What animal do you think
it represents?**

Mansa Wali began the tradition among the ruling Keita
clan of being very religious. He made a *hajj,* a holy
pilgrimage to the Moslem capital at Mecca on the Arabian
peninsula.[3] In this way Wali sought to establish broader
contact between his empire in the Sudan and a world
across the Sahara.

Mansa Wali ruled from 1255 to 1270. On his death he
was succeeded by another of Sundiata's sons, Mansa
Karifa. Karifa became insane and amused himself by
shooting arrows at his subjects!

Mali fell upon sad times. After Karifa, a long period of
struggle for power saw a series of rulers of average talent
take the throne of Mali. For a time it appeared that the
empire founded by Sundiata might never fulfill its great
promise.

But once again, when Mali was in desperate need of
strong leadership, the right man came onto the scene at
the right time. His name was Musa. As Mansa Musa I, he
became the most famous ruler in the history of the western
Sudan.

The Fabulous Hajj

Musa came to the throne of Mali in 1307. He was a grandson
of one of Sundiata's sisters. Because his mother's
name was Kongo, he is often referred to as Kongo Musa,
which means "Moses, son of Kongo." (Musa is the Arabic
version of the name Moses.)

He ruled the empire of Mali for twenty-five years. In
that quarter of a century the fame of Mali spread across
the Sahara to the Middle East, and across the Mediterranean
Sea to Europe. Mansa Musa's name was known
throughout the world.

Mansa Musa's achievements were many. He extended
the boundaries of Mali by diplomacy and war. He promoted
trade and commerce. He encouraged the spread of
learning. He was a lover of the arts (designs, architecture,
literature). Above all Mansa Musa was devoutly religious.

---

3. **Arabian peninsula:** the large peninsula between Africa and the Red Sea to the
   west and the Persian Gulf and Iran to the east.

Several of the Moslem rulers of Mali, starting with Mansa Wali, had made pilgrimages to Mecca, the holy city of Islam. The hajj, as these pilgrimages are called, is one of the five basic observances[4] of the Islamic faith. If it is possible, every believer in Islam should make this journey to the holy city at least once in his lifetime.

Mansa Musa made his hajj in 1324, in the seventeenth year of his reign. The fact that he made the pilgrimage was not unusual. But the way he made it was.

For Mansa Musa's hajj was one of the grandest grand tours[5] ever recorded. The spectacular wealth displayed by his entourage[6] so dazzled the people on his line of march that their descendants still talked about it one hundred years after it occurred.

As the ruler of the richest empire in West Africa, possibly in the world, at that time, Mansa Musa could easily afford the expenses involved. Even so, it was a hard journey. Arabia, where Mecca is located, was thousands of miles from Musa's capital city, Niani. His caravan would be traveling across some of the most barren wastelands on earth.

Mansa Musa's hajj was one of the grandest grand tours ever recorded.

Months before the journey, the Mansa's officials and servants went through the empire to collect the necessary food and supplies for the trip. To make sure that the Mansa would have plenty of money, they assembled some 80 to 100 camel-loads of gold dust, each load weighing about 300 pounds.

By the time the caravan was finally assembled, it had become possibly the biggest moving crowd that Africa had ever seen. Mansa Musa was accompanied by thousands of

---

4. **observances:** customary acts or ceremonies.
5. **grand tours:** trips taken by wealthy young men to complete their education.
6. **entourage** (än′too•räzh′): large group of advisors and aides that travels with an important person.

descendants (dē•sen′dənts): offspring; children and their children.

Timbuktu U.

The great city of Timbuktu in Mali was founded in 1100 near the Niger River on a major trade route. By the mid-1400s, Timbuktu had become a world center, with a world-class university. Traders, scholars, and travelers from far and wide visited the city. About one hundred thousand people lived there—and a fourth of them were scholars. Many of Mali's kings prized learning as much as wealth, and libraries flourished. In 1591, however, forces from the nearby country of Morocco captured Timbuktu. With many of its scholars arrested, exiled, or killed, the city and its university went into decline.

followers. Some sources say that the caravan consisted of 60,000 people!

Included in the entourage were many members of Mansa Musa's family, his close friends, doctors, and teachers, and the most important of the local chiefs of his empire. The Mansa took these chiefs along not only to honor them but to keep them from interfering with his son, whom the Mansa had left behind to rule the empire while he was away.

Mansa Musa's glittering caravan entered Cairo, Egypt, in July 1324, and he was an immediate sensation. The Sultan of Cairo honored the distinguished visitor from the western Sudan with <u>elaborate</u> ceremonies. He spared nothing to make the visitors comfortable. The Sultan even went to the trouble of making preparations for the remainder of the Mansa's journey to Arabia, so that he would be honored and his caravan kept supplied wherever they went.

Mansa Musa's generosity was probably as impressive as his religious faith. He freely gave gifts in the holy cities of Mecca and Medina, and he also gave generously to all

elaborate (ē·lab′ə·rit): having many parts or details.

SIDELIGHT

"The Sultan [Mansa Musa] holds court in his palace on a great balcony called *bembe* where he has a great seat of ebony that is like a throne fit for a large and tall person. On either side it is flanked by elephant tusks turned towards each other. His arms stand near him, being all of gold, saber, lance, quiver, bow and arrows. He wears wide trousers made of about twenty pieces [of material] of a kind which he alone may wear. Behind him there stand about a score of Turkish or other pages bought for him in Cairo. One of them, at his left, holds a silk umbrella surmounted by a dome and a bird of gold: the bird has the figure of a falcon. His officers are seated in a circle about him, in two rows, one to the right and one to the left; beyond them sit the chief commanders of his cavalry. In front of him there is a person who never leaves him, who is his official executioner. . . ."

—Ibn Fadl Allah al-Omari, Arab scholar (1324)
   in *Great Civilizations of Ancient Africa*
   by Lester Brooks

those who performed some service for him. On his return trip from Arabia to Mali, Mansa Musa passed through Egypt once more and reportedly "spread the waves of his generosity all over Cairo. There was no one, officer of the court or holder of any official job, who did not receive a sum of gold from him." Indeed, the Mansa was so free with his gifts that two embarrassing things happened.

First, he ran out of money. Even 80 to 100 camel-loads of gold were not enough to keep up with his generous ways. He was forced to borrow from the leading merchants of Cairo. They didn't hesitate to lend money to him because the Mansa was obviously a good credit risk.

And second, the Mansa put so much gold into circulation that he almost ruined the Cairo gold market. Suddenly gold was not so scarce in Egypt anymore and its price fell sharply. A writer in the service of the Egyptian sultan reported that the Cairo gold market had still not fully recovered from Mansa Musa's visit twelve years after the Musa's hajj.

Wolfgang Kaehler Photography

▲ This mosque in Djenne, Mali, is the largest mosque built with adobe, a type of clay.

✓ Reading Check

1. For how long did Mansa Musa rule Mali?

2. Name at least three of Musa's accomplishments as a leader.

3. Why did Musa make a pilgrimage to Mecca?

4. List at least three details of Musa's great pilgrimage.

5. What two things went wrong with Musa's return trip from Arabia to Mali?

These days, who would think of starting a band without a set of drums? Drums might just be the most universal instrument. Nearly every culture throughout time has created its own drums. Archaeologists have even discovered a drum used in 6000 B.C.! Drums come in many different shapes and sizes—and, as it turns out, with different voices, too. Read on to find out how the drums of certain African cultures can "talk"—in drum language, of course.

Talking Drums and Talking Gongs
from *Faces*

by ENID SCHILDKROUT

© James Marshall/CORBIS

▲ Asante drums.

When Europeans first went to Africa, they were amazed to discover the existence of what they called a bush telegraph—drums that could send messages over long distances. Wherever they went, they discovered that the Africans were expecting them. The talking drums, as the Europeans called them, could send messages as important as a call to battle, a birth, or a death or as trivial[1] as a request to bring [merchandise] to the next village.

Talking drums are found in many parts of Africa. Though made in several different ways, all have two tones, one high and one low. A drum consists of a membrane, or skin, stretched over a resonator[2] (a hollow form that intensifies sound) made of wood, pottery, metal, or some other material. The membrane can be struck forcefully or gently, but it has only one tone. To produce two tones, the African drummer must have either two drums or a drum with two skins. Both these methods are used in West

---

1. **trivial** (triv′ē•əl): unimportant; minor.
2. **resonator** (rez′ə•nāt′ər).

Africa. People in Zaire, in central Africa, use several other instruments, such as gongs, whistles, horns, and even human voices, to send two-tone messages over long distances.

In Ghana, West Africa, the Asante have two kinds of drums. One, the hourglass drum, or *fontomfrom*, is commonly used in other parts of West Africa as well. This drum has two skins, one at each end of its hourglass-shaped[3] resonator. Leather thongs[4] join the two goatskin membranes that cover the ends, and the drummer tightens and loosens the thongs as he squeezes the drum under his arm (most African drummers are men, although there are some women drummers in northern Nigeria). The Yoruba of Nigeria call these drums *dundun* drums and make them in different sizes; the biggest one is called the mother drum. Some also have bells around the drumhead that jingle when the drum is played.

The other type of talking drum used by the Asante is the *ntumpane*. This large drum has a membrane covering only one end. This type of drum comes in pairs, referred to as husband and wife. The two drums are set at different tones; the drum with the lower tone is the husband.

Constructing an Asante *ntumpane* drum involves making sacrifices and praying to the spirit of the tree that provides the wood. Only chiefs can own these special drums, and they give the drum makers gifts . . . when they order new drums. Before he cuts down a tree, the drum maker—who is not a drummer—must soothe the spirit of the tree by throwing an egg against the trunk while he asks for the tree's forgiveness. When the drum is finished and the skin of a female elephant ear has been stretched

> ## You Need to Know...
> For centuries, West Africans have used drums to send news, tell stories, narrate religious ceremonies, and accompany dances. African drumming is very different from the drum music created elsewhere in the world. Western music uses a simple drum rhythm. The rhythms of African drumming, on the other hand, are as complicated as any spoken language and take years to learn. It is no wonder that talented drummers are considered great artists in Africa.

© James Marshall/CORBIS

▲ Ghanian *djembe* drum.

---

3. hourglass-shaped: two chambers connected by a narrow opening.
4. thongs: strings or straps.

"Ear" Witnesses

Drumming has been used in Africa to send messages to villages that were miles apart. According to eye—or ear—witnesses, drums could be heard many miles away. Drummers in one village would pick up their drums and repeat the message to the next village. Sending a message across large distances did not take as long as you might think. In 1899, British traveler A. B. Lloyd commented, "I was told that from one village to another, a distance of over 100 miles, a message could be sent in less than two hours, and I quite believe it possible for it to be done in much less time."

emphasis (em'fə•sis): special stress given to make something stand out.

over the top, it is given to the drummer, who also must break an egg on the carved "eye" of the drum to bless it and make it safe for him to beat.

Many rules govern the Asante drummers. An *ntumpane* drummer must never carry his own drums; women should not touch these drums; a drummer should not teach his own son the art of drumming; and the drummer must always walk behind the chief.

In Zaire, the instruments most often used to send messages over many miles are wooden gongs carved from a single piece of wood. A gong can be as small as a fireplace log or as large as a fireplace. Sometimes it has carvings of animals at each end. To achieve the two-tone effect, the carver first makes a slit in the center of the log. He then scrapes out the inside of the gong so that one side of the instrument is thicker than the other, thus producing a different tone. As with the Asante husband and wife drums, the thicker, lower-tone side usually is referred to as the male and the thinner, higher-tone side as the female. Sometimes the side whose sound carries farthest is referred to as the male.

To understand how these two-tone drums can talk, you must recognize that many African languages are tonal. In this type of language, the relative tone of a word—high or low—determines its meaning. In English, we use tone for emphasis—for example, to indicate whether we are making a statement or asking a question. Try saying "You like spinach." Then say, "You like spinach?" In the statement, the "spinach" tones go from high to low, while in the question, the "spinach" tones go from low to high. In either case, however, "spinach" means spinach. In many African languages, tones are much more important. In Lokele, a language of Zaire, *liAla* means fiancée, but *liala* means rubbish heap. The word for copper, *bosongo*, also can mean river current or pestle,[5] depending on which syllables are high and which are low. As one writer pointed out, if a man says *aSOoLAMBA bolli* instead of

---

5. **pestle** (pes'əl): short, stubby tool used to mash or grind something in a bowl called a mortar.

▲ Musicians from the Sahara use a variety of instruments. ❓ **For what village events might these musicians be performing?**

aSOolaMBA bolli in Lokele, he is saying that he is boiling his mother-in-law rather than watching the riverbank!

Since drums have only tone and volume as <u>variables</u>, they cannot produce word-for-word imitations of speech. Rather, drummers know certain set phrases, and as long as the listeners know the same language, they will be able to recognize the phrases. It takes about eight times as many syllables to say something in drum language as it does in speech, since in speech we can <u>convey</u> our meaning with other sound elements besides tone. "Spinach" and "spinning" sound different, for example, because of the different combinations of vowels and consonants.

While a drummer could imitate just about any sentence in drum language, certain subjects are part of his special <u>repertoire</u>. These usually consist of the praise names of chiefs, notices of approaching danger such as enemies or fire, the history of towns or villages, the death of a noted individual, the approach of a stranger, or, in the old days, a summons to take up arms in war. The Dagomba drummers of northern Ghana and the Yoruba "hourglass"

variables (ver′ē·ə·bəlz): things that can change.

convey (kən·vā′): make known; communicate.

repertoire (rep′ər·twär′): group of songs or musical pieces ready to be performed.

drummers recite long histories of the ancestors of chiefs. They follow the chiefs in processions and sing their praises. When people get married or name a new baby, the drummers sing the family's praises. In Zaire, drummers and villages have special gong names that identify them and commemorate great events in their history, such as the founding of the village or a victory in battle.

It is sad that as telephones and modern communications spread throughout the world, this great art—an ancient telegraph system—might be forgotten. For the moment, however, talking drums and talking gongs can still be heard beating in Africa wherever tonal languages are found.

✓ Reading Check

1. What kinds of messages are sent by talking drums?

2. Describe one type of drum used by the Asante.

3. The writer lists some of the rules that Asante drummers must follow. List two of these rules.

4. Why does a drummer take more than eight times more syllables to say something in drum language than in speech?

5. Why does the author think the art of drumming is threatened in the modern world? What do you think keeps drumming alive?

Cross-Curricular ACTIVITIES

■ SCIENCE/MUSIC/SPEECH

The Science of Drumming The drummers of West Africa are able to produce amazing sounds with their drums. The way that the drums are made has a lot to do with the sounds they can make. Find out as much as you can about how drums work. You may also want to learn about the science of sound waves. Prepare a brief oral presentation for the class based on the information you find. It will help your audience if you have props that show clearly what you are discussing.

■ HISTORY/DRAMA

Griots Live! Imagine that you are a griot—a master storyteller—with a story to tell from the history of your culture. Select a scene from history, and perform it the way a griot might. You could include music, dance, or visual images in your performance. Work out how you will present your characters, and then practice telling your story. Try using your voice and gestures in imaginative ways to tell your tale.

■ LANGUAGE ARTS/ GEOGRAPHY

The View from a Camel's Back You are a merchant transporting luxury items by camel caravan to market. You want to keep a journal of your current trip for your son, who will soon begin leading his own caravan along the same route. Tell him what he needs to know, such as where your caravan starts and ends, what items your camels carry, and how to survive desert travel and raiders. Include a map showing the cities where the caravan would stop. Sometimes you may want to make a journal entry each day, but other times an entry each week or month may be enough.

■ ART/ARCHITECTURE

The Beauties of Al-Andalus Fabulous examples of medieval Islamic art and architecture can still be seen in Spain. By doing research in libraries and on the Internet, learn all you can about a particular palace or religious building in Andalusia. Then, take your classmates on a "virtual tour" of the area. Make note of the interesting works of art or building techniques that you find. Be sure to offer illustrations to accompany your tour of medieval Spanish art and architecture. You can sketch designs that are particular to Islamic art or draw blueprints of buildings showing the locations of courts and fountains.

■ MATHEMATICS/SCIENCE

Whose Discovery? You've read about some of the important scientific advances made by Muslim scholars during the Middle Ages. Now, have a "round-table" debate featuring some of the finest minds of the time. Have each person in a small group take the part of a different Islamic mathematician, astronomer, doctor, or geographer. Then, take turns describing your particular contribution, using diagrams, charts, or maps if necessary. Whose findings were most important? Who had the biggest impact on history? Let the class listen in on your debate and ask questions.

READ ON: FOR INDEPENDENT READING

■ NONFICTION

The History of Counting by Denise Schmandt-Besserat (William Morrow, 1999) describes how early counting techniques evolved into our system of "one, two, three." This book by a famous archaeologist tells how the Arab travelers brought Hindu numerals from India and developed the numbers that are now used around the world.

The Adventures of Ibn Battuta: A Muslim Traveler of the 14th Century by Ross E. Dunn (University of California Press, 1989) retraces Ibn Battuta's remarkable journeys through Egypt, Russia, and China. Follow his progress and, with the help of maps and commentary, get an eyewitness account of how the world worked in the fourteenth century.

The Usborne Book of World Religions by Susan Meredith (EDCP, 1996) focuses on six major world religions in the order that they developed. Learn about Mohammed and the writings of the Koran, as well as Islamic festivals and works of art, in an illustrated text that provides maps and a time chart.

Kings and Queens of West Africa by Sylviane Anna Diouf (Franklin Watts, 2000) tells the exciting stories of West Africa's strongest rulers who changed the history of their nations for generations to come. From the emperor of Mali, Mansa Musa, in the fourteenth century, to the queen of Senegal in the nineteenth century, over five hundred years of West African history is told in dramatic stories and rich illustrations.

■ FICTION

Leo Africanus by Amin Maalouf (Ivan R. Dee, 1992) tells the story of the real-life Arab geographer Hasan al-Wazzan, exiled from medieval Spain by the conquest of Granada. Christened "Leo Africanus" by the pope, this traveler takes us on a tour of the Mediterranean world, showing us the West from the Muslim point of view.

The Beduins' Gazelle by Frances Temple (HarperCollins, 1998) is a romantic adventure that re-creates the nomadic Beduin (Bedouin) culture, a tradition rich in poetry and storytelling. This award-winning author illustrates the great university at Fez in the fourteenth century while weaving a tale of desert intrigue.

Shabanu: Daughter of the Wind by Suzanne Fisher Staples (Knopf, 1989) tells the modern-day story of a daughter in an Islamic family of nomadic camel herders. Shabanu must cope with an arranged marriage and new religious obligations. Her solution is to run away, but to where exactly can she run? This Newbery Award book tells the story of a young woman exploring her world and her conscience to learn a new kind of courage.

Kings, Gods and Spirits from African Mythology by Jan Knappert (Schocken Books, Inc., 1986) contains thirty-five stories from the Ashanti, Zulu, Bantu, Swahili, and other African cultures. Each story is readable, dramatically told, and accompanied by color illustrations. Passed down through the oral tradition, many of these stories are still being retold in Africa today.

CHAPTER 3
Looking to the East
China and Japan   A.D. 600–1500

Anything but Smooth

From China to Europe, luxurious silk traveled over 4,000 miles west across a series of dangerous caravan routes called the Silk Road. Actually, the Silk Road wasn't a road at all—just a long, long set of directions. It passed through the Taklamakan, one of the driest deserts in the world, whose name means "if you go in, you won't come out." It crossed over the treacherous Pamir mountains, or the "Trail of Bones." It moved into the wild, ungoverned country east of the Oxus River, where bandits on horseback roamed free. Most Chinese merchants sold their silk along the way and turned back. A few, however, pushed on all the way to Baghdad and earned fantastic fortunes.

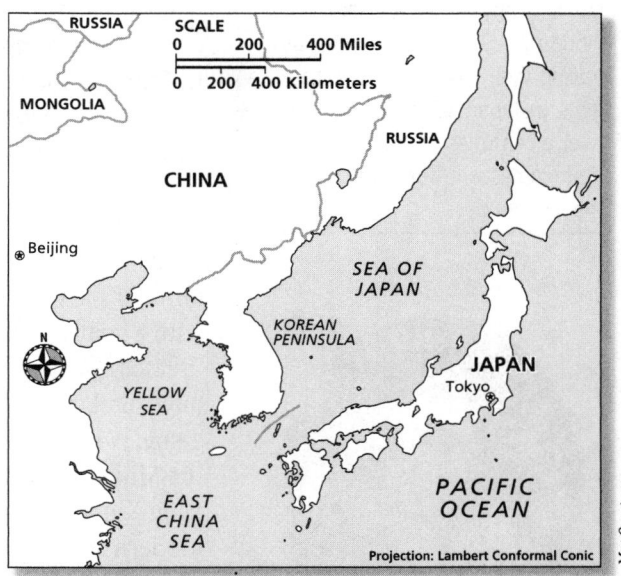

▲ China and Japan.

Dressing to Impress

Most westerners know the kimono as a simple, one-size-fits-all robe tied around the waist with a sash. Actually, *kimono* is just the Japanese word for "clothing." (*Ki* means "wear" and *mono* means "thing," so *kimono* is "the thing worn.") A thousand years ago, "the thing worn"—at least by ladies of Japan's royal court—was much more than a simple robe.

The layered look was definitely in: seven layers, at least, of loose, flowing garments, from scarlet trouser-skirts at the bottom to a jacket on top. When it came to showing off, though, what really mattered were the lined silk robes. They came in colors like

INVESTIGATE: What foreign goods did Chinese merchants bring back into China after selling their precious cargo of silk along the Silk Road?

The Tang dynasty, the Sung dynasty, the Ming dynasty—all are names used to describe long periods of time in China. A *dynasty* (dī′nəs•tē) is a series of rulers from the same line or family. Many dynasties around the world have justified long rules by tracing their bloodlines back to gods. In Japan, for example, twelve centuries of emperors claimed descent from Amaterasu, the sun goddess.

© Bettmann/CORBIS

▲ Marco Polo.

Memorable Quote

"I have not told half of what I saw. . . . Its abundant delights . . . might lead an inhabitant to imagine himself in paradise."

—Marco Polo, commenting on his travels to China

"plum blossom" (dark red cloth shining through thin white gauze) and "cherry blossom" (light purple under white). The right color combo meant the difference between being in style and being . . . well, history.

Just Kickin' Around

Soccer has only recently become really popular in this country, especially if compared to China. In China, 2,500 years ago, people played a game very much like soccer—kicking a ball made of stone. In the Tang and Sung dynasties, the golden age of ancient China, the game took on a more familiar form: Two teams, each with a goalie, faced off with an inflated leather ball. Soccer was a huge hit. Even emperors loved the game. Women played, too. During the Ming dynasty a woman named Peng Xiuyun was famous for using her whole body, just like modern soccer players—head, chest, back, and knees, as well as feet. (Good thing they'd quit playing with stone balls by then!)

© Christopher Liu/ChinaStock

▲ Chinese soccer players.

Tell the Truth, Marco Millions

When Marco Polo returned to his native Italy in the year 1295, after twenty-six years traveling through Asia, nobody would believe a word he said. Pears weighing ten pounds each? A city with twelve thousand bridges? Huge serpents called crocodiles, with claws like tigers' and jaws wide enough to swallow a man? People laughed at his outrageous claims and called him "Marco Millions" for the many giant numbers that filled his tales.

   Not everyone was so amused. When Marco lay on his deathbed at the age of seventy, his friends begged him to save his soul by taking back all those terrible lies. Marco Polo wouldn't budge. In fact, he said, "I have not told half of what I saw."

Who do you think invented the compass, fireworks, and organic gardening? The following article explains how much we owe to the Chinese and their many inventions.

Land of Discovery

from *Scholastic Update*

by PHIL SUDO and JEAN CHOL

Seventeenth-century British philosopher Francis Bacon[1] once argued that three inventions had done more to propel the world into the modern era than any others: the printing press, the magnetic compass, and gunpowder. The first promoted learning and literacy; the second led to exploration and discovery; and the last brought the capability of mass destruction.

All of these inventions came from China.

In fact, the list of Chinese contributions to world culture and development is staggering: Matches. Masts and sailing. The decimal system in mathematics. The use of petroleum and natural gas as fuel. The umbrella. Paper money. The wheelbarrow. The mechanical clock. The fishing reel. Playing cards. The parachute. Kites. The seismograph.[2] The list goes on and on.

"Possibly more than half of the basic inventions and discoveries upon which the 'modern world' rests come from China," says historian Robert Temple, author of *The Genius of China: 3,000 Years of Science, Discovery, and Invention.*

Many Chinese inventions, such as mechanical printing,

▲ The Chinese compass. The spoon that always pointed north became the magnetic compass.

© Christopher Liu/China Stock

You Need to Know...

During the Middle Ages, Chinese officials called mandarins encouraged their people to invent things—and they did. People in the West benefited from these inventions, too, as travelers and merchants took Chinese technology back to Europe.

---

1. **Francis Bacon** (1561–1626): English philosopher, essayist, and scientist.
2. **seismograph** (siz′mə•graf′): instrument that measures earthquakes and vibrations within the earth.

▲ The mechanical water clock. Three hundred years before the Europeans, the Chinese invented a clock that chimed the hours. **⁇ What else did the Chinese invent?**

adhere (ad·hir′): hold fast; firmly support.

surge (sɥrj): sharp increase; something that moves forward like a wave.

have been incorrectly credited to Europeans, who either came upon them independently at a later date or "borrowed" the idea from travelers who had been to China, Temple says. As a result, "the technological world of today is a product of both East and West to an extent which until recently no one had ever imagined."

Here are a few of China's contributions to the world, many of which remain quite foreign to Westerners:

Medicine

By the year 200, long before the concept of nutrition was recognized in the West, Chinese doctors discovered that certain human diseases—scurvy, rickets, beriberi—resulted from vitamin deficiencies.[3] In the 14th century, dietitian Hu Ssu-Hui wrote, "Many diseases can be cured by diet alone."

Even today, the Chinese adhere to their belief in medicinal foods, using such folk remedies as crushed sea horses and sliced deer antlers the way a Westerner reaches for aspirin. Typically, the Chinese use these elements in soups or teas.

In recent years, with the surge of Chinese immigrants to the U.S. and the growing American interest in natural medicines, herbal remedies have been gaining in popularity here.

The Chinese also pioneered the practice of acupuncture, a 3,000-year-old treatment for pain relief and other health problems. In acupuncture, doctors stick hair-thin needles into precise points on the body to enhance the flow of what they call *qi*, the body's natural energy system.

Acupuncture has gained wide acceptance throughout Asia; Chinese surgeons even use it in place of anesthesia when performing brain surgery. But Western medical

---

3. deficiencies (dē·fish′ən·sēz): shortages or lack; inadequate amounts.

experts have traditionally viewed the practice with suspicion; after all, there is still no definitive explanation for why acupuncture works. Recently, however, a growing number of doctors here have begun to accept acupuncture as a legitimate alternative to Western medicine, using it, for example, to ease withdrawal from addictive drugs.

Agriculture

The Chinese began planting crops in rows in the sixth century B.C. Now taken for granted, this practice gave the crops more room to grow, and thus mature more rapidly.

Around the same time, the Chinese also invented the hoe, which helped preserve soil moisture and cut down weeds, and the iron plow, whose design was far sturdier and more efficient than plows developed in Europe.

When European farmers finally adopted these practices in the 18th century, the European agricultural revolution began.

"Since the agricultural revolution of Europe is generally thought to have led to the Industrial Revolution, and to the West's superior power over the rest of the world," Temple writes, "it is ironic that the basis of it all came from China."

Martial Arts

To the ancient Chinese, there was no such thing as exercising to build muscles. One could only attain a healthy body—and a healthy life, they believed—through a system that developed strength, self-discipline, and self-knowledge. Thus were born the martial arts.

Many Westerners picture the martial arts as simply a way of fighting. While many of the arts center on combat styles, the rigorous training they require is usually undertaken as a means toward attaining wisdom. The ultimate goal, writes Deidre S. Laiken in *Mind, Body, Spirit,* is to produce "a calm mind in a strong, healthy body."

The arts have since spread throughout much of Asia, and evolved into hundreds of different styles. The main systems in China are known as kung fu, which means

legitimate (lə·jit′ə·mət): true, logical, or reasonable.

You Read It Here First . . .

Why would anyone buy a sheep bladder full of ants, put the ants in an orange tree, and then build tiny bamboo bridges to help the ants move from one tree to another? Believe it or not, this practice, common in ancient China, would today be called natural pest control. The ants fed only on insects that were harmful to the young orange fruit. Chinese pest control officials monitored destructive insects, and Chinese farmers found ways to use specific plants and animals to their advantage. Frogs, for example, were so prized for their insect consumption that people were forbidden to eat them.

rigorous (rig′ər·əs): strict or difficult.

Spiritual Training and Self-Defense

Legend says that 1,500 years ago an Indian monk named Bodhidharma found that Buddhist monks in a Shaolin temple were too weak to endure the long hours of meditation. He taught them kung fu—body-strengthening exercises. Eventually, the monks became famous for their martial arts skills, which they also used to combat bandits. When practiced for exercise rather than defense, kung fu resembles t'ai chi ch'uan, which uses flowing, rhythmic movements resembling those of six animals—bear, bird, deer, monkey, tiger, and snake. T'ai chi ch'uan is the most popular form of exercise in China today.

pervades (pər·vādz′): spreads throughout.

▲ Modern martial arts.

"skill" or "ability," and t'ai chi ch'uan. The other main forms have evolved out of Japanese and Korean adaptations. These include karate, judo, and tae kwon do.

Over the last 20 years, the martial arts have become increasingly popular in the U.S., spurred by the films of such martial arts performers as Bruce Lee, Chuck Norris, and Jean-Claude Von Damme, and such movies as *The Karate Kid* and *Teenage Mutant Ninja Turtles*.

Warfare

Long before the Chinese invented gunpowder, they had invented the crossbow, the most deadly weapon of its era. The crossbow, which dates back to about the fourth century B.C., was so feared for its ability to pierce through armor that contemporaries thought it would end civilization.

Gunpowder, invented in the ninth century, was even more destructive. Ironically, its inventors were said to have been seeking a chemical mix for the secret to eternal life.

Following the invention of gunpowder, the Chinese developed a whole series of explosive devices; in the 10th century alone, they introduced flares, fireworks, bombs, grenades, land mines, and sea mines. In succeeding centuries, they invented guns, cannons, mortars, and repeating guns. "No nation in the world could match the Chinese expertise in warfare for two millennia," says Temple.

Philosophy

Simply put, the Chinese philosophy of Confucianism has influenced more people over the ages than any other way of life the world has known. It pervades virtually all aspects of Chinese society and has spread widely throughout Asia.

The principles of Confucianism came from a man named K'ung Fu-tse, or Confucius. Born in 551 B.C., he was a teacher who advised rulers and taught students so they might become advisers to the Chinese government. The China of his day was a corrupt society, and Confucius sought to establish high moral standards. He believed that if people followed simple rules of kindness, respect, selflessness, and obedience, China could be a harmonious society.

One of his basic principles he called *shu*, or reciprocity. Through shu, Confucius meant: "What you do not want done to yourself, do not do to others."

Confucius did not talk about God. In contrast to Western religions like Christianity, Confucianism considers the human being, not an invisible god, the highest form of life. In Confucian philosophy, there is no worship or prayer dedicated to any spirit or gods.

The ancient Chinese believed that the world was completely unified, containing interacting forces they called *yin* and *yang*, which roughly translate as positive and negative. All objects, they said, have both yin and yang. The unity of yin and yang together make up *tao*, or the ultimate way of the universe.

Confucius taught that if people cultivate the tao in themselves, society will achieve harmony in five areas: (1) rulers will rule their people wisely, and the people will be loyal to their rulers; (2) parents will be kind to their children, and children will honor their parents;

SIDELIGHT

The sayings of Confucius (551–479 B.C.), found in the book *Analects,* emphasize that improving one's moral character will, in turn, improve one's community and country. Here are examples of the sayings of Confucius:

- Never disobey.
- A person of true wisdom knows what he knows and knows what he does not know.
- A man who commits a mistake without correcting it is committing another mistake.
- Don't criticize other people's faults, criticize your own.
- Do not do to others what you do not want others to do to you.

—from the *Analects,* in "The Analects" by Carolyn Gard from *Calliope* (October 1999)

▲ Confucius.

Stapleton Collection, UK/Bridgeman Art Library, New York/London

(3) husbands will take care of their wives, and wives will obey their husbands; (4) older children will set a good example for younger children, and younger children will respect older children; and (5) friends will be responsible for the way they behave with one another.

From those simple teachings, the philosophy spread through all classes of Chinese society, and later, throughout Asia. Today, the people of Korea, Japan, and Vietnam all have incorporated Confucian ideals into their institutions and daily lives.

With such a tremendous following, Confucius is often perceived today as the leader of a religion, even though he himself never believed in a god.

✓ Reading Check

1. Why were some Chinese inventions thought to have been created by Europeans?

2. For what purpose do doctors in China use acupuncture? Why has the practice not been used more widely in the West?

3. What is the advantage to farmers of planting crops in rows?

4. What is the purpose of martial arts, such as kung fu or t'ai chi ch'uan?

5. Why did Confucius seek to improve the moral standards of his students?

The Great Wall of China has been called "the longest ceme-
tery in the world." It was built by millions of people, many
of whom died and were buried within the structure itself.
The following article will tell you even more interesting
facts about this wall of wonders.

The Biggest Wall of All
It Stretches Across
China ... and Across Time
from *National Geographic World*

by MARGARET McKELWAY

O ut of the desert they would ride, fierce warriors on
fast horses. They would attack peaceful settlements, snatch up <u>loot</u> and slaves, and dash off
again. These <u>invaders</u> from nomadic tribes of Asia <u>plagued</u>
the people living to the south, in what is now China, some
2,000 years ago. Finally the settlers decided to build a barrier of earth and stone that horses could not cross. Over
time they extended the barrier into a long wall from
which their soldiers could launch arrows and spears down
onto enemies. The wall protected the settlers and let them
live in peace for long periods throughout history. Parts of
it still stand today—the
Great Wall of China.

China and its Great Wall
share a common birthday.
By an ancient account,
both began in 221 B.C.,
when the leader of a small
state in eastern Asia joined
several neighboring states
together into one empire.
The new emperor—Qin
Shi Huangdi—sent

loot (lo͞ot): stolen goods.

invaders (in•vād'ərs): those who
enter forcibly; intruders.

plagued (plāgd): troubled.

You Need to Know...
The Mongols were one of several nomadic tribes that lived in
the enormous grasslands north of China. They spent their time
herding sheep and horses. As nomads, they did not settle in one
place. They were constantly moving their few possessions as
they searched for water and pasture. The Mongols were also
excellent riders and archers. To get the iron and grain they
needed from their Chinese neighbors, the Mongols thought
nothing of raiding farms and even plundering cities to the south.
To protect themselves, the Chinese built "the biggest wall of all."

continuous (kən·tin′yōō·əs): unbroken; attached together.

gorges (gôrj′iz): narrow, deep passages of a canyon; ravines.

Fantastic Facts and Figures

- The Great Wall was constructed over a period of 1,865 years.
- Towers built into the wall number 25,000.
- No one has ever seen the entire Great Wall, and so no maps agree on its true course.
- The wall is long enough to surround much of Europe—ten countries from France to Romania.
- With the soil, brick, and stone contained in the Great Wall, you could build a wall around Earth's equator that would be eight feet tall and three feet thick.
- Astronauts can see the Great Wall from Earth's orbit.

300,000 troops to fortify the country's northern borders. They did so by connecting a series of existing local fortifications into one <u>continuous</u> barrier. By 204 B.C., the wall guarded about a thousand miles of China's frontier.

The original wall wore away. But later emperors rebuilt and lengthened it. In the 1300s, as the threat of yet another invasion emerged, a new period of wall building began. It resulted in the stone-and-brick barrier you can see today.

How far did the wall finally stretch? Estimates vary. Some experts say as long as 2,500 miles, almost the distance across the United States. But there's no doubt about this: The Great Wall of China is the largest structure ever built.

Some describe the Great Wall as the Eighth Wonder of the World. Snaking along steep mountain ridges, through river <u>gorges</u>, and across empty deserts, the wall stands 40 feet tall in some places. It's enough for ten men to walk

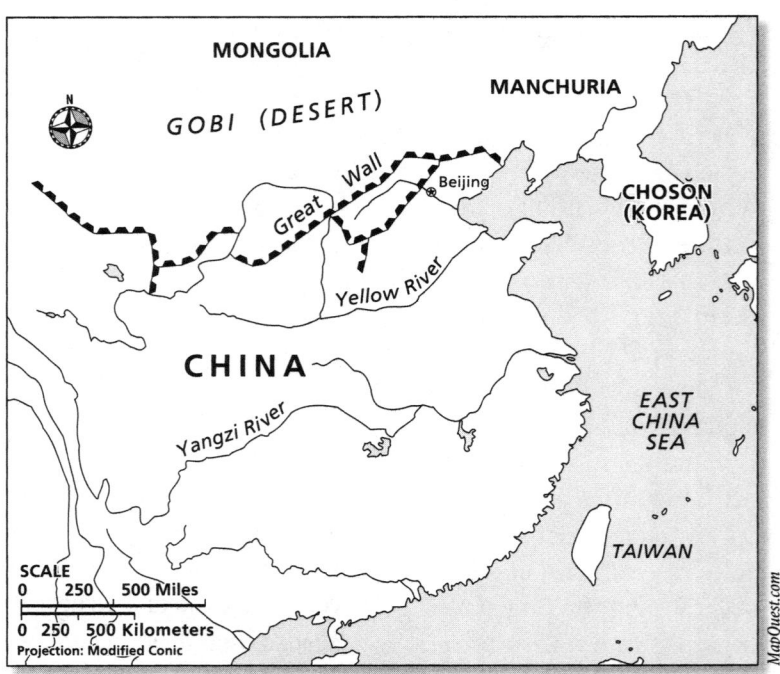

▲ The Great Wall of China. **?** **Why did the Chinese build a wall as long as the Great Wall?**

side by side along its top. Towers for troops and supplies, as well as signal platforms, are built into it.

In spite of its size, the Great Wall did not always protect China. Sometimes invaders overran it. But the wall still stands, a monument to the millions of workers who built it.

▲ The Great Wall.

✓ Reading Check

1. Why did settlers in early China begin building fortifications?

2. When and how was the Chinese Empire formed?

3. How did the Chinese use existing defenses in building the Great Wall?

4. What defensive features are built into the Great Wall?

5. Was the Great Wall an effective defense for China? Explain.

The Granger Collection, New York

▲ Genghis Khan.

resounding (ri•zoun′din̄):
echoing; making a loud sound.

plunder (plun′dər): goods or
belongings taken in warfare.

Where would you look for clues to discover a treasure
buried in a tomb for eight hundred years? The following
article reveals that finding the lost tomb of Genghis Khan
begins with studying events in the emperor's life.

from The Search for Genghis Khan

from *Current Events*

To begin, here's an exercise for your imagination: In
your mind, travel back in time more than seven
centuries—to the year 1227.

That may not seem like an awfully long time ago—not
like going back to the time of the dinosaurs, for example—but in some ways the world of 1227 might seem as
strange to modern Americans as the age of the dinosaurs.
For one thing, the world 700 years ago would be strangely
quiet to modern ears. There were no cars, trucks, planes,
lawn mowers, or motors of any kind. There was no radio,
no TV, no electric lighting. Most of the world went to bed
when it got dark and rose when the sun came up.

In 1227 much of the world was at war, resounding with
the hoofbeats of warhorses, the clash of swords, and the
screams of battle. (Gunpowder, although probably invented, was not yet used in warfare.) Throughout Asia and
Europe, armies fought to the death, some in the name of
God, others simply for glory or plunder.

A Funeral Procession

Now that your imagination is firmly planted in the world
of the 13th century, focus your mind's eye on a rocky
mountain path in what is now Mongolia, a country north
of China. On August 18, 1227, a huge oxcart carrying a
yurt, or Mongolian tent, makes its way to a remote location. Surrounding the cart are 2,500 people and a mounted bodyguard of 400 soldiers.

It is no ordinary procession. Inside the yurt is the dead body of the most feared, most powerful, most hated, and most admired man in the world—Genghis Khan. In the space of 20 years, Genghis Khan's armies had conquered much of the known world, killed millions, and sent shudders of fear from Japan to Germany.

Legend has it that Genghis Khan's bodyguards killed every person encountered by the funeral procession in its journey into the mountains. After the great khan's body was placed in its grave, the soldiers turned on the other members of the funeral procession, killing all 2,500 of them. When the soldiers returned to Karakorum, Genghis Khan's capital, they, in turn, were killed by other soldiers so that they could not reveal the location of the tomb.

encountered (en·koun'tərd): met unexpectedly or accidentally.

Maury Kravitz

Now, a Chicago millionaire, Maury Kravitz, accompanied by a team of scientists and historians, has mounted a $1.2 million expedition to look for the lost tomb. . . . A Japanese team had begun a three-year search in 1990 and had come up empty-handed. Kravitz, however, believes he has knowledge that will give his team a better chance of finding the tomb.

For Kravitz, 68, having the opportunity to search for Genghis Khan's tomb is a dream come true. Genghis Khan has fascinated Kravitz since, at age 20, he read a book about the ruthless conqueror. He has now read 500 to 600 books about the Mongol ruler.

To gain a better understanding of where the burial place may be, Kravitz and his team are retracing the main events of Genghis Khan's life.

▲ Genghis Khan. ❓ **What events in his young life made him become a cruel leader?**

reputation (rep′yo͞o·ta′shən): public opinion about someone's character.

renounced (ri·nounsd′): gave up, or disowned.

delegation (del′ə·gā′shən): group of people sent to speak for others.

Temujin

Genghis Khan was born in about 1167 and was given the name Temujin, after an enemy chief whom his father had captured in battle. At that time, the Mongols were a collection of nomadic tribes constantly at war with one another and not taken seriously by the Chinese.

In 1176, Temujin's father was poisoned by the Tatars, a powerful tribe in eastern Mongolia. Enemies within Temujin's tribe then robbed his family of much of their flocks and left the family to face the harsh Mongolian winter with almost no resources. Over the next few years, Temujin, his strong-willed mother, and his brothers and sisters rebuilt the herds and acquired a reputation for bravery. Others renounced their own families and became members of Temujin's clan.

By the time he was 30, Temujin dominated a major part of northeastern Mongolia. By the end of 1202, he had defeated nearly all of his enemies in Mongol lands, wiping out the Tatars as a people. In 1206, at a *kuriltai*, or great assembly of Mongol tribes, Temujin was proclaimed *khan* (leader) of all the Mongols. Temujin selected for himself the name Genghis, probably derived from a Turkish word meaning "ocean." The implication was that his power spread over the world like a great body of water.

The Prince of Wei

In 1207, a delegation from Beijing made its way to Genghis Khan to inform him that a new emperor—the prince of Wei—had ascended to the throne of China. On hearing this, Genghis stated that an emperor "must be an eminent personage, designated by heaven." He then asked: "How can an imbecile[1] like the prince of Wei perform such a role?"

Before the astonished ambassadors could make any reply, the khan spat on the ground and rode off.

The insult marked the beginning of a Mongol attack on China. Chinese armies, which were used to fending off scattered attacks from these tribal people, were not prepared for the new Mongol army of Genghis Khan.

Genghis proved to be a military genius who turned the Mongol tribesmen into the world's best-trained and best-led army.

The favorite tactic of the Mongols in battle was to send a "suicide corps" galloping toward the enemy ranks. The corps would then stop short and fake a retreat to tempt the enemy into a disorganized chase. Then the entire Mongol force would charge at them according to a set plan. Enemies fell victim to this tactic again and again.

Chinese Defeated

Genghis Khan's army quickly defeated the armies of Chinese rulers sent to defeat it, including the Xi Xia kingdom of northwestern China. After conquering Xi Xia, Genghis returned to Mongolia to build his new capital, which he named Karakorum. In 1218, he returned with his armies to conquer the Kara Khitai empire, located between the modern nations of China and Kazakhstan.

Now that his realm stretched west to the border of the rich Khwarizm empire, Genghis sent gifts of jade, ivory, gold, and white camel wool to its ruler, Shah Muhammed. Genghis also proposed trade between the

eminent (em′ə·nənt): important or highly respected; outstanding in character or performance.

fending (fend′iŋ): resisting.

tactic (tak′tik): special military arrangement.

realm (relm): kingdom or region.

Rules for a Warrior People

Despite their ruthless battlefield tactics, the Mongols had rules that punished wrongs, tied together the nomadic clans, and demanded people's loyalty to their leader. The Mongol Code, or *Yasa*, declared that liars, spies, and thieves would be killed. It also ordered the rich to help the poor and children to respect their parents. The *Yasa* even stated that Mongols should believe in one god. At first, these rules of government were spread by word of mouth. When Genghis Khan captured people who could write, he ordered them to write down the Mongol Code.

---

1. imbecile (im′bə·sil): silly or stupid person.

two empires and sent a caravan of 450 merchants to Muhammed. When the caravan reached the Khwarizm city of Utrar, however, that city's governor accused them of being spies and executed them. When Genghis sent an ambassador to demand that the shah hand over Utrar's governor for punishment, Muhammed killed the ambassador and sent his head back to Genghis.

A Bad Decision

It was not a good decision for Muhammed or for his empire.

An enraged Genghis sent the Mongol army into Shah Muhammed's territories. Muhammed, however, remained

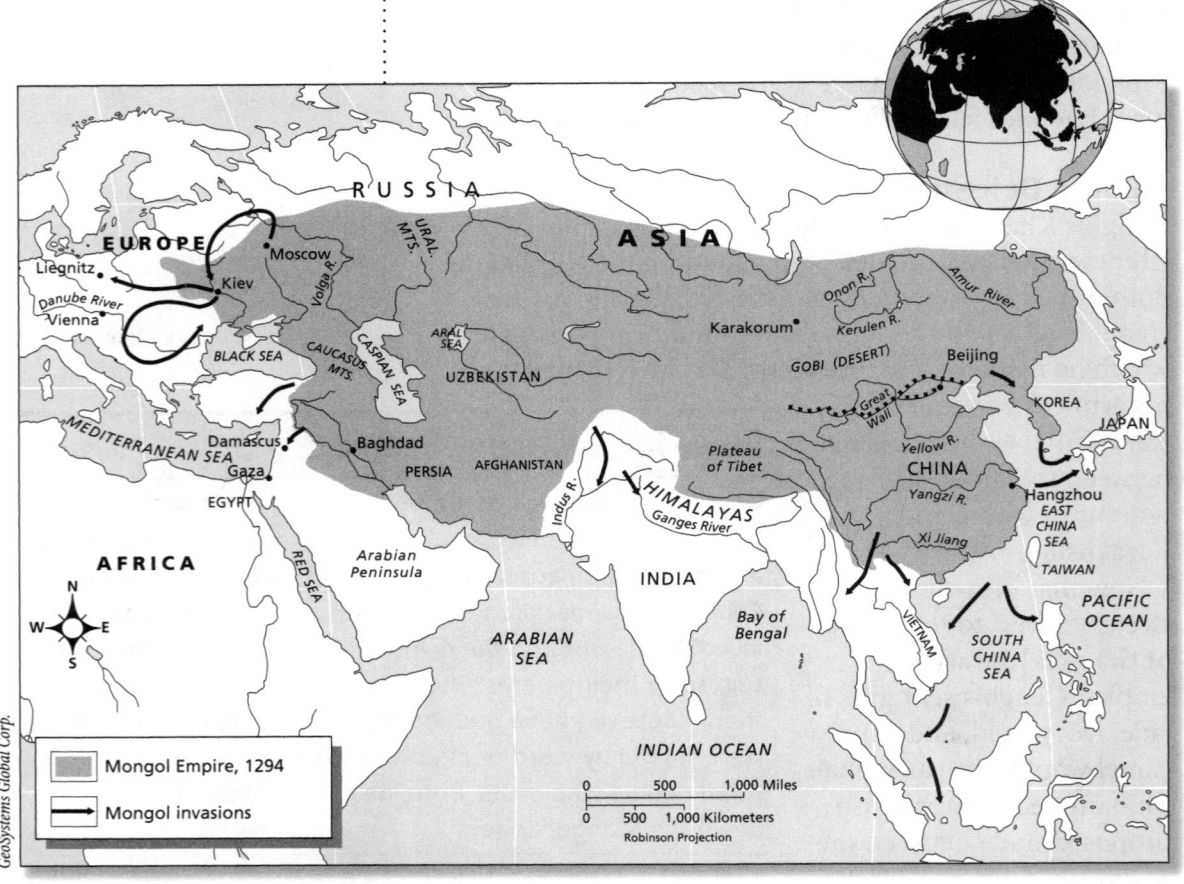

▲ The Mongolian Empire.

confident. He had 400,000 troops, whereas Genghis's army numbered barely 100,000.

It turned out to be no contest. Genghis split his army into two parts and surrounded Muhammed's forces. Utrar fell after a siege of a few months. The Mongols captured the governor and killed him by pouring molten silver into his eyes and ears. The Mongol army then destroyed the city of Merv. In the city's rubble a Muslim holy man spent 13 days counting corpses, which reportedly numbered 1.3 million. Terrified, the city of Balkh also surrendered. The Mongols killed all its inhabitants anyway.

"The Punishment of God"

After capturing the city of Bukhara, now in Uzbekistan, Genghis told the terrified inhabitants, "I am the punishment of God. If you had not committed great sins, God would not have sent a punishment like me upon you."

Samarkand surrendered to the Mongols after a brief siege, but Muhammed's forces defended the Khwarizmian capital of Urgench to the end. The Mongol army set the city on fire, house by house, and slaughtered all its inhabitants.

After the utter defeat of the Khwarizm empire, the Mongol army reached the Caspian Sea[2]—and the gates of Europe. Two of Genghis's best generals, Jebe and Subedei, with 20,000 picked troops, crossed into Europe.

The Mongols defeated two large Russian armies sent to meet them. News of the Mongol invasion spread terror throughout Europe as far away as England. People told of terrifying invaders from the East who had the heads of dogs and who ate their defeated enemies.

2. **Caspian Sea** (kas'pe•ən): inland sea north of Iran, between Europe and Asia.

Dressed for Success

What did the fearsome army of Genghis Khan wear on the battlefield? A soldier's first layer of defense was a thick silk shirt. If an arrow struck a soldier, it pushed the silk into the wound. When the doctor removed the silk shirt, the arrow came with it. Mongol soldiers also wore horsehide armor that had been hardened in animal urine. Warriors protected their faces with small leather shields. They carried as weapons a lance, a dagger, a strong bow, up to three quivers of arrows, and as many as six different kinds of arrowheads. A special arrowhead whistled when it was shot—terrifying the Mongols' opponents.

The Granger Collection, New York

▲ Mongol warrior shown with his battlefield weapons.

"In the countries that have not yet been overrun by them, everyone spends the night afraid that they may appear there too," wrote Ibn al-athir, an Arab historian.

But the two generals led only an exploratory mission. They soon turned back and rejoined Genghis in central Asia with a vast amount of plunder.

Private Collection/Bridgeman Art Library, New York/London

▲ Mongol warriors.

Xi Xia Revolt

Meanwhile, the Xi Xia kingdom had tried to revolt against Mongol rule. In 1226 Genghis led his army south again into China. It was during this campaign that he fell from his horse, causing injuries that led to his death.

The Xi Xia king offered to surrender, but as Genghis Khan lay dying, he ordered the king killed and the total destruction of the Xi Xia kingdom: "As long as I can eat food and still say, 'Make everyone who lives in their cities vanish,' kill them all and destroy their homes. As long as I am still alive, keep up the slaughter." Ever obedient to the leader who had built the world's most powerful empire, the Mongols wiped the Xi Xia kingdom, its cities, and its people from the Earth.

After Genghis's death, control of the empire went to Ogadei, his third son by his first wife. By the next century, however, the empire broke apart and disappeared as thoroughly as the remains of its remarkable founder.

A Fabulous Treasure?

Kravitz believes that the great khan was buried with a fabulous treasure collected from all the Mongol conquests.

"Not one single bejeweled dagger, not one artifact has surfaced," Kravitz told reporters. "Nothing. One has to conclude that this stuff has gone into the ground with [Genghis Khan's body]."

If he succeeds in finding the tomb of the great conqueror—and he admits it's a long shot—Kravitz says the find will make unearthing King Tutankhamen's[3] tomb in Egypt seem minor by comparison. "It would be the find of finds," he said. "There would be enough to study for hundreds of years."

---

3. **King Tutankhamen's** (tŏŏt′äŋk·ä′mənz): (c. 1355 B.C.) Egyptian king whose tomb was discovered almost intact in 1922.

Private Collection/Bridgeman Art Library, New York/London

▲ Subedei, one of Genghis Khan's best generals, crossed into Europe with his men but soon turned back.

✓ Reading Check

1. Why does Genghis Khan's burial site remain a secret?

2. What was the relationship between the young Genghis Khan (Temujin) and the Tatar tribe?

3. What incidents began the conflict between the Mongol people and the Khwarizm empire of Shah Muhammed?

4. How did the people in Europe react to the news of Genghis Khan?

5. What happened to the Mongol Empire after Genghis Khan's death?

Imagine passing your friends notes written on big leaves or scratched on rocks! A world without paper would be a strange one indeed. The following article explains how the invention of paper by the Chinese gave us everything from books to bags.

The Paper Revolution
from *Faces*

by JOHN S. MAJOR

China Stock

▲ The ancient Chinese wrote on long bamboo slats tied together side by side.

In China 2,500 years ago, people had a choice of materials to write on—one cheap but clumsy, the other elegant but expensive. Most ordinary documents were written on narrow slats of wood or bamboo[1] tied together with string like miniature snow fences. (These long, narrow strips are the reason the Chinese write in up-and-down lines.) The wooden strips were cheap but very awkward to carry around, and they could easily get mixed up if the string broke. The other choice was silk cloth—strong, light, and easy to write on but too expensive for everyday use.

Writing was invented independently by several different ancient civilizations beginning more than 5,000 years ago. Among these civilizations were those in Babylon,[2] Egypt, Greece, India, and Mexico. The materials people in these places used to write on were either heavy and clumsy (such as stone, clay tablets, or pieces of bone) or fragile and perishable (such as tree bark or strips of palm leaves).

You Need to Know...

What do you get when you mix tree bark, rags, and old fishnets? The Chinese discovered that these items, combined in a certain way, form paper. The development of paper brought about a long list of other new inventions. The most important was the invention of printing, which helped encourage reading and writing and the spread of knowledge around the globe.

perishable (per′ish•ə•bəl): easily spoiled.

---

1. **bamboo** (bam•bo͞o′): treelike, tropical plant, often with hollow stems.
2. **Babylon** (bab′ə•län′): capital of ancient Babylonia, and part of ancient Mesopotamia, located in what is now central Iraq.

Gradually, people began to discover more suitable writing materials. The ancient Egyptians used papyrus,[3] made from flattened reeds glued together to form sheets. (Our word "paper" comes from "papyrus.") The Romans used parchment, made from sheepskin. Papyrus broke easily; parchment was strong but expensive.

In early China, where the ability to read and write was the most important qualification for a successful career, there was a strong demand for better writing materials. Responding to that demand, the Chinese discovered how to make the perfect companion for writing: paper.

People used to believe that paper was invented by a man named Ts'ai Lun, who was an official in the <u>imperial</u> government workshops around A.D. 100. In recent years, however, Chinese archeologists have discovered several fragments of paper that date from at least 250 years before that time. Perhaps what Mr. Ts'ai did was to improve the process of papermaking.

The first paper was made from rags. Later papermakers preferred to use plants with long, strong <u>fibers</u>, such as hemp, flax,[4] bamboo, and the inner bark of the mulberry

imperial (im·pir′ē·əl): related to an empire; of the highest authority.

fibers (fī′bərz): thread-like tissue from plants or animals.

---

3. **papyrus** (pə·pī′rəs): writing material made from a tall water plant native to the Nile River.
4. **hemp:** Asian plant with a tough fiber used to make rope and cloth; **flax:** plant whose fibers are used to make linen thread.

SIDELIGHT

Marco Polo (1254–1324) was the first European young man to visit China, where he lived for a time at the court of the emperor Kublai Khan. To Europeans, whose money was made of gold and silver, the paper money used in China must have seemed strange.

"This paper currency is circulated in every part of the Khan's dominions, and no person, at the peril of his life, dares to refuse to accept it in payment. All his armies are paid with this currency, which to them is of the same value as if it were gold or silver. It may certainly be said that the Khan has a greater command of treasure than any other ruler in the universe."

—Marco Polo, from *Adventures and Discoveries of Marco Polo* by Richard J. Walsh

tree. To make paper, the plant materials were boiled and beaten with wooden hammers to soften and separate the fibers. Then the fibers were mixed with water. A screen made of woven split bamboo held in a wooden frame was used to scoop up a thin layer of wet fibers. When dried, that layer became a sheet of paper.

The first paper was made from rags.

At first paper was made only in plain white sheets. But soon papermakers began to decorate it with colored dyes and block-printed designs. By the time of the T'ang dynasty (A.D. 618–907), wealthy people enjoyed using luxurious note paper to write letters to friends and relatives. This custom also was followed in Japan, where people often folded their letters in fancy shapes. This idea led to the Japanese art of origami, or folded-paper figures.

The invention of printing in China in the eighth century greatly increased the demand for paper. Printing made it possible to produce books in large quantities. Chinese and Japanese artists also found paper perfect for ink painting.

Wonderfully suited for writing and printing, paper soon began to be used for many other purposes as well. Made waterproof with oil or wax, it was used for raincoats, umbrellas, and windows. Many decorative items such as fans, lanterns, and kites and other toys were made of

luxurious (lug·zhŏŏr′ē·əs): expensive; costly.

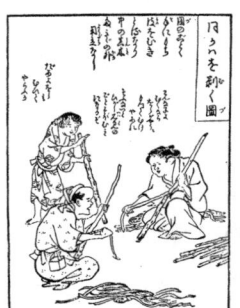

The Granger Collection, New York

▲ Steps in making paper. These Japanese woodcuts show how paper was made from strips of bark. **❷ What are the steps in creating paper from the strips?**

paper. Layers of paper, strengthened with lacquer,[5] were even made into armor. The Japanese also used paper in their houses, where they made interior walls of paper glued to lightweight wooden frames.

Paper was so useful that it quickly spread from eastern Asia to the rest of the Old World. By A.D. 750, there was a papermaking workshop in Baghdad (in present-day Iraq). Later, paper was introduced to Egypt and then to Spain, Italy, and the rest of Europe. The availability of paper helped <u>spur</u> the invention of the printing press in Europe in the 15th century. Printed books in turn brought great changes to education in Europe.

The earliest European paper was made of cotton or linen rags. It was very strong but also rather expensive. By the 19th century, people used machines to make inexpensive paper from wood fiber. Today paper is made on giant machines, sometimes as long as a football field, that take in pulp at one end and spit out huge rolls of paper at the other.

We still use paper for writing and printing, of course—everything from notebooks to newspapers, books to computer printouts, post cards to photocopies—but we also use it in many other ways as well. Think of a trip to the supermarket. Almost everything in the store arrived there packed in corrugated[6] cardboard boxes. Dozens of products are sold in paper packages. We can buy paper plates and cups, paper towels and tissues, toilet paper and wrapping paper. When we are finished shopping, we pay for our purchases with paper money, get a paper cash register receipt, and often carry what we bought in paper bags.

When you think about it, it is hard to imagine life without paper.

The Granger Collection, New York

▲ A Chinese print shop. The shop had many drawers in the background walls that probably held some of the thousands of Chinese characters necessary for printing.

spur (spur): to urge to action.

---

5. **lacquer** (lak′ər): coating, such as varnish, that dries leaving a tough finish.
6. **corrugated** (kôr′ə‧gāt′id): shaped in parallel wrinkles or ridges.

Too Much Type to Move

Since Chinese inventors developed the technology for both making paper and printing, why do Europeans get credit for inventing the printing press? For one thing, the Chinese handwriting is complex. It uses about 80,000 symbols, or ideograms. Medieval Chinese texts could require as many as 60,000 individual pieces of type—every single one of which had to be carved by hand, taking years of labor. In Germany, Johannes Gutenberg invented a mold for movable type and a printing press in 1450. These inventions revolutionized printing because Gutenberg was able to use an alphabet with a limited number of letters. Even in modern times, no printer ever has a complete set of type that includes every Chinese character.

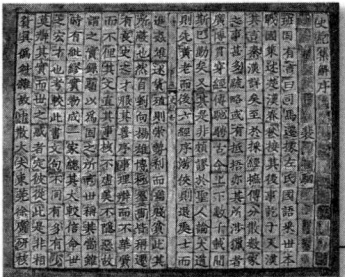

China Stock

▲ Wooden type used in printing Chinese book. This page is read from top to bottom and from right to left. The columns match the bamboo slats the Chinese first used as paper.

✓ Reading Check

1. In ancient China, what were the advantages and disadvantages of writing on slats of wood or bamboo?

2. What types of writing materials did other early civilizations use?

3. Why was there a demand for improved writing materials in China?

4. How did the Chinese decorate and improve plain white paper?

5. What other countries learned about papermaking from China?

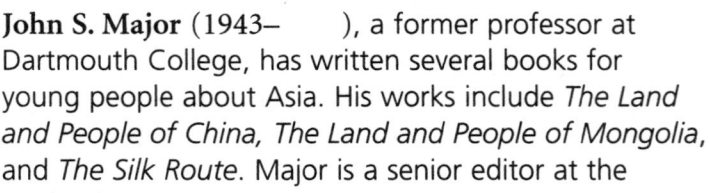

MEET THE *Writer*

John S. Major (1943–   ), a former professor at Dartmouth College, has written several books for young people about Asia. His works include *The Land and People of China, The Land and People of Mongolia*, and *The Silk Route*. Major is a senior editor at the Book-of-the-Month Club.

What might happen when a teenager is put in charge of an empire? The following excerpt explains how Prince Taishi Shōtoku created a peaceful and prosperous Japan.

from Prince Taishi Shōtoku
Japan, A.D. 574–622
from Heroes: Great Men Through the Ages

by REBECCA HAZELL

Thirteen hundred years ago, Japan was a rustic island empire on the eastern edge of Asia. Its rulers claimed to be descended from the sun goddess, Amaterasu. Although these leaders were worshipped almost as gods by the masses, they were often powerless against ambitious wealthy nobles. Because there was no clear way to choose a new ruler when an emperor or empress died, civil war often broke out between rival clans, causing suffering for the whole nation. In 593 these clans were able to agree upon a new empress, a member of the most powerful clan. However, she was a mere figurehead, since the real power was held by her nephew, Prince Taishi Shōtoku, who was married to a woman from another influential clan.

rustic (rus′tik): rural; unsophisticated.

You Need to Know...
Prince Taishi Shōtoku is greatly respected as the father of Japanese culture. His influence changed the people of Japan profoundly—in their thinking as well as in their lifestyles. Shōtoku borrowed cultural and political ideas from China. He encouraged the Japanese arts to blossom, and he restructured the Japanese government. Perhaps his greatest accomplishment was his *Seventeen Article Constitution*, a code for the ruling class that stressed the importance of unity and morality.

influential (in′floo•en′shəl): able to use power over someone or something.

When Prince Shōtoku became regent[1] of Japan, he was only nineteen years old. Unlike many rulers, this remarkable young man was not interested in power for its own sake; he wanted to help his country. To do this he had to

---

1. regent (rē′jənt): person who rules while a monarch is absent, disabled, or too young to govern.

prosperity (präs•par′ə•tē): wealth;
good fortune.

inherited (in•her′it′id): received from
ancestors.

© *Bettmann/CORBIS*

▲ Prince Taishi Shōtoku.

keep the rival clans at peace with each other while pro-
moting Japan's <u>prosperity</u>.

Prince Shōtoku knew that Japan's political institutions
were not very sophisticated, so as the Japanese had done
in the past, he looked far over the sea to China for inspiration. First he reformed and centralized his government
based on the teachings of the Chinese sage Confucius.[2]
Confucius taught that everyone must be responsible for
one another's welfare. He said that governments should be
run by able people regardless of their background, and
not only people who had <u>inherited</u> power, as had been the
case in Japan. Inspired by these ideals, Prince Shōtoku
persuaded the ambitious nobles to give up some of their
powers to capable commoners, a policy that improved the
efficiency and quality of Japanese government. The prince
also introduced the Chinese calendar and writing system
to Japan.

Then the prince sent out messengers across five hundred
miles of stormy seas to study Chinese culture. They
brought back many artists, craftsmen, and scholars. From
them Japanese artists and craftsmen learned new skills
that they adapted to form a brilliant new culture. Prince
Shōtoku did still more for his people. He built highways
and irrigation[3] systems. He started social programs. He
erected temples and established a new court near the city
of Nara. (These buildings are among the oldest surviving
wooden structures on earth.) The prince also wrote a
history of Japan, which sadly no longer survives.

Prince Shōtoku also helped spread a new religion,
Buddhism. Until this time, the Japanese religion, called
Shinto, was based on rituals that showed love and respect
for nature. Buddhism taught people a way of life
based on caring for each other as well.
Buddhism did not replace Shinto—the
Japanese practiced both religions, as they still
do today—but it did deeply affect the way

---

2. **Confucius** (kən•fyoo′shəs): (c. 551–c. 479 B.C.) Chinese philosopher and teacher.
3. **irrigation** (ir′ə•gā′shən): artificial system of watering by means of canals or
   sprinklers.

people lived. Buddhist values of compassion helped reduce the amount of violence in Japanese society.

Sometimes people do not like change, but the Japanese welcomed Prince Shōtoku's improvements. During his reign, Japan became more peaceful and prosperous. Its contact with the Chinese enriched and stimulated its culture. The changes Prince Shōtoku brought to Japan continue to affect its history and even now, the Japanese honor him as a great Buddhist saint.

A New Culture

Although Japan borrowed many ideas from China, its people soon <u>adapted</u> them to their own ways. During Prince Shōtoku's reign, new forms of architecture, music, sculpture, painting, textile design, and dance developed. Some still flourish in their ancient form, such as gagaku, a type of Japanese dance.

The Japanese also created their own unique art forms, expressed in mediums such as wood-block prints, paper, and fabrics, that are now world famous, like origami, the Japanese art of paper folding. Japanese Buddhists developed other art forms like the tea ceremony, flower

adapted (ə·dapt′id): adjusted to new circumstances; made to fit.

Would You Believe?

Japan borrowed Chinese arts and Chinese science. The Chinese had developed beautiful goldfish from the carp—small, dull-colored, freshwater fish—by using the principles of genetics to create many new kinds of fish. One gold-tinged carp kept in the same fishbowl with another gold-tinged carp had produced offspring even more brightly colored than their parents. By A.D. 1500, the fish arriving in Japan no longer resembled carp. In fact, they were such regal-looking goldfish that the commoners in Japan were forbidden to keep these animals as pets.

© Klaus Paysan/Peter Arnold, Inc.

◀ Japanese carp.

© Burstein Collection/CORBIS

▲ Japanese landscape painting.
❓ **In addition to art, what else did the Japanese borrow from China and adapt to their own culture?**

arranging, and archery as well. Each combines a simple activity with strict discipline to create an atmosphere of simplicity and calm.

Eventually, the Japanese integrated Chinese writing symbols (kanji) with their own traditional script (hiragana). They loved calligraphy (decorative handwriting) and wrote masterful poetry and novels. One type of poetry, the haiku, has only seventeen syllables, yet can make its readers see, hear, and feel as the poet does and has inspired poets around the world.

Many of the arts that flowered during the reign of Prince Shōtoku are still practiced in Japan today. The present imperial family is descended from the prince and the other early "divine" rulers, making it the longest unbroken line of rulers in the world.

✓ **Reading Check**

1. Why was medieval Japan often involved in civil wars?

2. What changes did Prince Taishi Shōtoku make to Japanese government?

3. How did Prince Shōtoku make sure that Japan would learn from Chinese ideas?

4. How did Japanese religion change during the time of Prince Shōtoku?

5. What Japanese artistic traditions arose without the influence of Chinese ideas?

Feeling a little cramped in your social life? Lady Murasaki Shikibu so longed for a livelier crowd that she secretly created an entire cast of friends to entertain herself. Read the following excerpt to find out more about this outrageous woman of the Middle Ages.

from Murasaki Shikibu

from *Outrageous Women of the Middle Ages*

by VICKI LEÓN

Murasaki Shikibu, whose name means "purple wisteria[1] blossom," was born in the ancient capital of Kyoto,[2] Japan. Back then, it was called Heian-kyo or "capital of peace and tranquility." Like Washington, D.C., Shikibu's city was famous for its spring flowers—above all, the cherry blossoms. Like pink and white clouds, the cherry trees floated up nearby hillsides, nearly hiding the many Buddhist temples from view. Heian-kyo was full of aristocrats[3] and officials, nicknamed "cloud dwellers" by those not so fortunate.

> ### You Need to Know...
>
> Murasaki Shikibu is the pen name of a talented writer who lived in tenth-century Japan. Her book, *The Tale of Genji*, took her decades to complete. It is the first novel written in Japanese. Shikibu's ironic story about a smart, charming, "shining prince" has entertained readers for a thousand years with its tales of Japanese court life and dozens of interesting characters.

Young Shikibu came from a family with little money; they, however, took comfort from their <u>modest</u> connections with the high and the mighty. The Murasakis could claim a distant kinship with the powerful Fujiwara clan, who dominated court politics during the Heian period, from 800 to 1100 or so. The Murasaki household was a literary place, where as a child Shikibu often heard her parents recite poetry they had composed.

modest (mäd′ist): humble; quiet.

---

1. **wisteria** (wis·tir′ē·ə): climbing woody vine with drooping, fragrant flowers, native to East Asia.
2. **Kyoto** (kē·ō′tō): capital of Japan until 1869, and a cultural, religious, and artistic center.
3. **aristocrats** (ə·ris′tə·krats′): members of the nobility.

conceited (kən·sēt′id): vain; having too high an opinion of oneself.

elegance (el′ə·gəns): gracefulness; refinement.

prestige (pres·tēzh): impressive reputation.

prompt (prämpt): prod into action; remind.

In her diary, Shikibu described herself as unsociable, conceited about her looks, fond of old stories, and gentle. Judging by her life, she was also stubborn as a mule about going after her goals in life.

Born about 978, she lived in an era of peace, prosperity, elegance, and slow pace. By her day, a number of Japanese women had made their marks as writers and poets. Even so, girls had a tough time getting an education—and making use of it.

Most people said, "Japanese writing is good enough for women—that is, if they're going to read and write at all."

Shikibu's brothers, however, got to study the high-prestige subjects: Chinese poetry, literature, and the beautiful and complex art of Chinese brush-writing. She was shut out; fortunately, no one stopped the young girl from hanging about during the daily lessons of her older brother.

As Shikibu later recalled, "My father was anxious to make a good Chinese scholar of my brother Nobunori, and often came to hear him read his lessons. On these occasions, I was always present, and so quick to pick up the language that I soon could prompt my brother whenever he got stuck."

SIDELIGHT

Murasaki Shikibu may have been familiar with the following poem by the Chinese poet Zhang Ji, who lived during the Tang dynasty (618–907), an age that produced some of China's best classical poetry.

Maple Bridge

The moon drops, a crow cries, frost fills the air.
By a fishing lamp beneath the river maples I try to sleep.
Then from Cold Hill Temple outside of Ku Su Town
The sound of the midnight bell reaches my drifting boat.

—from *Maples in the Mist*
translated by Minfong Ho (© 1996)

Her father would sigh and say to Shikibu: "If only you were a boy, how proud and happy I should be!"

Like today, scholars in Shikibu's time sometimes got labeled as eggheads or nerds. Shikibu wrote in her diary: "It wasn't long before I repented of having distinguished myself. Person after person assured me that even boys generally become very unpopular if it's discovered that they are fond of their books. For a girl, of course, it would be even worse."

Shikibu began to keep her knowledge hidden. She put away the ink and brushes used to write the symbols for Chinese. "I was careful to conceal the fact that I could write a single Chinese character," she confessed to her diary. "This meant I got very little practice. To this day, I am shockingly clumsy with my brush."

Sometime between her sixteenth birthday and her twentieth, Murasaki Shikibu married a distant cousin of hers, a dashing lieutenant in the Imperial Guard. Within a few years, the couple had two daughters. Quietly, stubbornly, Shikibu shared her education with them, teaching her youngsters to read, write, and appreciate poetry.

Shikibu shared her education . . . teaching her youngsters to read, write, and appreciate poetry.

In 1001, her family life shattered like a fancy porcelain vase. Her husband died unexpectedly—possibly of the plague. It just wouldn't do for a widow of the Fujiwara clan to live independently, the family argued.

"You shall marry again, and well," her father promised. Before he could act on his promise (or threat), he was offered the job of governor for a distant province[4] to the north of Kyoto. The family was newly worried. The chances of finding a good catch for Shikibu there were slim.

---

4. **province** (präv′ins): territorial district.

月落烏啼霜滿天　江楓漁火對愁眠　姑蘇城外寒山寺　夜半鐘聲到客船

Illustrations copyright © 1996 by Jean and Mou-sien Tseng. Used by permission of HarperCollins Publishers.

▲ The poem "Maple Bridge" written in Chinese. Each set of Chinese characters represents a line of the poem.

from Murasaki Shikibu　**95**

By now, however, others knew about Shikibu's keen mind and literary talents—even though she'd kept a low profile. After her husband's death, Shikibu had started writing a romantic and complex story. She called it *The World of the Shining Prince* or *The Tale of Genji*.

The Emperor of Japan himself heard about Shikibu's as yet unfinished book. He had chapters read to him, and said, "This lady must be terribly learned."

His daughter, the Empress Akiko, got very excited. "I want this woman as a teacher!" she said. At sweet sixteen, the empress was a hard-core student, a tireless learner—and a bit of a prude. No boyfriends or flirtations for her—or for the ladies of her court, either. She wouldn't let her attendants dress in stylish gowns. Behavior as well as clothes had to be dull and modest.

Soon it was all arranged; Shikibu's father agreed that his daughter would serve the Empress Akiko at the Imperial Court. (Her children evidently were cared for by servants in the parents' household.)

Now about twenty-six years old, Lady Murasaki gamely[5] did whatever young Akiko ordered. As time went on, she looked with longing at the livelier court held by Princess Senshi, the emperor's aunt. "The princess and her ladies are always going off to see the sunset . . . or to hear a nightingale among the flowering trees," she wrote in her trusty diary. Oh, to be one of the Senshi gang!

"In her court, I'd be allowed to live buried in my own thoughts like a tree stump in the earth," she wrote wistfully. "At the same time, they wouldn't expect me to hide from every man I hadn't yet met. And even if I made a few remarks to such a person, I shouldn't be thought lost to all shame. Indeed, I can imagine myself under such

Mary Evans Photo Library, England

▲ A Lady of the Court. Unlike the women in Empress Akiko's court, this lady may wear many layers of silk: trouser skirts; unlined dress; lined robes; gown; mantle; train; jacket.

? **What else did ladies of the court do besides wear beautiful clothes?**

---

5. gamely (gām′lē): in a resolute manner.

circumstances becoming, after a certain amount of practice, quite lively and amusing!"

Her social life may have been cramped. But Shikibu did have a daring—even dangerous—assignment. Young Empress Akiko had a secret passion. It didn't involve the opposite sex. It involved language. She burned to learn Chinese—the main subject forbidden to Japanese women. "Too difficult!" proclaimed the male scholars. Shikibu and the empress knew better. Eventually Akiko talked Shikibu into giving her lessons, working from books in the library of Chinese literature that Murasaki had inherited when her husband died. No one ever learned of their "mission impossible," either—until many years later, when Shikibu's diary was published.

Private Collection/Bridgeman Art Library, London/SuperStock

▲ Scene from *The Tale of Genji.*

Meanwhile, the writer continued to work on her own secret project: finishing *The Tale of Genji.* She probably had trouble figuring out where to store her manuscript; the romantic tale kept getting longer and longer. All told, the manuscript had fifty-four chapters! (In one of its English translations, the book runs more than 1,100 pages—over a million words.) . . .

There are many mysteries about the author of *The Tale of Genji.* Her masterpiece, although very long, appears unfinished. It's thought that Shikibu went into a nunnery[6] in her later years, but accounts don't agree. We don't know

---

6. **nunnery** (nun·ər·ē): convent; religious community.

Past to Present: *Tale of Genji* Remakes

The Tale of Genji remains squarely within the culture of modern Japan. High school students learn the old story to prepare for college. The novel is much more than just required reading, though: A recent edition sold more than two million copies. Shikibu's story of a handsome prince is also available on CD-ROM and has become the subject of numerous Web sites. A novel that was originally written by hand, copied by court writers, and read into the ear of an eager Japanese emperor has been made into a television series and several films, including one animated version. The novel's name was even borrowed by a popular musical group that called themselves Hikaru Genji—"Shining Genji."

▲ Murasaki Shikibu's signature.

how her daughters grew up, or what they were like. But there is no mystery about Murasaki's talent or fame, which continues to bloom as brilliantly as the wisteria flowers still do each spring in Japan.

✓ Reading Check

1. What languages did Japanese girls of Shikibu's time learn to read and write?

2. How did Murasaki Shikibu learn Chinese?

3. Why did Shikibu begin to hide her knowledge?

4. What secret assignment did Shikibu receive from the Empress Akiko?

5. What was Shikibu's own secret project?

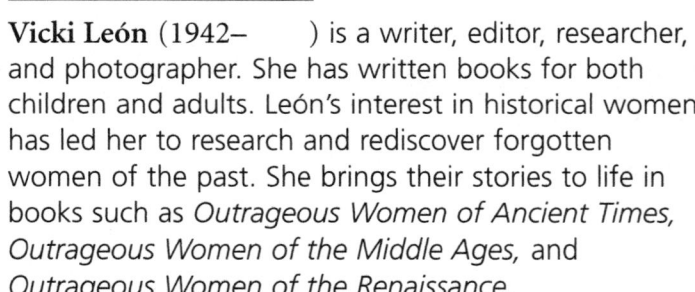

MEET THE *Writer*

Vicki León (1942–   ) is a writer, editor, researcher, and photographer. She has written books for both children and adults. León's interest in historical women has led her to research and rediscover forgotten women of the past. She brings their stories to life in books such as *Outrageous Women of Ancient Times, Outrageous Women of the Middle Ages,* and *Outrageous Women of the Renaissance.*

Cross-Curricular ACTIVITIES

■ HISTORY/ART

Mongolian Murals From the Mongols' perspective, the Great Wall might have looked like a perfect surface for a mural. What pictures or feelings might Mongols have painted on the Great Wall? How would they depict themselves, their leader Genghis Khan, or the Chinese emperor? With a partner, sketch or paint two or three ideas for a Mongol mural. Then, share your mural with the rest of the class, explaining how your mural reflects ideas or information you read about here or in other sources.

■ LANGUAGE ARTS/SCIENCE

Try It—You'll Like It! Get the word out about a terrific new Chinese invention or discovery. Select an invention—such as paper, acupuncture, or row planting—and design an informational brochure. Include pictures of the new invention, and explain how it works. Emphasize how using the invention will make people's lives easier or different. Present several reasons why someone would want to try this new invention.

■ HEALTH/DRAMA

Medicine in the Empire Work with a partner to determine how a common ailment might have been treated in medieval China. Gather information about the types of treatments and medicines that might have been used to diagnose and help cure a broken leg, a cold, or an infection. With one of you performing the role of a "doctor" and the other performing as a "patient," re-create a medical consultation as it might have occurred hundreds of years ago.

■ SCIENCE/MEDIA

Get Out Your Papers In a small group, create a video about the modern-day process of making paper. First, conduct research to find out about the materials and machinery needed to make paper. Then, film a demonstration of the steps in the production process, showing how raw materials become a finished product. You might choose to demonstrate the papermaking process by crafting your own paper or by explaining the industrial papermaking process. Present your video to the class.

■ SCIENCE/ART

Smooth as Silk Become an expert on the life cycle of the silkworm from egg to moth, and create a how-to manual for someone interested in raising silkworms. Include drawings of each stage of the silkworm's life, and make notes of the approximate length of time for each stage. You might also add details to your manual that explain how the silk is unwound from the cocoon and spun into silk thread.

■ ART/MATHEMATICS

The Empress's New Clothes Imagine that Murasaki Shikibu has asked you to design a new outfit for a special occasion in the Japanese court. Do research in libraries or on the Internet to gather ideas about typical designs for that era. Create a colorful pattern for a new kimono for Shikibu or the empress, including measurements for the various parts of the garment. Then, chart out the kimono's design on graph paper, adding colors to create special effects. Post your creation on a bulletin board in the classroom.

READ ON: FOR INDEPENDENT READING

■ NONFICTION

One World, Many Religions: The Way We Worship by Mary Pope Osborne (Random House, 1996). Are you still curious about Confucius, China's famous philosopher and teacher? This introduction to seven of the world's major religions contains color photographs and a brief overview of the history, rituals, and traditions of Confucianism. An NCTE Orbis Pictus Honor Book.

The Cultural Atlas of Japan by Martin Collcutt, Isao Kumakura, and Marius Jansen (Facts on File, 1988). Take a complete tour of Japan without ever leaving your room! With this atlas you can compare the beauty of Ice Age Japan with the Japan of today. Over 300 illustrations (most in color) and historical maps help you discover the culture of Japan—its history, geography, arts, and archaeology.

Walls: Defenses Throughout History by James Cross Giblin (Little, Brown, 1984). China's Great Wall is long enough to stretch from New York to San Francisco—and back again to Salt Lake City. Read this book by an award-winning author to learn how walls are built as defenses and why. You will amaze your friends with your knowledge of facts and legends about the Great Wall and other historic walls.

■ FICTION

The Weaving of a Dream: A Chinese Folktale by Marilee Heyer (Penguin Putnam, 1989). Have you ever lost something beautiful that meant a lot to you? In this traditional Chinese folktale, a widow loses her gorgeous woven tapestry because it is stolen. Each of her three sons searches for it. Follow their quests, which are brought to life in illustrations of old China's landscapes, costumes, and animal life. A Bring History Alive! book.

Mysterious Tales of Japan by Rafe Martin (Putnam, 1996). These Japanese mysteries are eerie and filled with unusual events that reveal Nature's spiritual power. In these tales a samurai falls in love with a willow tree, and a priest changes into a carp. Adding to the atmosphere of the mysteries are the color illustrations, haikus, and tiny sketches. A 1997 ALA Notable Book.

Maples in the Mist: Children's Poems from the Tang Dynasty translated by Minfong Ho (HarperCollins, 1996). Imagine writing a poem to get a job, or learning to read by reciting two-thousand-year-old poetry, as some young people in China have done! Here, sixteen short, classical Chinese poems are translated into English, with illustrations and Chinese characters. A 1997 ALA Notable Book.

The Hunter: A Chinese Folktale by Mary Casanova (Simon & Schuster, 2000). In the strange world of *The Hunter,* a snake is really a princess, rubies and emeralds are not the real treasure, and things are not always what they appear to be. Illustrated by dust-colored paintings and Chinese characters, this folk tale of sacrifice is a 2001 ALA Notable Book and a Parents' Choice® Gold Award winner.

CHAPTER 4
The Making of the Middle Ages
Europe and Japan A.D. 500–1500

Family Ties

What do you want to be when you grow up? Now there's a question young people in the Middle Ages probably never heard. Medieval society in Japan and western Europe was governed by the feudal (fyoo´l) system, in which people were born into well-defined social classes. This system didn't offer many choices. In Europe, lords (men of noble birth) owned land and lived in castles along with their families and servants. They depended upon knights (called samurai in Japan) for protection. Peasants farmed the lords' land for a share of the crops and sometimes had to fight their wars. Strict laws kept the lower classes in their place. Peasants could almost never work their way up in the world or even leave the village where they were born.

The Granger Collection, New York

▲ Medieval castle and peasant workers.

Food for the Feast

If you think you've ever eaten too much at a party, check out the food bought for a royal feast in 1387: 16 oxen; 14 calves; 120 sheep; 11,000 eggs; 60 dozen hens; 120 gallons of milk; 1,200 pigeons; 8 dozen young rabbits; 210 geese; 50 swans; and 140 piglets.

Of course, along with good food, you would need good manners at such a special occasion. Here are a few rules for fine dining in the Middle Ages: Don't carve the table with your knife.

The Granger Collection, New York

▲ A medieval feast is a high-protein meal.

Memorable Quote

"In the world of 999, on the eve of the first millennium, time moved at the speed of an oxcart or, more often, of a sturdy pair of legs. . . ."

—from "Life in 999: A Grim Struggle" by Howard G. Chua-Eoan in *Time Magazine*

In 1095, Pope Urban II, who was head of the Catholic church, urged Christians to defend their faith by traveling to the Holy Land and rescuing Jerusalem from the Muslims. After his speech, Christian warriors were given crosses to carry with them. The medieval Latin word *cruciata*, "marked with a cross," gave these military expeditions their name: the Crusades. Crusaders set out from Europe a number of times, making eight major trips before 1291. The word *crusade* gradually came to describe any "holy war" begun for religious reasons.

INVESTIGATE: When and where did each of the Crusades take place? What was the result of each one?

Don't spread your butter with your thumb. Don't throw bones on the floor. When you set down your spoon, make sure it doesn't get stolen!

Saint George, the Dragon Slayer

The real Saint George was an early Christian who stood up to a cruel Roman emperor. The emperor, known for killing Christians, had George tortured, dragged through the streets, and beheaded. During the Middle Ages, many legends describing Saint George as a warrior-saint became popular. Knights returning from the Crusades to the Holy Land—and even King Richard the Lion-Heart of England—reported seeing a vision of Saint George during an important battle. No wonder Saint George became the patron saint of soldiers and of England. The famous story about this warrior-saint killing a dragon may have developed to symbolize how Saint George rescued the church (a beautiful princess) from evil (the dragon).

Victoria & Albert Museum, London/Art Resource, NY

▲ Saint George and the Dragon.

The Other 1492

When Christopher Columbus and his ships reached the Americas, Luis de Torres, a Jewish translator, was the first to set foot on dry land. Shortly before Columbus had set sail, King Ferdinand and Queen Isabella of Spain had declared that every Jew in Spain must convert to Christianity and be baptized—or leave forever. Jews had lived in Spain for nearly fifteen hundred years. Some chose to be baptized, but 200,000 left after being forced to turn over their life savings and everything else of value to the royal treasury. Few ended up as well as Luis de Torres.

What if you had to sail thousands of miles in an open ship over rough, cold oceans just to talk to your family? Some brave Vikings, expert and fearless sailors, did just that. Read how they turned accidents on the high seas into discoveries of new lands.

NONFICTION BOOK

GEOGRAPHY •

HISTORY •

from Viking Luck

from *Accidental Explorers*

by REBECCA STEFOFF

▼ Viking helmet.

P. Belzeaux/Photo Researchers, Inc.

In [986], . . . the third of the Vikings' three great accidental discoveries took place. This time they found America itself.

The discoverer was Bjarni Herjolfsson, who traded between Norway and Iceland in his knörr. He reached Iceland in the summer of 986, expecting to <u>dispose</u> of his cargo and spend the winter with his father, who lived there. To his surprise, he learned that a few weeks earlier his father had sold the family home and left the island. He had gone off with Erik the Red to live in Greenland. Herjolfsson decided to follow.

Like Naddod and Gunnbjorn Ulfsson before him, Herjolfsson was caught in a gale[1] and blown off course. After the gale subsided, the knörr was surrounded by fog, and when the fog cleared, Herjolfsson was hopelessly lost. Two days later he sighted land, which

You Need to Know...

Centuries before Christopher Columbus arrived in the Americas, sailors from Scandinavia landed in North America quite by accident. In the middle of the ninth century, a Viking outlaw named Naddod was sailing north of the British Isles and was blown off course. His *knörr*, a high-sided sailing ship suitable for deep-water voyages, reached the island we today call Iceland. Around 900, a similar accident happened to another Viking, Gunnbjorn Ulfsson. He was on his way to Iceland when his boat was carried as far west as Greenland. Although tossed about by bad weather, these Vikings managed to find their way home again. Soon, other Vikings returned to these islands and even dared to sail further west, landing at last on the North American continent.

dispose (di•spōz′): distribute or transfer; sell.

---

1. gale (gāl): very strong wind, sometimes whistling or howling.

Viking Longships

During the Middle Ages, Vikings sailed fearlessly through the known world. They sailed up the rivers of Russia, traded in Baghdad and Rome, and probably reached Africa. How were they able to travel such distances? They had developed the longship. Low and light, longships were easy to manage during quick raids. They could be powered by oars to slip into rivers or to land on beaches. The longship's square sails were also easily raised and lowered, helping sailors catch the wind for fast getaways. Vikings often buried their dead inside a longship deep in the ground. Today, archaeologists are uncovering Viking graves and learning more about these awesome longships.

exploited (ek•sploit′id): made use of; used to advantage.

he described as "level and well-wooded." Before leaving Iceland he had heard enough descriptions of Greenland to know that this was not it. He headed north. Twice more he sighted land—once a flat, rocky shore and once an ice-covered mountain. But these lands were in the west, the wrong direction to be the Greenland settlement, which was on the eastern side of the sea approach. His crew wanted to land and look around, but Herjolfsson refused, saying, "This land looks unwinsome and ungainsome." This is the first recorded opinion about North America—that it looked neither pretty nor profitable.

▲ Viking longship with round shields lined up for protection.

The Granger Collection, New York

Herjolfsson decided that he had been blown west past Greenland. He turned east, and four days later he arrived at his father's home near the southwestern tip of Greenland. Herjolfsson settled in Greenland, and it seems that he had no desire to explore the lands he had sighted. Some Greenlanders, however, *were* interested in his story, perhaps because he reported seeing trees, and wood was always in short supply in the colony. Just as Erik the Red had exploited Ulfsson's accidental discovery of Greenland, so also did his son Leif decide to investigate this new find of Herjolfsson's. Around 1001, Leif Eriksson bought Herjolfsson's knörr and sailed it west with thirty-five men.

Eriksson and his men were the first Europeans to walk the soil of North America. They landed in three places, which were later described in *Erik the Red's Saga*. The first they called Helluland, which means "land of flat stones." It was cold and bleak,[2] and most scholars believe it was either the southern coast of Baffin Island, a large island that lies between Greenland and Canada, or the northern part of Canada's Labrador peninsula. South of Helluland the Vikings made their second landing, at a place they called Markland, or "wooded land"; this was probably the southern Labrador coast. The third landfall[3] they called Vinland, which could mean "wine land," "vine land," or "fruitful land."

Modern geographers and historians have argued for years about the location of Vinland. Some placed it in

---

2. **bleak** (blēk): bare; treeless; subject to wind and cold.
3. **landfall** (land′fôl′): landing after a voyage.

No Wonder Vikings Were Scary

In 793, Vikings suddenly appeared at the monastery of Saint Cuthbert, a holy site on the island of Lindisfarne off England's north coast. They grabbed gold objects and silk altar cloths, killing anyone who opposed them and taking the rest as slaves. With the raid on Saint Cuthbert's, the Viking reign of terror began. Not all Vikings robbed and pillaged, though: Most Scandinavians were primarily herdsmen and farmers. Nor were the Vikings lawless barbarians. Their general assembly, the *Althing*, is the world's oldest surviving parliament, or public council. Nevertheless, the monks at Saint Cuthbert's finally abandoned their monastery in 875, taking the body of Saint Cuthbert with them.

---

sojourn (sō′jərn): visit; temporary stay.

ancestry (an′ses′trē): line of family members.

Canada, on the shores of the Gulf of St. Lawrence. Others thought it was in Maine, in Massachusetts, in Rhode Island, or even as far south as North Carolina. But most experts now agree that Vinland was probably the northern tip of Newfoundland Island. There, in 1961, at a place called L'Anse aux Meadows, archaeologists uncovered the nine-hundred-year-old remains of a small Viking settlement. Perhaps those ruins are all that remains of the huts Leif Ericksson and his men built during their visit to America.

Eriksson and his men were the first Europeans to walk the soil of North America.

Leif Eriksson and his party had sailed from Greenland in the summer. They explored the three landfalls during late summer and fall, and they spent the winter in Vinland, returning to Greenland the following summer. Leif never went back to Vinland, but his brother Thorvald led an expedition there in 1002 and stayed in the huts Leif had built. This time the Norsemen encountered native inhabitants, either Inuit[4] or forest Indians, and fought with them. Thorvald Eriksson was killed in the fight, and his men retreated to Greenland.

In the years that followed, other relatives of Leif Eriksson tried twice to establish permanent settlements in Vinland. During the first sojourn, a woman named Gudrid gave birth to a boy who was named Snorri. He was the first child of European ancestry born in America. The Norse[5] bartered with the local Native Americans for furs and meat, but fighting broke out again, and the Norse were driven back to Greenland. The final attempt to settle Vinland was led by Freydis, Leif Eriksson's half-sister. It ended in a bloody battle among the settlers, and once again the survivors retreated to Greenland.

---

4. **Inuit** (in′o͞o·it): Eskimo people; native peoples of North America who inhabit Greenland, Canada, and Alaska.
5. **Norse** (nôrs): people of Scandinavia.

That was the end of the Vikings in America, although a few later captains may have landed briefly in Vinland or elsewhere to take on water or cut timber. As the Greenland colony declined and fell out of touch with the rest of the world, Vinland <u>receded</u> into the misty borderland between history and legend. But in the centuries that followed, it was not utterly forgotten. Tales of Leif Eriksson and the western land continued to be told in Iceland, England, and northern Europe, where they may have come to the attention of later explorers—perhaps even Christopher Columbus himself.

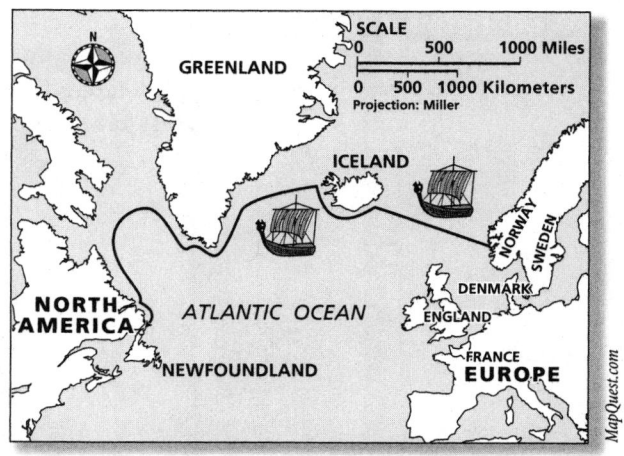

▲ Vikings sailed west from Scandinavia and established settlements in North America. ❷ **Why did these settlements fail to flourish?**

receded (ri•sēd′id): became fainter or more distant.

✓ Reading Check

1. When Bjarni Herjolfsson was blown off course, how did he know that he was not near Greenland?

2. Why would reports of seeing an area with trees have interested people who lived in Greenland?

3. Who were the first Europeans to set foot on North America?

4. What difficulties did the Viking colony encounter in Vinland?

5. How were the tales of Vinland remembered after the Viking colony disappeared?

MEET THE *Writer*

Rebecca Stefoff (1951–   ) has written over sixty books for young readers about nature, geography, exploration, history, and people of other cultures. Her recent books include *Exploring the New World*, *Colonies*, and *First Frontier*. In 1997, her *Finding the Lost Cities* won the Smithsonian Notable Book award.

It was called a curse of God, "bad air," and even the Great Plague. As the following excerpt describes, no one knew what caused the killer disease or how to stop the spread of its black death.

from Plague

from Invisible Enemies:
Stories of Infectious Disease

by JEANETTE FARRELL

▲ *Rattus rattus.*

The Black Death

Anyone who dared to venture out upon the streets of Florence in the summer of 1348, even someone who slipped out in the gray light of early dawn to avoid the death carts and the corpse robbers and the plague-inspired bandits, could not avoid the dead. In doorway after doorway they lay in rude[1] piles, father, mother, and children. They had been dragged out and dumped by their neighbors: no one was friend enough to bury the plague dead. By the end of six months, for every resident of Florence still living, at least one would have died. The young as well as the old, the strong as well as the weak all succumbed.[2] In their groins or their armpits rose the painful lumps they called buboes;[3] some grew big as a fist. Black splotches appeared on their skin. From their

> ### You Need to Know...
>
> Take a European black rat, scientific name *Rattus rattus*, a rodent that lives close to humans and doesn't stray far from home. Add some fleas—rat fleas, *Xenopsylla cheopis*. Combined with crowded and poor living conditions, these elements can produce a deadly outbreak of *Yersinia pestis*, a disease better known to us as the plague. In the fourteenth century it was called the Black Death, and it killed three-quarters of the population in certain areas. Estimates indicate that one-fourth of Europe's population—about twenty-five million people—died in this outbreak.

---

1. **rude** (rōōd): rough; coarse.
2. **succumbed** (sə·kumd'): died; were overcome.
3. **buboes** (byōō'bōz): swollen or inflamed lymph glands, especially in the armpits or groin area.

suffering bodies rose a horrible <u>stench</u>: their sweat and their urine smelled vile. None of the popular treatments, neither bleeding—which was considered beneficial in the mistaken belief that corrupt[4] body substances could be bled out—nor herbal potions, seemed to be of any use. Victims could be dead in a day.

In the fourteenth century, plague moved slowly around the world, beginning sometime around 1330 in the Gobi Desert of Mongolia. This was the second of three plague pandemics[5] in recorded history. The first, beginning in A.D. 541, spread throughout the Mediterranean civilizations. It appeared to those who experienced it to stretch to "the ends of the habitable world." The Black Death was to travel even farther in this second pandemic, making its way east to China, as well as south to India, and west through the Middle East, and on into Europe, in less than twenty years reaching as far as London.

Faster even than the disease traveled the news of it. First, stories of great natural disasters in China made their way to Europe: a drought had scorched the earth, then torrential floods drowned four hundred thousand people. There were deadly earthquakes one after another, and scourges[6] of locusts.

By the end of 1346 people across Europe had heard that these horrible <u>calamities</u> had been followed by the most deadly plague ever known. Death strode across Asia, leaving behind nothing but piles of bodies. Ships were found drifting aimlessly about the sea, their entire crews having perished from the disease.

A year after news of the disease had swept Europe, plague entered cities along the Mediterranean and appeared in Alexandria, Egypt. Along roadsides in Egypt the piles of corpses grew so high bandits used them as cover for ambushes. One traveler in Jerusalem came across a group having a feast in the midst of all this dying. The host explained that he had vowed to hold a feast if the

---

4. **corrupt** (kə·rupt′): contaminated; unwholesome.
5. **pandemics** (pan·dem′iks): epidemics that occur over a wide geographic area.
6. **scourges** (skʉrj′iz): means of inflicting suffering or punishment.

stench (stench): foul odor; stink.

"Ring Around the Rosey"

Remember holding hands, marching in a circle, chanting "Ring Around the Rosey," and dropping suddenly to the ground? This nursery–rhyme game actually re-creates each stage in a victim's death from the plague.

- "Ring around the rosey" describes a rash—the plague's first symptom.
- "A pocket full of posies" refers to flowers or herbs thought to be protection from disease.
- "Ashes! Ashes!" was originally "A-tishoo! A-tishoo!" a word copying the sound of the victim's violent sneezing.
- "We all fall down" describes the tragic end—a quick death for most of those infected.

calamities (kə·lam′ə·tēz): great misfortunes; disasters.

plague should lighten enough for one day to pass without a friend or relative dying. One such day had occurred, so now, for the moment, they feasted.

In 1347 plague entered the port of Messina on the island of Sicily. From there it was a short step to the mainland of Italy. By 1348 it was in Paris, by the end of the year in London. An Italian, Agnolo di Tura, wrote the following about his life in the year 1348:

> *The mortality in Siena began in May. It was a cruel and horrible thing; and I do not know where to begin to tell of the cruelty and the pitiless ways. It seemed that almost everyone became <u>stupefied</u> by seeing the pain. And it is impossible for the human tongue to recount the awful truth. Indeed, one who did not see such horribleness can be called blessed. And the victims died almost immediately. They would swell beneath the armpits and in their groins, and fall over while talking. Father abandoned child, wife husband, one brother another; for this illness seemed to strike through breath and sight. And so they died. And none could be found to bury the dead for money or friendship. Members of a household brought their dead to a ditch as best they could, without priest, without divine offices. Nor did the death bell sound. And in*

stupefied (stoo′pə•fīd): stunned; astounded.

The dreadful plague. ▶
? Why were people so afraid of the plague?

many places in Siena great pits were dug and piled deep with the multitudes of dead. And they died by the hundreds, both day and night, and all were thrown in those ditches and covered with earth. And as soon as those ditches were filled, more were dug. And I, Agnolo di Tura, called the Fat, buried my five children with my own hands. . . . So many died that all believed it was the end of the world.

Sudden death all around them disordered the living. So many were sick and dying that there were too few people to tend the crops, or run the courts, or police the streets. The healthy, too, abandoned their responsibilities, some to flee or hide, others to live in revelry, drinking and partying away what they thought could be their last days. Some took advantage of the chaos to plunder the homes of the sick or the dead and gather up what wealth they could. They would come upon a house, silent with death, and boldly rob the corpses. There was much to plunder: stores stood empty, riderless horses roamed the streets.

chaos (kā'äs'): disorder; confusion.

"So many died that all believed it was the end of the world."

In Florence, Italy, some of those paid to carry away the dead, emboldened[7] by their great risk of death, became fearless brigands.[8] They would burst into the homes of the living and threaten to carry them away along with the dead if they were not appeased with bribes. Between fear of their vicious attacks and fear of the disease, few upright citizens braved the streets of Florence: an expectant quiet settled over the city, broken only by the rattling of the wagons on their rounds to pick up the dead, and the carriages of the wealthy as they hurriedly fled to the country. Behind their closed doors, in their stuffy rooms, everyone wondered: What is killing us, and how can I be saved? . . .

appeased (ə•pēzd'): satisfied or calmed; bought off.

---

7. **emboldened** (em•bōl'dənd): given courage.
8. **brigands** (brig'əndz): robbers; roving bandits.

▲ No one noticed the rat.

quarantined (kwôr′ən•tēnd′): isolated from human contact for a required period of time to prevent spread of disease.

epidemic (ep′ə•dem′ik): rapid spread of contagious disease.

Strangely enough, no one seems to have noticed the rats. Hardly one of the plague chroniclers[9] mentions these rodents, which must have been lying dead in the dark back streets, and in the walls of poor homes, and occasionally swept by a disgusted mother out of a kitchen. No one seems to have noticed that many rats were dying—rats that could have nimbly[10] found their way ashore even from a quarantined boat.

The Shrinking World

About one hundred and fifty years before the Black Death, the empire of Genghis Khan and his Mongol warriors began to stretch across Asia, eventually to encompass much of China and Russia. The empire bound together these vast lands with a network of messengers and traders broader and swifter than any that had been seen before. Caravans traveled new northern routes across the great dry plains of Central Asia known as the steppes, and messengers on swift ponies traveled one hundred miles a day. They made the world smaller and brought into contact people and creatures that had never before met.

It seems very possible that, borne in the saddlebags of these swift Mongol ponies, and in the sacks of grain carried to feed the traders on their way, and in booty stolen by ransacking Mongol warriors, traveled the plague.

The plague has a nimble home: when the bacillus[11] that causes the disease is not infecting a dying human, or some other larger creature, it lives in the body of a flea. A plague epidemic depends upon the presence of rats and fleas because bubonic plague—the most common form of the disease, named for the buboes it causes—cannot spread from person to person without a flea to carry it. Occasionally, the type of flea that likes to bite humans can be the culprit, but most of the time it is the rat flea, and the plague must go from rat to flea to human.

The rat flea prefers the body of a creature like a rat to bite for its dinner of blood, but if another body—such as

9. **chroniclers** (krän′i•klərz): historians.
10. **nimbly** (nim′blē): very quickly and with agility.
11. **bacillus** (bə•sil′əs): microorganism, especially one that causes disease.

a human one—is within leaping distance, it will do. The flea leaps and bites, and in its bite it <u>disperses</u> the plague. In fact, the flea is eager to bite because the plague has made it very hungry. Plague germs multiplying inside the flea block its stomach, leaving the flea insatiable.[12] It bites and bites, drinking feverishly, as it tries to satisfy itself. For plague, this is ideal, since the blocked flea vomits the blood it desperately drinks right back into the wound it has made in its host's flesh, and along with the blood, plague germs. The flea bite becomes an injection of plague bacilli.

It appears that plague lived in the burrows of wild rodents near the mountainous intersection of China, India, and Burma. Plague traveled from rodent to rodent, carried by the flea. If all the rodents in an area died of the disease, leaving all the fleas to starve to death, plague could still survive in the dirt of the rodent burrows for as long as five years. . . .

The rats that ran off the sailing ships arrived in a Europe that had swollen to the bursting point. Europe's population had grown by leaps and bounds in the previous few centuries, so that there were now more people than there was food to feed them or wood to house them. And in the years approaching the 1340s, bad winters had decimated[13] food crops, leaving even less food for an already hungry continent.

When the first plague-infested ship landed at Messina on the island of Sicily, there were as yet uninfected rats onshore to host the fleas, and starving humans to succumb to the plague. The Black Death had arrived.

Plague bacilli are terrible little <u>toxin</u> factories. The heat of the human body signals the thousands of bacilli injected by the flea to go into special production: they began to make poisons specifically designed to help them bore their way into human cells. If the human's immune-system cells manage to kill some of them, the germs release more poisons from their dying bodies. Meanwhile, they work their

disperses (di·spʉrs′iz): spreads widely.

Artist Unknown: Correr Civic Museum, Venice, Italy/ET Archive, London/SuperStock

▲ The plague doctor. The doctors wore gloves and carried canes so that their hands would not touch the sick. They also wore bird-like masks and filled the beaks with sweet-smelling herbs.

toxin (täk′sin): poison.

---

12. **insatiable** (in·sā′shə·bəl): impossible to satisfy; always wanting more.
13. **decimated** (des′ə·māt′id): killed in great numbers; largely destroyed.

Cover Your Mouth When You Bark!

The next time you're sick, you might ask your dog how it feels, too. Humans share sixty-five different diseases with dogs, fifty diseases with cattle, and forty-two with pigs! For many diseases, such as malaria and typhus, animals pass infections along to humans. The infection may harm humans more than animals because bacteria and viruses become more deadly as they pass from one type of host to another. Bubonic plague, however—one of the thirty-two diseases that we share with rats and mice—is as deadly for rodents as it is for humans. In this case the flea is to blame.

▲ The bite of a tiny flea (shown here in magnified form) spread the Black Death across Europe.

inexplicable (in′eks•pli′kə•bəl): not easily explained.

way into the body's fluid drainage system, called the lymphatic system, to travel. If the flea bite was on the leg, the lymph drainpipes carry plague to the lymph nodes in the groin. If the bite is on the hand, plague rides the pipes to the armpit nodes. In the nodes, the filtering centers of the lymphatic system, a massive battle begins to take place. The bacilli excrete toxins, the body sends immune-system cells, and the node swells with the dead of both armies and coagulated[14] blood. It forms a bubo, a hard lump that can reach the size of an orange, a lump that can last for several days and is so painful it can almost drive one mad. If the person is lucky, the bubo will burst, leaving a horrible open wound, somewhat relieving the pain and perhaps marking the beginning of recovery.

Even without treatment, as many as one quarter to one half of bubonic plague victims will survive. But in an unlucky one out of twenty victims the bacilli will find their way to the lungs and become pneumonic[15] plague. The lungs are an excellent place for plague to grow, and it will rapidly infect the entire lung surface. One day the victim has a headache and fever and the next is coughing up bloody sputum.[16] The lungs are so rapidly destroyed the body cannot get enough oxygen and the hands and feet begin to turn black. Without treatment, the patients will certainly die that very day or the next. And every cough from the victim's infected lungs will disperse plague bacilli into the air. Unlike bubonic plague, this form of infection needs no flea. All those who inhale those bacilli are vulnerable to developing plague in their own lungs.

To the witnesses of the plague, living in their small towns, none of this was evident. They didn't even notice the dead rats, much less the tiny fleas. They only saw the horrible <u>inexplicable</u> deaths of those people around them. While plague would return again

---

14. **coagulated** (kō•ag′yōō•lāt′id): changed from liquid to solid state; clotted.
15. **pneumonic** (nōō•män′ik): affecting the lungs.
16. **sputum** (spyōōt′əm): matter, including saliva, that is coughed up and spit from the mouth.

and again to ravage people in Europe, Asia, and Africa, it would be hundreds of years before they were to consider that such devastation was wrought by the tiny invisible living creatures we know as germs.

✓ **Reading Check**

1. What are the symptoms of the Black Death?

2. In addition to their fear of catching the Black Death, what other terrible conditions did the people living during the time of the plague face?

3. How is the plague passed from one person to another?

4. Where did the plague seem to originate?

5. How does the plague work its way through the human system? Where will the germs collect?

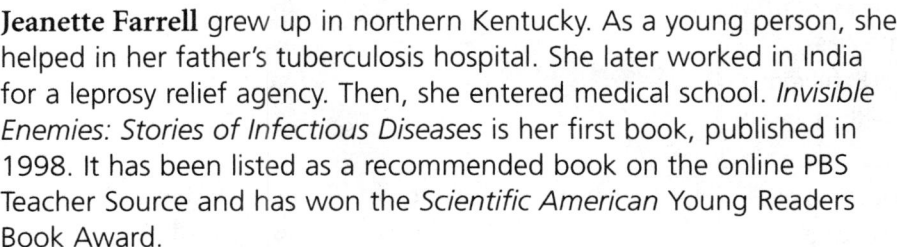

MEET THE *Writer*

Jeanette Farrell grew up in northern Kentucky. As a young person, she helped in her father's tuberculosis hospital. She later worked in India for a leprosy relief agency. Then, she entered medical school. *Invisible Enemies: Stories of Infectious Diseases* is her first book, published in 1998. It has been listed as a recommended book on the online PBS Teacher Source and has won the *Scientific American* Young Readers Book Award.

Sometimes a person's last words in life form a perfect expression of his or her character. This was especially true of one of the most famous figures of the Middle Ages, Saint Francis of Assisi. Among his last words was a *canticle*, or a song of praise, showing how he saw all of God's creations as his brothers and sisters.

Brother Sun ... Sister Moon

from *Brother Sun, Sister Moon: The Life and Stories of St. Francis*

by MARGARET MAYO

All praise to you, most high, all powerful, all good Lord.
To you alone, all praise belongs.
Praise to you, through everything
you have made . . .

All praise, my Lord, through Sister Moon and the Stars,
set in the sky, so wonderful and bright.

All praise, my Lord, through Brothers Wind and Air,
and all the weathers, cloudy, calm, or stormy,
by which you <u>nourish</u> all you have made.

You Need to Know...

Saint Francis (1181/82–1226), whose original name was Francesco di Pietro di Bernardone, was born into a wealthy family. As a young man, inspired by his religious beliefs, Francesco gave up all his material goods and family ties to live in poverty. For the rest of his life, he cared for people suffering from illness and poverty. His preaching attracted many followers whom he organized into three Franciscan orders of monks and nuns.

nourish (nŭr′ish): feed; support or help develop.

All praise, my Lord, through Sister Water,
so precious, useful, humble, and pure.

All praise, my Lord, through Brother Fire,
who lights up the night.
How joyful he is! How beautiful and strong!

All praise, my Lord, through Sister Earth,
our mother who feeds us
and gives us fruits and herbs and colored flowers.

Praise and bless my Lord.
Thank Him and serve Him
With great <u>humility</u>.

▲ Saint Francis preaching to the birds.

Brother Wolf, Sister Lark

Many legends tell of Saint Francis's ability to communicate with animals. He supposedly tamed a wolf that was terrifying a village by arranging a truce between the village and the wolf. The gentle monk also was especially fond of "Sister Lark," a plain bird with a beautiful voice. On the day Francis died, legend says, larks gathered above his resting place, then flew above him in a great circle, singing him his final song.

humility (hyōō•mil′ə•tē): lacking pride; the quality of being humble.

✓ Reading Check

1. What aspects of the world does St. Francis choose to praise?

2. What does St. Francis's song ask his audience to do?

How would you like to be an eyewitness to a dramatic and unforgettable event that affects thousands of lives? All that teenager Anna Comnena had to do was look out her window and see history in the making. Read on to find out what she saw, and how she wrote it all down to become the first female historian.

Anna Comnena

from *Outrageous Women of the Middle Ages*

by VICKI LEÓN

The First Crusade, which began on August 15, 1096, wasn't reported in any newspaper. It did, however, have an eyewitness reporter to document it—Anna Comnena. A princess of the Byzantine Empire, Anna was the oldest child of Empress Irene and Emperor Alexius I. She lived in Constantinople, the city we now call Istanbul.

The Crusades were often made out to be noble pilgrimages by fair and gallant knights, traveling from Europe to take back the holy city of Jerusalem from the infidels. Anna Comnena knew better. She saw the crusaders in action. Many of them were unwelcome, unwashed, and ungallant invaders who came for reasons far from holy.

You Need to Know...

Anna Comnena had more than enough ambition and education to rule the Byzantine Empire. When her brother was made emperor instead of her, Anna turned her talents to writing a biography of her father, Emperor Alexius Comnenus. This became a fifteen-volume history book called *The Alexiad*. In this enormous work, Anna drew on royal archives, military reports, and diplomatic correspondence to provide insight into a major event that affected not only her father's life, but the entire history of the Middle Ages as well—the First Crusade.

Anna's father was one of the key people who got the First Crusade off the ground. Ambitious Alexius was very short of manpower, and anxious to reconquer Turkey, Syria, and other lands once governed by his Byzantine Empire. He decided to ask the pope in Rome for troops. "Send us help," he said to Pope Urban. "The Infidels (he meant non-Christians, mainly Muslims) are nearly at our door. Together let's chase them out of these lands—and from Christianity's holy places!"

The pope liked this SOS[1] from Alexius. It gave him an excuse to form a papal[2] army. "A holy war!" he declared. "It's our duty to march to the rescue of the Christians in the East." To make the Crusade more attractive to Europeans, the pope proclaimed that anyone could do <u>penance</u> for sins by fighting the holy war, or giving money to it. "What about taking lives?" people asked. Officials had a good answer for that, too. It would only be a sin if Christians were killed, they said.

▲ Crusaders on their way to the Holy Land. **❓ How would you describe the Crusaders as shown in this illustration?**

Bettmann/CORBIS

Soon Anna heard the bad news about the "Franks," as she and her fellow Byzantines called the Europeans. To Anna and her family, the Franks were barely civilized. Anna's father wasn't happy about the troops that were being sent to him, either. "Instead of the trained soldiers I asked for, the pope has gotten everyone stirred up!" he exclaimed.

Religious enthusiasm soon got completely out of hand. The first wave to arrive in Constantinople was a motley[3] crew of untrained peasants, French and German, plus a few foot soldiers and knights, who'd already attacked and killed four thousand innocent Hungarians along the way. They were led by a <u>fanatic</u> monk riding a donkey who called himself Peter the Hermit. (Anna nicknamed him "Cuckoo Peter.")

As the summer heat shimmered off the walls of Anna's city, thousands of people milled around. The singing, chanting crusaders, the boiling dust they raised, the long slender palm branches and crosses they carried, made a

penance (pen′əns): act of devotion done to show sorrow for a wrong-doing.

fanatic (fə•nat′ik): extremely devoted to a cause.

---

1. **SOS** (es′ō′es′): international signal of distress, as sent by radio code.
2. **papal** (pā′pəl): relating to a pope.
3. **motley** (mät′lē): diverse; composed of clashing elements.

Adventure on the Second Crusade

In 1147, another famous woman—Eleanor of Aquitaine—set out for the Holy Land on a crusade with her very religious husband (King Louis of France). Queen Eleanor did not travel light. She took along many chests of silk dresses and fur-lined robes, jewelry, and cosmetics. She also invited many friends, who brought their maids, singers, and pet falcons. When food supplies gave out, the falcons hunted down game birds for the nobles to eat. In the end, though, the Second Crusade was not the sort of adventure Eleanor had hoped for. Winter storms blew the ladies' tents over, soaking their fancy clothes, and the sight of dead Crusaders along the roads brought them face to face with the terrible reality of war.

▲ Eleanor of Aquitaine.

Bettmann/CORBIS

destitute (des′tə·tōōt′): poor; lacking basic necessities.

tremendous impression on the princess. From her perch atop the great stone walls of Constantinople, Anna saw it all: "Full of ardor and enthusiasm, the Franks thronged[4] every highway. With these warriors came a host of civilians, outnumbering the grains of sand on the seashore, carrying palms in their hands and bearing crosses on their shoulders. There were women and children, too, who had left their own countries. Like tributaries[5] joining a river, they streamed in all directions toward us."

It was a terrifying logistics[6] problem. These ragtag arrivals were short on food, water, and good behavior. And behind them were eighty thousand more crusaders, led by powerful princes from the west. Besides supplying food and water, and helping with the big job of transporting them across the waters of the Bosphorus[7] that divided Constantinople in two, Anna's father was worried about violence. He'd seen the Franks in action already. As Anna later wrote, "He feared the incursions[8] of these people, for he had already experienced the savage fury of their attack, their fickleness[9] of mind, and their readiness to approach anything with violence."

Anna thought it would take a miracle to move the waves of crusaders through Constantinople and get them safely on their way. As it turned out, the flood of people headed for Jerusalem lasted nine months.

A teen when the First Crusade began, Anna was twenty-four when it ended. Jerusalem was now in Christian hands. As predicted, countless knights and civilians had straggled back into the Queen of Cities, as Constantinople was nicknamed. Many were hurt, ill, or simply destitute.

---

4. **thronged** (thrônd): crowded.
5. **tributaries** (trib′yōō·ter′ēz): streams that flow into a larger body of water.
6. **logistics** (lō·jis′tiks): relating to the management of an event, the people, and their lodging and supplies.
7. **Bosphorus** (bäs′fə·rəs): narrow waterway dividing the European and Asian sections of present-day Turkey.
8. **incursions** (in·kʉr′shənz): invasions; raids.
9. **fickleness** (fik′əl·nis): instability; the quality of being changeable.

Anna worked with her father to establish and run an enormous hospital and convalescent[10] center in the heart of Constantinople. Called the Orphanage, it had special facilities for the mutilated,[11] the blind, and the poor. As many as ten thousand lived there, it was guessed. As Anna wrote, "The buildings stood in a double circle . . . so large was the circle that if you wished to visit these people and started early in the morning, it would be evening before you were done."

▲ Crusaders embarking for the Holy Land.

The hours she spent at the Orphanage were not a make-work job to occupy the spare time of a princess. Anna had a natural talent for medicine, brought along by a fabulous education. She'd studied the wisdom and literature of the ancient Greeks and Romans. She'd tackled geometry, mathematics, astronomy, and medicine. As a cultured Byzantine princess, naturally she knew the Christian scriptures well, played music and sang acceptably, and had an understanding of geography and history.

An all-around intellectual, Anna had <u>formidable</u> skills as a healer. She followed the teachings of Galen, the renowned physician and teacher of Roman days. She also understood the effects of the mind on the body. When her father became ill with the gout,[12] she began to research that disease and its possible cures. Eventually she wrote a book about it. Later in life, when her father was on his deathbed, she was called in as one of the medical experts.

A bookworm since childhood, Anna Comnena was, sad to say, consumed by another worm as well. It was called jealousy. Anna always craved the family limelight. In 1091, eight-year-old Anna had been the center of attention. With great pomp, she became engaged to Constantine

formidable (fôr′mə·də·bəl): impressive; awe-inspiring.

10. **convalescent** (kän′və·ləs′ənt): slowly and gradually recovering from injuries.
11. **mutilated** (myo͞ot′il·āt′id): crippled; damaged or injured.
12. **gout** (gout): condition resulting in the painful swelling of the joints, especially in hands and feet.

momentous (mō·men′təs): important; significant.

Ducas, the boy who would inherit the throne from her father. After a <u>momentous</u> ceremony, she went to live in the palace of her new fiancé's family, as was the custom.

Then, like a series of slaps to her face, dreadful events began to happen. Without warning, her five-year-old brother John was named the new heir; Anna's engagement with Constantine was abruptly broken off by one or both sides; and Constantine died in 1097.

Angry and feeling cheated, Anna was married off that same year to Nicephorus Bryennius. She was fourteen. She grumbled at the time, "I would prefer to remain unwed." Nicephorus was as nice as his name, however. Handsome, hardworking, and a whiz on the battlefield, he made points with Anna's dad and little by little, with Anna herself. They had four children together and many years of marriage before he died from illness. Despite the happiness she enjoyed with her family, Anna's heart still looked for revenge.

When her beloved father died in 1118, brilliant Anna gave in to her dark side. Twice she devised plots and conspired with others to assassinate her brother John, now Emperor of the Byzantine Empire. When the plots failed, John forgave his big sister. But Anna didn't get away scot-free. John banished her from the court and exiled her to a nunnery.

Oddly enough, out of her punishment and her continuing bitterness came a wonderful legacy. Now in her late thirties, Anna Comnena put her mind to a new labor—one that would occupy the rest of her life. She began to write *The Alexiad*, a history of her father and her family. Sheer luck decreed that Anna's book survived the lottery of time. In *The Alexiad*, we have more than a family memoir. *The Alexiad* is a precious,[13] sometimes melodramatic account of the Byzantine world of the eleventh and twelfth centuries. It shows the Crusades from the perspective of a woman, a civilian, and a keen-eyed reporter who saw and remembered it all.

The Granger Collection, New York

▲ Anna's father, Alexius I Comnenus (1048–1118). This detail from a mosaic shows the Byzantine emperor as a respected monarch.

---

13. precious (presh′əs): overly refined in behavior or language.

"Lightning From Heaven"

Without giving away its secret formula, Anna describes a Byzantine weapon that struck fear into the bravest of hearts. "Greek fire," or "lightning from heaven," was first used to save Constantinople from Arab invaders in A.D. 673. It was invented by Callinicus, a refugee from Syria. The exact composition of Greek fire is still a mystery. Anna Comnena reports that the deadly mixture was blown through reed tubes to burst into flame at the tube's end, like a flamethrower. Containers of it hurled at enemy ships would explode on impact. It set fire to anything it hit and even burned in water.

✓ Reading Check

1. When did the First Crusade begin? How did Emperor Alexius I help start it?

2. What did Anna Comnena and her family think of the European crusaders who arrived in Constantinople?

3. What were some of Anna's observations about the people she saw crowding the streets of her city?

4. Why was Anna especially well suited to help run Constantinople's hospital?

5. What events in Anna's life made her feel that she was treated unfairly by her family? What was a positive result of Anna's treatment by her brother John?

MEET THE *Writer*

Vicki León (1942–   ) is a writer, editor, researcher, and photographer. She has written books for both children and adults. León's interest in historical women has led her to research and rediscover forgotten women of the past. She brings their stories to life in books such as *Outrageous Women of Ancient Times*, *Outrageous Women of the Middle Ages*, and *Outrageous Women of the Renaissance*.

During the Middle Ages, an army of children set out from Europe on a long, dangerous journey to the Middle East. Read on to discover what inspired them to risk their lives and what happened to them along the way.

The Children's Crusade

from *Renaissance*

by CRISTINA PELAYO

zeal (zēl): enthusiasm; eagerness.

The religious fervor[1] brought about by the Crusades eventually captivated Europe's children. Seized with a fanatical zeal, thousands of youngsters believed that they, too, should join this noble cause and help save the Holy Land. Two separate groups of children started out on these Crusades. Unfortunately, both ended in disaster.

The first of these Crusades was spurred by a ten-year-old German boy called Nicholas, who managed to lure thousands of children between the ages of six and eighteen to run away from home. Nicholas assured his young band of followers that God would help them redeem Jerusalem from the Saracens,[2] and like their adult counterparts, they took vows to reach and defend the Holy Land.

The Church neither sanctioned[3] nor approved of the children's quest, and despite the fact that all

You Need to Know...

In 1095, the head of the Catholic Church in Rome, Pope Urban II, sent out a plea to the Christians of Europe. He claimed it was their duty to wage war against Muslims occupying Jerusalem and other places in the Middle East that were considered holy to Christians. (See "Anna Comnena," page 118.) The pope's call for help set off a series of disastrous military expeditions that came to be known as the Crusades. For two hundred years, Crusaders set out to conquer Jerusalem. Even children were swept up in the cause during the Children's Crusade in 1212. In the end, the Crusaders never accomplished their goal.

redeem (ri·dēm'): take back; restore.

---

1. **fervor** (fʉr'vər): intense emotion; passion.
2. **Saracens** (sar'ə·sənz): term used especially at time of the Crusades to describe Arab or Muslim peoples.
3. **sanctioned** (saŋk'shənd): given permission. *Sanctioned* has two contradictory meanings—"given permission" and "punished."

responsible authorities—both clerical and lay[4]—<u>deplored</u> it, the children marched off to Italy where they intended to board a ship bound for Jerusalem. As they traveled from town to town, their enthusiasm attracted more <u>impressionable</u> children along the way, and their numbers steadily increased to about 20,000.

But the route was treacherous and difficult. By the time they reached Mainz,[5] many of the younger and weaker children had succumbed to fear and starvation. Weary and sick from exhaustion, they tried to find their way back home. The rest continued across the Alps to Italy, only to be separated; some continued toward Venice while the main body of about 7,000 children headed for Genoa, only to be refused passage to the Holy Land and forced

deplored (dē·plôrd′): disapproved of; regretted.

impressionable (im·presh′ən·ə·bəl): easily influenced.

▲ The Children's Crusade.

Artist unknown/SuperStock

---

4. **clerical and lay** (kler′i·kəl): Clerical relates to the clergy, or religious officials. Lay refers to secular offices not related to the Church.
5. **Mainz** (mīnts): city of western Germany, located on the Rhine River.

SIDELIGHT

A historian writing during the time of the Children's Crusade describes its beginnings.

"About the time of Easter and Pentecost, without anyone having preached or called for it and prompted by I know not what spirit, many thousands of boys, ranging in age from six years to full maturity, left the plows or carts which they were driving, the flocks which they were pasturing, and anything else which they were doing. This they did despite the wishes of their parents, relatives, and friends who sought to make them draw back. Suddenly one ran after another to take the cross. Thus, by groups of twenty, or fifty, or a hundred, they put up banners and began to journey to Jerusalem. They were asked by many people on whose advice or at whose urging they had set out upon this path. . . . They briefly replied that they were equal to the Divine will in this matter and that, whatever God might wish to do with them, they would accept it willingly and with humble spirit."

—from *Chronica Regiae Coloniensis Continuatio Prima*
translated by James Brundage,
from *The Crusades: A Documentary History*

to abandon their Crusade. Several made their way to Rome to ask the Pope to release them from their vows, but most of the group simply scattered across Italy, confused and penniless. A few may have succeeded in taking passage on ships bound to Jerusalem, but sadly, a great majority simply disappeared without a trace.

A great majority simply disappeared without a trace.

Meanwhile, in France, a shepherd boy named Stephen initiated a similar movement after claiming that Christ had appeared to him in a vision and commanded him to raise an army to aid the Crusaders in the Holy Land. Like Nicholas in Germany, the glamour of Stephen's quest drew a horde of followers that included adults as well as children.

The group headed to Paris to try to convince the king to sanction their Crusade, but the king refused their request and told them to return to their homes. Undaunted, thousands of children continued to rally behind Stephen.

Close to 30,000 children eventually reached Marseilles,[6] where it is said that two disreputable merchants offered them free passage to Syria, all the while intending to sell them as slaves to Saracen princes and slave merchants. Different accounts suppose that seven ships carrying the children were destroyed in a storm, killing all aboard. Whatever remaining ships managed to reach Alexandria and Algeria delivered the captive children into sinister hands. Many were killed and most certainly enslaved.

horde (hôrd): traveling crowd; large throng.

Bettmann/CORBIS

▲ The ill-fated Children's Crusade. ❓ **Why was this Crusade so unsuccessful?**

---

6. **Marseilles** (mär·sā′): port city in southeast France.

The Children's Crusade illustrates the thirteenth-century passion engendered[7] by holy causes. Unfortunately, the children's emotional response to crusading fervor achieved nothing, and instead ended in a tragic tribute to the grip that the Holy Land held on all classes of the European imagination.

---

7. **engendered** (en·jen′dərd): produced.

Reading Check

1. How did the first Children's Crusade begin? About how many children joined this Crusade?

2. What happened to the young Crusaders when they reached Genoa?

3. Why did the French shepherd named Stephen begin a crusade?

4. What message did the French king give the young Crusaders?

5. What might have happened to the children who reached Marseilles, seeking passage to the Holy Land?

What is your most prized possession? In Japan of the Middle Ages, the samurai's greatest treasure was his sword. Read the following article to discover how important making a flexible, sharp sword can be.

The Sword of the Samurai

from *Calliope*

by CAROLYN GARD

▲ Samurai sword.

Araldo de Luca/CORBIS

"**A** sword is a samurai's most prized possession and should be chosen with care," advised Katsu Kokichi, a samurai and sword dealer, who knew a samurai's sword was not only a weapon but also a symbol of a warrior's power and position in society.

A samurai's long sword (*katana*) expressed the owner's courage, honor, and obedience. Good swords had a spirit that reflected the owner's character. A sword could bring its owner good fortune, virtue, or sickness. A samurai slept with his sword under his pillow, for if he lost his sword, he also lost his honor.

Because swords meant so much to the samurai, the Japanese held the swordsmith (*kaji*) in high esteem. The swordsmith took his work very seriously. Before he started making a blade, he prayed, fasted, and purified himself with cold water. For some parts of the process, he wore a white robe.

You Need to Know...

From the twelfth to the mid-nineteenth centuries, the samurai (sam′ə•rī′) made up the highest of four castes (social classes) in Japanese society. As warriors, the samurai owed absolute loyalty to their lord, or *daimyo* (dī′myō′). The lords were rich landowners who used the samurai as a private army for protection. In medieval Japan only the samurai were allowed to carry swords. The samurai warriors believed that their swords were sacred because the swords reflected their inner thoughts and symbolized their souls.

obedience (ō•bē′dē•əns): willingness to obey authority.

virtue (vʉr′chōō): honor; respectability.

esteem (ə•stēm′): favorable opinion; high regard.

fasted (fast′id): ate very little or no food at all.

purified (pyōōr′ə•fīd′): made clean by special rituals or ceremonies.

The swordsmith started the blade by welding steel strips together to make a bar about six inches by two inches by one-half inch. He heated this bar and cut it almost in half, folded it over, and beat it out again. He repeated the heating, folding, and beating as many as twenty times. This gave the blade more than a million layers of steel.

This gave the blade more than a million layers of steel.

After shaping the metal bar into a blade, the smith tempered it. The sword had to be hard at the edge to stay sharp in battle, but flexible in the body so it did not break. The swordsmith covered the entire blade with a clay mixture and scraped the clay off of the edge. He heated the blade in a charcoal fire. When the metal glowed the right color, he plunged the red-hot blade into cold water. The edge cooled quickly and became hard. The part of the blade protected by the clay cooled slowly and stayed soft.

After tempering, the sword had to be polished and sharpened, a process that often took several weeks. Some people say swords made by the greatest swordsmiths never needed to be sharpened.

The Japanese named seventeen men master swordsmith (*meijin*). The most important of these was Masamune, who lived in the early fourteenth century. Another swordsmith of the fourteenth century, Muramasa, also made excellent swords, but his swords had a reputation for casting an evil spell. Samurai who

▲ Samurai in full armor. ❓ **In addition to a samurai's sword, what else helped the warrior defend himself?**

Chain Mail and Scary Masks

A samurai's armor weighed only twenty-two pounds. Made of Japanese chain mail—metal panels sometimes laced together by silk threads—the armor allowed the samurai to be quick on his feet. A samurai's helmet and neck guard were just as important, since defeated samurai were often beheaded. A steel mask (*menpo*) protected the warrior's face and frightened the enemy with its fierce features—sometimes including a huge mustache made of hemp (long fibers usually used to make rope). A helmet with tall horns (*kabuto*) made the samurai look even more frightening. A hole (*tehen*) at the top of the helmet allowed the warrior's hair, braided into a pigtail, to pass through.

Samurai Goes Hollywood

Akira Kurosawa, a Japanese film director, set several of his movies in medieval Japan. The strict code of honor for the samurai warrior interested him. Kurosawa's 1954 epic *Shichinin no samurai (Seven Samurai)* not only inspired the 1960 Hollywood western *The Magnificent Seven*, but also led other directors, such as George Lucas, to model heroes in their films on the samurai. In these films the samurai warrior became a "western-ized" Hollywood hero.

used them became blood-thirsty or brought evil onto their families. One samurai who had a Muramasa blade became a robber.

Masamune and Muramasa had a contest to see who could make the best blade. Muramasa put his sword upright in a stream. Every leaf that struck the sword was cut in two. When Masamune put his sword in the stream, the leaves passed around his blade and floated by unhurt. Thus, it was said that Masamune's sword had power over the leaves and would have power over its owner's enemies as well.

▲ A samurai warrior on horseback.

Culver Pictures Inc/SuperStock

✔ Reading Check

1. Why would a samurai sleep with his sword under his pillow?

2. How would the swordsmith prepare himself to make a sword?

3. How did a swordsmith form the shape of a sword's blade?

4. How could a sword have both a hard, sharp edge and a flexible body?

5. Why were the swords of Masamune thought to be better than those of Muramasa?

How long does it take you to get ready in the morning? If you had to put on a suit of armor before going to school, you might have to ask for help in order to attach all the pieces—or even just to carry the heavy metal of the suit—as the following excerpt explains.

Getting Dressed
from *Armor*

by CHARLOTTE and DAVID YUE

Francis G. Mayer/CORBIS

▲ Suit of armor. The tonlet, or iron skirt, gave a knight added protection for fighting on foot.

Armor became heavy and uncomfortably hot when worn for any length of time. The knight did not put it on until he was ready to go into battle. It did not take long to put on a suit of armor, but it did require the help of a squire.[1]

Under his armor a knight wore an arming doublet. This was a close-fitting jacket lined with satin or silk. Metal armor rubbed and wore through fabric easily, so the doublet was constructed of sturdy material, such as cotton canvas or corduroy. The smooth lining kept the roughness of the other material away from the knight's skin and helped prevent chafing. He wore a pair of thick woolen hose tied to the arming doublet. Usually these were separate leggings, but sometimes the two legs were sewn into a single garment.

Pieces of mail were attached by laces called arming points at any place that was not well protected by the plate armor. Vulnerable places were under the armpits, at the bend of the elbow, and at the bend of the knee.

You Need to Know...

Knights in the thirteenth century needed to protect themselves from newly developed weapons, such as maces (clubs with spiked, metal heads) and longbows. They switched from wearing chain mail (metal rings laced together) to wearing plate armor made of solid metal. Constructed with as many as two hundred pieces and weighing as much as sixty-five pounds, plate armor was a knight's state-of-the-art defense for three hundred years.

---

1. **squire** (skwīr): attendant for a medieval knight.

vulnerable (vul'nər•ə•bəl): easily injured or hurt.

Designer Armor

In the Middle Ages, craftsmen called armorers used their skill to turn iron ore into tough, well-fitting armor. Armorers were highly respected because a knight's safety depended on their craft. The best armor bore a signature mark (a design stamped into the metal) as proof that the armorers had performed a test of the armor's strength. Usually the test was to shoot a short, heavy arrow, called a bolt, at the armor from a crossbow. Armorers were richly rewarded for their engineering skills. They could make a suit of armor that was hard, yet flexible—steel on the outside and bendable iron on the inside.

▲ Armorer's workshop. ❓ **What was the relationship between the armorer and the knight?**

The Granger Collection, New York

Sometimes, pads of blanketing were fastened at the knight's knees to prevent chafing from the knee guard. He wore stout leather shoes.

Parts of the plate armor were usually tied to the arming doublet. This helped distribute the weight of the harness and helped keep the armor securely in place and less likely to shift as the knight moved.

Arming a man was a serious business; an improperly attached piece of armor could prove fatal. Since a suit of armor was such a complicated defense, it was easy for a fastening to break or a hinge to work improperly. When arming a knight, the squire began at the feet and tried, as far as was possible, to dress his knight so that each piece overlapped the one beneath it. This created a glancing[2] surface.

The foot defenses were put on first. They covered only the top of the foot and were strapped to the sole of the shoe. The leg armor was strapped on next—greaves, knee guards, and cuisses. Then a skirt of mail, called a brayette, was attached around the waist to protect the groin. If the neck defense, or gorget, was worn under the body armor, it was put on next. Otherwise, the breast- and backplates were buckled on with the taces and tassets, the attaching plates which protected the knight from his waist to his thighs. A leather belt was usually buckled around his waist to make sure the body defenses stayed secure. After this, the arm defenses were put on and fastened to the arming doublet just below the shoulder. In some suits they were kept as three pieces that were strapped on separately. If the gorget was worn over the body armor, it went on next. The sword was buckled on the left side and the dagger on the right. The helmet

---

2. glancing (glan′siŋ): hitting indirectly and going off at an angle; as used here, causing such an action when hit by a weapon.

and gauntlets[3] were put on last. These were the two parts of his equipment that the knight would take off at the first opportunity.

An improperly attached piece of armor could prove fatal.

Anyone who has ever worn a snowsuit in winter might wonder if a knight was able to relieve himself after all his armor was in place. It was possible, although inconvenient. Leg armor went up to the top of the thigh. The covering from waist to thigh was skirtlike. The hose underneath were just tied to the arming doublet.

The armorer had put a lot of effort into making movement as free as possible and in distributing the weight of armor as evenly as possible. A knight in full armor could bend, stoop, drop to his knee, fall to the ground, lie flat on his back, pick himself up, mount his horse, and move his arms enough to <u>wield</u> his sword without difficulty.

3. **gauntlets** (gônt′lits): protective gloves worn with armor.

▲ Medieval castle under siege.

Bettmann/CORBIS

Under Siege: Attack and Defend

Medieval battles sometimes included a siege to take over a castle or fort. During a siege, an army either directly attacked a castle or forced the defenders to surrender by cutting off their food supply. After surrounding the castle or fort, the attackers might build siege towers, tall structures that could be loaded with archers and wheeled right up to castle walls. Attackers sometimes used catapults to hurl four-hundred pound stones against the walls. They sometimes even threw dead animals over the walls to spread disease. As defense against a siege, a king or lord spent enormous sums of money to build a castle with thick walls, deep moats, and high towers. From atop the castle walls, defenders might drench the attackers with boiling water, burning oil, or hot sand.

---

wield (wēld): use a weapon or tool with skill.

agile (aj′əl): able to move quickly and easily.

hoisted (hoist′id): lifted into place, especially with the help of a pulley or other apparatus.

impairing (im·per′iŋ): hindering or undermining.

The medieval knight had special training in wearing armor. He began his training at boyhood, and literally grew up in armor. He exercised to keep lean and active and <u>agile</u> in full armor. Young men would even accustom themselves to wearing armor by turning somersaults in their suits. It is not true that a knight in full armor had to be <u>hoisted</u> into his saddle. Nor was he unable to get up if knocked off his horse. Some knights could vault into the saddle with armor on. But of course, knights varied in how agile they actually were in full armor. Unhorsed knights were frequently captured or killed in battle. This was often because the fall in heavy armor would stun the knight or shift his helmet, <u>impairing</u> his vision. Knights were known to swim to safety in full armor; others drowned trying.

✓ Reading Check

1. What was an arming doublet? Why was it made of two different types of material?

2. Where were additional pieces of mail attached to a knight's armor?

3. Why was it important that a squire attach a knight's armor carefully?

4. In what order did a knight put on his armor?

5. How well could knights move about once they were fully dressed in armor?

MEET THE *Writers*

Charlotte and David Yue have worked together as author and illustrator for a number of award-winning books, including *The Igloo* and *The Tipi: A Center of Native American Life*. *The Tipi*, published in 1984, was one of the *School Library Journal*'s Best Books of the Year; it also won the ALA Notable Book award, and was a Boston Globe–Horn Book Awards Honor Book.

When most people hear "Ice Age," they think of a frozen world long before human history began. Did you know there was another, smaller ice age that started a mere six hundred years ago, during the Middle Ages? Read on to find out about the effects of the "Little Ice Age" on the people of Europe.

SCIENCE ●

HISTORY ●

from The "Little Ice Age"
from *The Ice Ages*

by ROY A. GALLANT

Try to imagine looking out your bedroom window and seeing a huge wall of ice—the front end of a *glacier*—near your house. Only the length of two city blocks away, the wall is 50 feet (15 m) high and 600 feet (180 m) wide—and it is moving, though very slowly, toward you.

This was the view that people living around the year 1600 had from their homes in the village of Chamonix, in the French Alps. The mountain glacier was advancing in response to a cold period called the *Little Ice Age* that gripped Europe from about the year 1400 to around 1850.

The Little Ice Age began in a mild manner. Increased precipitation—rain, hail, mist, sleet, and snow—in the mountains caused glaciers to grow. As a result, there was an average lowering of the temperature.

glacier (glā'shər): large mass of ice and snow that flows slowly over land.

You Need to Know...

What happens when the sun's radiation decreases by just one percent? In the winter of 1708–1709, swift-flowing rivers froze. Ships changed their courses to avoid ice. Late frosts killed trees and vines. Crops failed because of the shorter growing seasons, and bread became more expensive to buy. As a result, people began to starve and die. By 1750, the earth's glaciers were more widespread than at any time since the Great Ice Age. The cold temperatures and advancing glacial ice dramatically affected the lives of people in Europe for about 450 years, beginning in the Middle Ages.

▲ Canadian glacier (center of photograph). This present-day photograph shows how close glaciers may come to civilization.

Midlatitude[1] winters gradually grew a bit longer and became slightly colder. Summers were somewhat shorter and cooler than before. But the average lowering of the temperature was not anywhere near the 10° F (−12° C) that accompanies a major ice age. Instead, it was only a few degrees.

But that's all it takes to shorten the growing season by about two weeks in the midlatitudes, for example, in southern Maine and Wisconsin in the United States and France and Germany in Europe. At higher latitudes, such as where Canada, Iceland, and Norway are, the growing season is shortened even more. Advances of glaciers took place in 1600, 1640, 1740, 1810, 1820, and 1850 with resulting drops in average temperature. It is important to realize that even small average changes in climate over long periods of time are very significant. This is especially so in high latitudes, where the growing season tends to be short even in good times.

> ## Even small average changes in climate . . . are very significant.

By the year 1600, several glaciers in the Alps had advanced and crushed houses, including some in the Chamonix Valley. Although a number of villagers abandoned their homes and moved elsewhere, others decided to stay and try to carry on, in hopes that the glacier would reverse its course. Many of these people starved to death, mainly because the shorter growing season prevented

---

1. **midlatitude** (mid'lat'ə·to͞od): temperate zone; an area midway between the equator and the North or South Poles.

What If the Gulf Stream Moves Again?

The Gulf Stream is a river of warm water that flows through the Atlantic Ocean northeast from the Gulf of Mexico to Europe. It acts like a warm blanket for Iceland, Scandinavia, and Britain. From 1600 to 1780, the Gulf Stream moved east and then southeast. That change in direction added to the effects of the Little Ice Age. Today the Gulf Stream has moved back to its nearly northeast course. However, some scientists warn that melting polar icecaps could change the course of the Gulf Stream again, once more threatening the loss of our warm ocean blanket.

▼ The Gulf Stream. **?** How does the Gulf Stream warm the cold countries of Iceland, Scandinavia, and Britain?

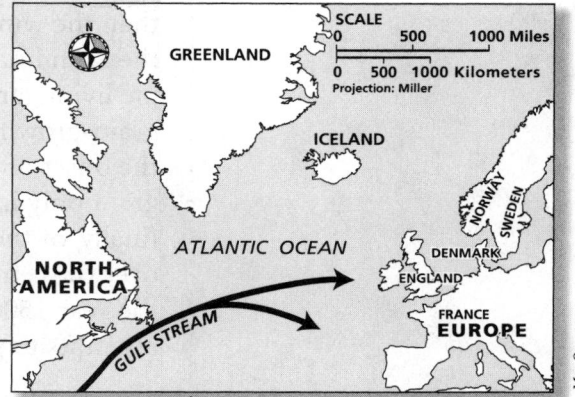

their crops from maturing. Those villages that survived the glacial advance of the Little Ice Age today have about half a mile (0.8 km) of woods and glacial <u>rubble</u> between them and the present forward wall of the glaciers.

rubble (rub′əl): rough, loose fragments of rock and debris.

Some winters of the Little Ice Age were especially fierce. The winter of 1709 was one of these. An Angers[2] priest of France described the winter in these words: "The cold began on January 6th and lasted in all its rigor until the 24th. The crops that had been <u>sown</u> were all completely destroyed. . . . Most of the hens had died of cold, as had the beasts in the stables. When any poultry did survive the cold, their combs were seen to freeze and fall off. Many birds, ducks, partridges, woodcock, and blackbirds died and were found on the roads and on the thick ice and frequent snow. Oaks, ashes, and other valley trees split with cold. Two-thirds of the walnut trees died."

sown (sōn): scattered for planting.

The year 1739 brought another fierce winter to Europe. Belgium was especially hard hit. According to diaries left by many people, there was no spring season that year, and bad weather lasted well into May. The summer was short, cold, and wet. A late wheat harvest was spoiled by rain;

---

2. **Angers** (än‧zhā′): a city in northwestern France.

wine grapes and other fruit harvests were destroyed by early frosts. Food was in such short supply that many of the poor rioted.

Although most winters of the Little Ice Age were not as severe as those of 1709 and 1739, they were more severe than the winters we have now. People living in Iceland and the Scandinavian countries were hit even harder than people living farther south. The Icelanders had been mainly a grain-growing people since about the year 900. But with the onset of the Little Ice Age, they were able to grow grain only in the southern regions of their country. And finally, of the different kinds of grains they had grown over the centuries, only barley could survive the cold. By the year 1500 the Icelanders had completely given up attempts to grow grain at all, even barley.

✔ Reading Check

1. When and how did the Little Ice Age begin?

2. How did the slightly lower temperatures affect the growing season?

3. During the Little Ice Age, what happened to homes and people in the Chamonix Valley?

4. What was significant about the Belgian winter of 1739?

5. How did weather changes affect the crops grown in Iceland?

MEET THE *Writer*

Roy A. Gallant (1924 –   ) is an award-winning writer who has published dozens of books and textbooks on science for young readers. His special interest is astronomy. Six times during the 1980s, he won the National Science Teachers Association Award for outstanding science books. He also won the John Burroughs Award in 1996 for *The Day the Sky Split Apart*.

Cross-Curricular ACTIVITIES

■ GEOGRAPHY/SCIENCE

Have I Got a Deal For You . . . The Little Ice Age shortened the growing season, and, as a result, people in northern Europe could not grow their crops. Suppose another Little Ice Age is coming again. Select a country or a region in southern Europe and find out the current climate, the annual rainfall, and the crops that can be grown in the area. Design a brochure for the people in northern Europe to advertise the advantages of the area you have chosen. Explain why they should relocate to your area.

■ HISTORY/HEALTH

Tracing the Path of the Black Death
Research how bubonic plague is transmitted from insects to animals and to humans. Design a flowchart that traces the course of the disease. Acting as a health official in a medieval town, present this important information to your class as if they are the townspeople. Present your flowchart and make suggestions about how to prevent the spread of disease.

■ LANGUAGE ARTS/MEDIA

It's A.D. 986 and You Are There The Vikings who sailed west and accidentally discovered Iceland, Greenland, and North America must have had some stories to tell. Imagine that you are a news reporter sent to interview a Viking sailor. Write a TV news story about the Viking's experiences on the open sea, especially when his boat was blown off course. Include a description of the new land he encountered and his activities in setting up a new camp. Perform or videotape your news story for presentation to the class.

■ HISTORY/ART

Armor, East and West Warriors in both medieval Europe and Japan wore armor. Create a fact sheet that lists what the medieval European knight and the Japanese samurai each wore for protection. Define each piece of armor and explain its importance. Illustrate your fact sheet with pictures or diagrams to compare armor of the samurai and the medieval knight. Share your fact sheet and illustrations with your classmates.

■ LANGUAGE ARTS/DRAMA

My Life as a Medieval Teen Some outstanding women during the Middle Ages were teenagers during the dramatic events that shaped their lives. For example, Anna Comnena, Joan of Arc, and Eleanor of Aquitaine all became important figures in history. Working in a group, research the lives of each of these three women. Then, present a panel discussion in which you explain the results of your research. You may choose to bring each woman to life by preparing a script and dramatizing events in their lives as teenagers.

■ ARCHITECTURE/MATHEMATICS

What Has a Moat, a Bailey, and a Keep?
With a group of your classmates, construct a model of a European castle. First, do some research to find out how a typical castle was constructed and what building materials were used. Then, recreate the various parts of a castle and its grounds. Label each part of your castle, and display your model.

READ ON: FOR INDEPENDENT READING

■ NONFICTION

Armor by Charlotte and David Yue (Houghton Mifflin Company, 1994). Did you ever wonder how medieval armor was made, or how knights got dressed? This book by award-winning authors shows you. It is filled with facts and illustrations, such as a South Sea Islander's version of armor.

Beyond the Myth: The Story of Joan of Arc by Polly Schoyer Brooks (Houghton Mifflin Company, 1999). In one year, this teenage girl from a peasant family led an army, united France, brought a king to power, then was accused of disobedience and burned at the stake. Named ALA's Best Book of the Year for Young Adults in 1990. For another biography, read Brooks's 1984 ALA Notable Book, **Queen Eleanor: Independent Spirit of the Medieval World** (J.B. Lippincott, 1983).

Cathedral: The Story of Its Construction by David Macaulay (Houghton Mifflin Company, 1973). This 1974 Caldecott winner shows how cathedrals were built. Also check out **Building the Book Cathedral** (Houghton Mifflin Company, 1999), in which Macaulay explains how he created his book and what he would do differently today.

A Samurai Castle by Fiona Macdonald (Peter Bedrick Books, 1995). Enter the world of the rich and powerful in medieval Japan, with the help of detailed pictures.

When Plague Strikes by James Cross Giblin (HarperCollins, 1995). Three of history's most deadly plagues—the black plague, smallpox, and AIDS—are explained. The woodcut illustrations add to the book's interest. A 1995 Orbis Pictus Award winner.

■ FICTION

Catherine, Called Birdy by Karen Cushman (Clarion Books, 1994). The diary of fourteen-year-old Catherine records her daily life in the year 1290. In her first entry, she writes that she is bitten by fleas and plagued by family. Catherine wants to go on a Crusade or charm warts or keep goats, but her father wants only to marry her off to the highest bidder. A 1995 Newbery Honor Book and ALA Notable Children's Book. For another book by Cushman about a teenage girl in the Middle Ages, read *The Midwife's Apprentice,* a 1996 Newbery Award winner (HarperTrophy, 1996).

The Road to Damietta by Scott O'Dell (Fawcett Books, 1988). Before Francis of Assisi was a saint, he was a high-spirited Italian boy who captured the heart of a girl named Ricca. Scott O'Dell's historical novels have won several awards, including the Newbery Medal and Hans Christian Andersen Medal.

The Sign of the Chrysanthemum by Katherine Paterson (Thomas Y. Crowell Company, 1973). Written by a two-time Newbery Award winner, this is the story of thirteen-year-old Muna, who searches for his samurai father through the crowded and dangerous city streets of twelfth-century Japan.

The Sword and the Circle: King Arthur and the Knights of the Round Table by Rosemary Sutcliff (Puffin, 1994). Storytellers retell the legend of the young boy who became king. Just as if you were a knight of the Round Table, you will share these adventures with your friends, too.

CHAPTER 5

Forces of Change
Renaissance, Reformation, and Scientific Revolution   1350–1700

When and Where

Italy in the mid-1300s and 1400s was the place to be if you really wanted to get in on the beginning of the great cultural awakening known as the Renaissance. Of course, you might have a little trouble finding Italy. Back then, it didn't exist as a united country—it was just a lot of competing (and sometimes warring) cities, such as Venice, Florence, and Rome.

Venice was a shopper's paradise, the center of trade. Merchants loaded their ships with silver, wool, and wine from Europe; silk and porcelain from China; and spices from the East Indies. Florence was the artistic center of the Renaissance. It was run by the powerful Medici family, art-loving bankers who paid artists to create new works. Rome was the center of the Catholic church, which was headed by the pope. The pope controlled even more wealth than the Medici family and also acted as a patron of the arts.

▲ Map of modern-day Italy.

It's 105° Outside, and I'm Freezing!

The burst of creativity that brought about new art and literature during the Renaissance also caused a revolution in science. One important invention was the first thermometer, made by Galileo Galilei in 1592. It was just a long-necked glass beaker turned upside down in a bowl of water. The water rose and lowered with a change of air temperature.

Other Renaissance scientists quickly grasped the idea and improved on the instrument. They marked numbers on their glass

Memorable Quote

"There is nothing more difficult to take in hand, more perilous to conduct, or more uncertain in its success, than to take the lead in the introduction of a new order of things."

— from *The Prince* by Niccolò Machiavelli (1469–1527), Italian statesman and writer

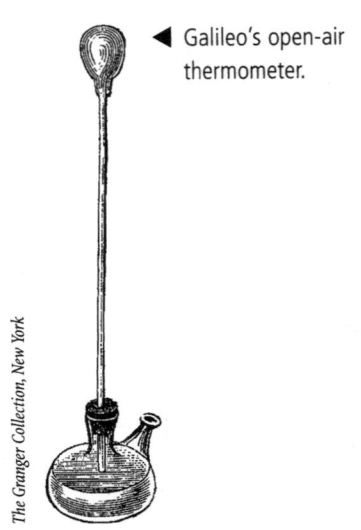

◀ Galileo's open-air thermometer.

The Granger Collection, New York

INVESTIGATE: The Chinese invented a printing press that used movable type centuries before the Europeans, but it was not a success. Why did it fail?

© 1996 North Wind Pictures

▲ The first printing press.

beakers, for example, so they could actually measure temperature. There was only one problem—all the scientists marked their thermometers differently. By the early 1700s, there were as many as thirty-five different temperature scales! Eventually two systems won out: one invented by a German physicist, Gabriel Daniel Fahrenheit; and one by a Swedish astronomer, Anders Celsius. In the original version of the Celsius scale, zero was the boiling point of water and one hundred was the melting point of snow.

VOCABULARY MATTERS

Renaissance (ren'ə•säns') is a French word meaning "rebirth." During the period of the Renaissance in Europe, many people believed that philosophy, science, and art were coming to life again after the violence and turmoil of the Middle Ages. If the Renaissance was a rebirth, though, when was the first birth? The Renaissance marked a rediscovery of the learning and achievements of ancient Greece and Rome during the classical era.

Pretty Im*pres*sive, Gutenberg

"As much may now be printed by one man in one day as could before scarcely be written by many in a whole year."

An ad for the latest high-speed laser printer? No. The high-tech equipment wowing this Renaissance writer was the printing press, invented by Johannes Gutenberg around 1440. Gutenberg used "movable type"—letters molded from metal and clamped into a wooden frame to spell out words. The printer rolled ink over the type and pressed paper on it, a page at a time.

The press printed as many as three hundred pages a day. That doesn't sound like much now, but before Gutenberg, the only way Europeans made books was by copying each one by hand. That could take months! Books were so rare and expensive that few people even learned how to read. Gutenberg's invention changed all that. Books could now be made by the millions much more quickly and cheaply.

By modern standards, Mona Lisa would not be considered beautiful, yet her mysterious little smile still fascinates those who look upon her. Her ageless image can be found on everything from socks and bathing suits to shower curtains and wristwatches. Leonardo da Vinci is perhaps best known for painting the *Mona Lisa*, but here you will discover the equally lasting mark he made across many fields of science.

BIOGRAPHY

SCIENCE ●

HISTORY ●

from *Leonardo da Vinci*

by DIANE STANLEY

▲ *Mona Lisa* by Leonardo da Vinci.

The world saw Leonardo as courtly[1] and charming. But at heart he was a solitary man. "If you are alone," he once wrote, "you belong entirely to yourself . . . . If you are accompanied by even one companion you belong only half to yourself, or even less." In the peace of his aloneness, Leonardo could imagine, create, and dream. It is easy to picture him, then, in his room by himself, writing in one of his famous notebooks.

He began them when he was about thirty. Over the years he filled thousands of pages with the outpourings of his amazing mind. There were drawings of grotesque faces, drafts[2] of letters, sketches for future paintings, lists of books he owned, plans for inventions, moral observations, pages copied out of books he had borrowed, notes of things to remember, designs for weapons, drawings of anatomy,[3]

> ### You Need to Know...
> Born in a small town near Florence in 1452, Leonardo da Vinci (lē′ə•när′dō dä vēn′chē) became one of the greatest thinkers of all time. He was a master painter, sculptor, architect, scientist, mapmaker, and military engineer. He has come to represent the very essence of the phrase "Renaissance man"—a person whose knowledge and talents cover a broad range of subjects. For over half of his long lifetime, da Vinci recorded ideas, plans, and sketches in a series of incredible notebooks. Though none of his sculptures and only a few of his paintings have survived, his notebooks remain to give us a rare glimpse into the mind of a genius.

1. **courtly** (kôrt′lē): dignified and polite; elegant.
2. **drafts** (drafts): first copies that will be revised.
3. **anatomy** (ə•nat′ə•mē): study of the human body.

grotesque (grō•tesk′): distorted; bizarre; ugly.

moral (môr′əl): relating to correct behavior or thinking; knowing the difference between right and wrong.

Bettmann/CORBIS

▲ Self-portrait by Leonardo da Vinci.

dissected (di·sekt′id): cut into pieces to be examined.

and observations of nature. On one page, for example, you can find geometry problems, a plan for building canals, and the note "Tuesday: bread, meat, wine, fruit, vegetables, salad."

All this was written in a peculiar backward script, going from right to left. You must use a mirror to read it. This has led to the myth that he wrote that way to keep his notebooks safe from prying eyes. In fact, Leonardo was left-handed and found it much easier to write that way. When he *really* wanted to keep something secret, he wrote in code.

Perhaps the most stunning drawings in Leonardo's notebooks are those that show his careful study of anatomy. During the Renaissance, painters often studied the human body so they could learn to draw it correctly. Leonardo did this too. But soon his interest had grown far beyond his work as an artist. He approached anatomy as a scientist. Over a period of twenty-five years he <u>dissected</u> some thirty bodies, making almost two hundred painstaking drawings of them. Besides that, he dissected bears, cows, monkeys, birds, and frogs, comparing their structures to that of humans.

He developed a way of drawing anatomy that medical artists follow to this day. To show the inside of the head,

Church Chants and Love Songs

Not only was Leonardo da Vinci an accomplished artist and scientist, but he could sing, too! Leonardo had a beautiful voice, and he played the *lira*, an early form of violin, with great skill. He also designed musical instruments. Music itself was changing in Leonardo's time. Earlier music was composed mainly for religious worship. Monks sang "plainsong" or "chant," in which all voices sang the same melody. During the Renaissance, people  began singing in harmony, combining different tones to produce a pleasing balance of sounds. In addition, musicians began writing new music, both sacred (for the church) and secular (for everyday life). Secular songs often told amusing stories or celebrated love. New musical instruments were invented, such as the lute, a sweet and gentle-sounding type of guitar. Another instrument is still popular today—the recorder, a wooden instrument that sounds like a flute.

for example, he drew a cross section. To clarify the organs in the abdomen, which lie on top of one another, he drew the ones in front as if they were transparent.[4] And he often drew features from several different views, as if he were turning them in his hand.

Over the years he filled thousands of pages with the outpourings of his amazing mind.

It is hard to imagine the fastidious[5] Leonardo doing such work. "If you have a love for this," he wrote, "you may be turned from it by disgust in your stomach; and if that does not deter[6] you, you may be afraid to stay up at night in the company of corpses cut to pieces and lacerated and horrible to behold." Not to mention the fact that the bodies began to <u>decompose</u> before he could finish examining and drawing them. Yet for Leonardo the human body was a wondrous thing. Though he was not a religious man, he wrote that the more he studied the body, the more he was struck by thoughts of God, "who creates nothing superfluous[7] or imperfect."

All nature fascinated Leonardo. His notebooks are filled with descriptions of his extraordinary scientific studies. Based on this evidence, he has been called the first modern scientist. In those days people answered questions by looking them up in the Bible or in the writings of the ancient Greeks. Leonardo said that people who did that were using their memories, not their minds. Instead he followed what today we call the scientific method.

First he observed things carefully—the movement of water, the arrangement of leaves on a stem, the flight of birds. That led him to ask questions. Why does a pot lid jump up and down when water starts to boil? Water must expand when it turns to steam, he decided. In attempting

decompose (dē′kəm·pōz′): to rot or decay.

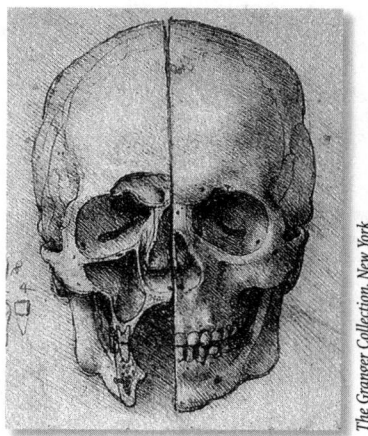

The Granger Collection, New York

▲ This pen-and-ink study done by Leonardo da Vinci appeared in one of his notebooks.

---

4. **transparent** (trans·per′ənt): able to be seen through.
5. **fastidious** (fa·stid′ē·əs): overly critical; easily disgusted.
6. **deter** (dē·tʉr′): stop; discourage from.
7. **superfluous** (sə·pʉr′flōō·əs): extra; unnecessary.

Going and Going and Going . . .

In the pages of his notebooks, Leonardo drew ideas for new machines, some of which were actually invented hundreds of years later. Here are a few examples:

- armored car
- giant crossbow
- glider
- flying ship
- parachute
- self-propelled automobile
- drilling machine
- pulleys
- machine for digging trenches
- floats for walking on water
- boat with paddle wheels
- deep-sea diving suit

hypothesis (hī·päth′ə·sis): possible reason or explanation meant to be tested.

to explain what he observed, Leonardo was making a hypothesis. But then he had to prove it, and often he wasn't satisfied until he had also measured it. So he set up an experiment. He made a glass cylinder and put water and a piston inside. Then he measured how far the piston rose when the water was heated to boiling. Leonardo was so keen on measuring things that he invented all sorts of devices for that purpose—to measure humidity, altitude, distance traveled, angle of inclination,[8] the speed of wind and water, and the intensity of light.

He often made astonishing mental leaps. When he threw a pebble into a pond, he noticed that circular waves formed around it, expanding steadily outward. From this it occurred to him that sound and light must also travel in waves through the air. What's more, he remembered that he always saw lightning before he heard thunder. He therefore concluded that light waves must travel faster than sound waves.

---

8. **angle of inclination** (in′klə·nā′shən): the measure of how steep or shallow a sloped or slanted surface is.

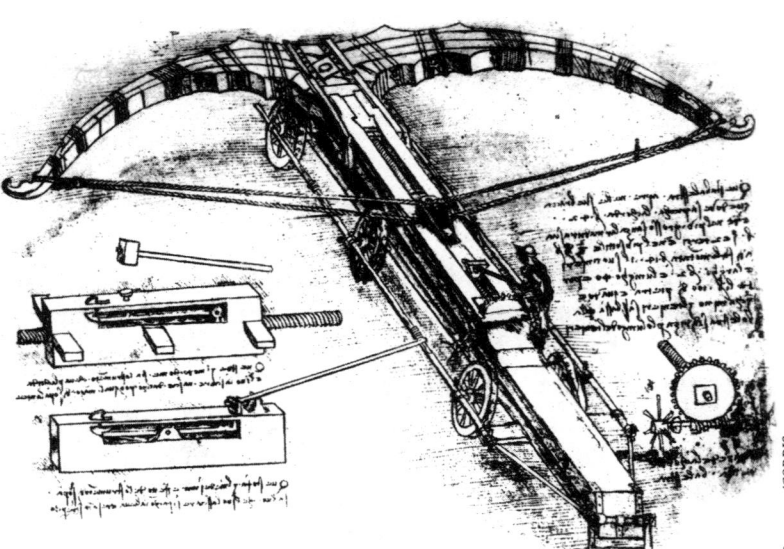

Bettmann/CORBIS

▲ Among the war machines Leonardo designed was this giant crossbow. **?** If **it had been built, how would this crossbow have worked? Does it seem like a practical invention? Why or why not?**

He trusted his own observations, even if others disagreed with him. For example, up in the mountains he saw fossils of shells, fish, and coral. How had they gotten there? The popular theory of the time was that they had floated up during the great biblical Flood. But Leonardo knew that shells were heavy and did not float. It seemed clear to him that the rock that now formed a mountain once lay at the bottom of the sea. Today we know that in this—as in so many other things—he was correct and far ahead of his time.

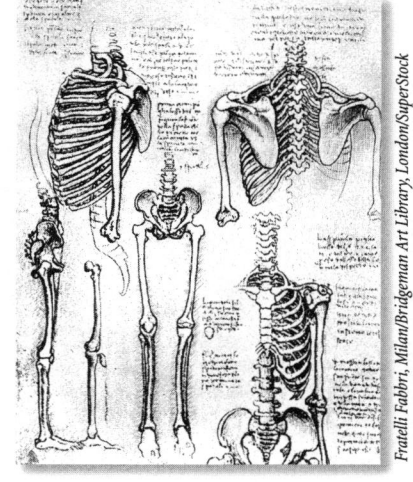

▲ Leonardo's study of human anatomy included all views of the skeleton.

✓ Reading Check

1. Why did Leonardo da Vinci prefer to be alone?

2. Why did he use "mirror writing" in his notebooks?

3. How did he learn so much about anatomy?

4. What steps did he follow in his scientific studies?

5. What was Leonardo's theory to explain why fossils of fish and shells were found on mountains? How did it differ from the usual thinking of his time?

MEET THE *Writer*

Diane Stanley (1943–   ) is an award-winning author who grew up in a house full of books. She has written and illustrated biographies of Peter the Great, Queen Elizabeth I, and William Shakespeare. She also enjoys creating humorous stories and has written her own version of the Rumpelstiltskin fairy tale, *Rumpelstiltskin's Daughter*.

ART •

HISTORY •

The author Irving Stone wrote a novel about the life of artist Michelangelo called *The Agony and the Ecstasy*, which was later made into a Hollywood film. As you read about Michelangelo's difficult personality, you may decide that he wasn't the only one who experienced both intense pain *and* happiness in connection with his artistic genius!

Michelangelo

from *Italian Renaissance* (*Living History Series*)

edited by JOHN D. CLARE

You Need to Know...

Like Leonardo da Vinci, Michelangelo Buonarroti (mī′kəl•an′jə•lō′ bwô′när•rô′tē) was a "superstar" during his own lifetime (see "from *Leonardo da Vinci*," page 143). Even today, long after his death in 1564, Michelangelo is still considered one of the greatest artists who ever lived. He is known for his incredibly lifelike sculptures, such as the *David* in Florence, Italy, the *Moses* in Rome, and the *Pietà* in St. Peter's Basilica in Rome. We know so much about Michelangelo's life and personality because not one, but two, biographies were written about him while he lived. After he disagreed with the first one, Michelangelo asked his own assistant to write the second biography! As a result of his fame, hundreds of his letters, sketches, and other mementos were preserved. Born in 1475, Michelangelo grew up in Florence but spent his last years in Rome.

stereotype (ster′ē•ə•tīp′): a rigid, too-simple notion held by many people about a person or group.

apprentice (ə•pren′tis): someone studying and working with a master to learn an art or a skill.

Even during his own lifetime, "the divine Michelangelo"—sculptor, painter, architect, and poet—was held to be a genius. Michelangelo Buonarroti's character fulfills our stereotype of a genius: brilliant yet difficult, outspoken, and unstable. He was often disheveled,[1] and he slept in his boots. He criticized other artists. Once he was so rude that an apprentice punched him and broke his nose. On another occasion, Leonardo da Vinci asked Michelangelo to explain a passage of poetry to some admirers. "Explain it yourself," snapped Michelangelo. He cared little for the wishes of his patrons,[2] and he often put a clause[3] in his

---

1. **disheveled** (di•shev′əld): untidy; rumpled.
2. **patrons:** wealthy supporters who pay the living expenses of their favorite artist, musician, or writer.
3. **clause:** part of a legal document or contract.

contracts that gave him the right to do the work "as it pleases the said Michelangelo." Once, when the pope would not see him, Michelangelo left Rome for seven months. According to the artist, when the pope asked why he had left, Michelangelo replied, "Not from ill will, but from scorn."

Michelangelo learned his skills while apprenticed to the painter Ghirlandaio in Florence. He sketched classical statues in the Medici gardens and imitated them so successfully that his sculpture of a sleeping Cupid was sold by a dealer as an antique.

Like Leonardo da Vinci, Michelangelo changed the way artists viewed their work. Although he understood the rules of perspective and foreshortening,[4] for example, he demanded the right to ignore them when he wanted to create a particular effect in a painting. "All the reasoning of geometry and arithmetic and all the proofs of perspective are of no use to a man without the eye," he remarked. After he had carved the tomb of Giuliano de' Medici (1534), it

▲ Michelangelo was featured in Giorgio Vasari's 1550 book about Italian artists. Vasari painted this portrait.

4. **perspective and foreshortening:** techniques of drawing that make the size and placement of objects in a picture look natural.

Art, Money, and Medicis

During the Renaissance, the powerful Medici (med′ə•chē′) family ruled the city of Florence. They gained their wealth through an international banking business. Cosimo de' Medici (1389–1464) was a shrewd businessman and a patron of the arts, meaning that he financed the work of artists. He collected ancient coins and statues and made his house a gathering place for painters, sculptors, and poets. Cosimo's grandson, Lorenzo (1449–1492), was also a man with many interests. He played sports, wrote poems and songs, and continued the family tradition of supporting artists. Some say that Michelangelo entertained Lorenzo's children by carving animals in the snow for them. Lorenzo was criticized for his harsh politics and his excessive lifestyle, but he also earned a memorable nickname: "Lorenzo the Magnificent."

▲ Lorenzo de' Medici.

▲ Among the many Biblical characters pictured on the Sistine Chapel ceiling is this image of the prophet Isaiah.

discarding (dis·kärd′iŋ): throwing away; getting rid of.

depiction (dē·pik′shən): portrayal; image.

was observed that the figure on the tomb did not look like the dead man. "A thousand years from now, nobody will want to know what he really looked like," retorted[5] Michelangelo. Out of this attitude came a new style of painting that art historians call mannerism; mannerists strove to define their own styles, even when that meant <u>discarding</u> the realistic <u>depiction</u> of nature.

Michelangelo was an example of the Renaissance universal man; his talents were broad ranging. He wrote poetry in a neat Renaissance italic script. His skills as an architect were so respected that in 1546 he was put in charge of the rebuilding of St. Peter's Church in Rome.

Like Leonardo da Vinci, Michelangelo helped change the direction of the Renaissance. Michelangelo's works were awe inspiring, but they were also solemn and religious. His later sculptures, particularly, conveyed a sense of human weakness, sin, sadness, and death.

The Sistine Chapel

In 1508, Pope Julius II (1443–1513) asked Michelangelo to paint the ceiling of the Sistine Chapel in the Vatican. Michelangelo had reservations; he claimed that he was a sculptor not a painter, but he accepted the commission.[6] His reservations were borne out when the first scene he painted was ruined before it was finished; in his inexperience, he had used too-damp plaster and had to start over.

Like Leonardo da Vinci, Michelangelo helped change the direction of the Renaissance.

The huge fresco[7] took Michelangelo four years to complete. Too ill-tempered to employ assistants, he worked mostly alone. In a poem written in 1510, he described how uncomfortable the work was:

---

5. **retorted:** replied showing annoyance or irritation.
6. **commission:** the performance, or doing, of a certain task at the request of someone in authority.
7. **fresco** (fres′kō): painting done on wet plaster.

My belly is shoved up under my chin . . .
My beard faces skyward and the back of my neck is
wedged into my spine . . .
My face is richly carpeted with a thick layer of
paint from my brush . . .
I don't want to be here and I'm no painter.

The relationship between the <u>temperamental</u> artist and the fierce pope was stormy. Julius frequently climbed up to inspect the work, and once, when Michelangelo told him he would finish "when I can," Julius threatened to throw Michelangelo from the scaffolding.[8]

temperamental (tem′pər•ə•ment″l): moody; excitable; unpredictable.

---

8. **scaffolding** (skaf′əl•diŋ): poles and planks made into a framework to support workers on projects high above the ground.

Sandro Vannini/CORBIS

▲ St. Peter's Basilica.

A Dome to Duplicate

Michelangelo was already in his early seventies when he took over as chief architect of St. Peter's Basilica in Rome. Others had been working on the project for forty years, and Michelangelo guided it for nearly twenty more. He got right down into the dust with the stonemasons and up on the scaffolds with the carpenters. His most visible contribution is the great dome he designed for the roof. He was inspired by a dome on a church in Florence, but it's Michelangelo's dome that has been copied for buildings all around the world—including the United States Capitol in Washington, D.C.

The Granger Collection, New York

▲ Michelangelo's portrayal of Moses is one of his most powerful sculptures. ❓ **What impression does this statue give about the strength and character of Moses?**

1. List four aspects of Michelangelo's personality that fit the stereotype of a genius.

2. How did Michelangelo learn his skills as an artist?

3. How did Michelangelo feel about following standard rules of drawing?

4. What were two of Michelangelo's talents besides sculpting and painting?

5. Why did Michelangelo not want to paint the ceiling of the Sistine Chapel? Why did it take him four years to finish it?

MEET THE *Writer*

John D. Clare loves history. "Michelangelo" is taken from a book he edited about the Italian Renaissance. He has also edited or written books about ancient Egypt, ancient Greece, ancient Rome, the Vikings, fourteenth-century towns, knights in armor, the Aztec civilization, and the First World War.

A monk named Martin Luther turned the world of the six-teenth century upside down. Just about everyone—popes, princes, ordinary people—ended up arguing about Luther's daring new ideas. Here you will find out why his thinking was so earthshaking, and how it shaped our world today.

from Martin Luther and the Reformation

from *Rats, Bulls, and Flying Machines: A History of the Renaissance and Reformation*

by DEBORAH MAZZOTTA PRUM

Not everyone in the church was happy with the way the church was growing and changing. During the Renaissance, as scholars studied classical[1] civiliza-tions and history, they learned about the early history of the church. Many devoted[2] monks and priests worried that the church was losing touch with the old ways. They feared that powerful and wealthy church leaders were not spiritual enough. Some people said that some of the practices of the church were wrong and needed to be fixed. They wanted to *reform* the church—which means they wanted to change it, to fix what was wrong.

In the early 1500s—about the time of the later years of the Renaissance—this

You Need to Know...
Today, Christians belong to many different churches. For exam-ple, they may be Baptists, Methodists, Lutherans, Presbyterians, or Catholics. Until the 1500s, however, there was only one Christian church, and it was very powerful: the Roman Catholic Church. By the Middle Ages, the Catholic church had come to control almost every aspect of life. The church owned a great deal of land, decided what should be taught in schools, influ-enced rulers, and even had its own military guard. Many popes and bishops lived more like princes than spiritual leaders. As a result, critics of the church wanted to see a return to the more spiritual values of the past. Martin Luther (1483–1546) launched the most forceful attack on the church in this move-ment toward a different way to worship.

---

1. **classical** (klas′i•kəl): relating to ancient Rome and Greece.
2. **devoted** (di•vōt′id): showing love and dedication.

▲ *Martin Luther* by Lucas Cranach the Elder (1472–1553).

movement to reform the church was sparked by the actions of a man named Martin Luther. Luther's actions and ideas were a major part of the great changes in the church and society which we call the *Reformation*.

A Lightning Flash

Martin Luther was one of eight children born to a poor German peasant family. Luther's father, a miner, worked hard to make sure his son could attend a university. Luther was an excellent student. When he was only twenty-one, he began to study law at the university. But he did not complete even a single semester.

What happened? As Martin Luther later told the story, he had a number of close brushes with death, which changed his attitudes about life. One such incident happened on a stormy summer night. As Luther walked home alone, thunder crashed around him, and lightning blazed across the sky. Suddenly a bolt of lightning struck, knocking Luther to the ground.

The storm raged around him. Terrified, Luther screamed, "St. Anne, help me!" He vowed that if he survived the storm, he would give his life to God and become a monk.

Luther did survive. True to his promise, but much to his father's dismay,[3] he quit studying law and entered a monastery.

Faith and Forgiveness

Like many Christians of his time, Luther believed that the only way to escape hellfire was to do good works, give to the poor, <u>confess</u> his sins, and live faithfully according to the ways of the church. But the more Luther thought about it, the more convinced he became that he could never be good enough to go to heaven. The somber[4] monk saw God as a stern judge who would most certainly <u>condemn</u> him.

confess (kən•fes′): tell a fault or crime.

condemn (kən•dem′): to penalize for wrongdoing; judge harshly.

---

3. **dismay** (dis•mā′): disappointment; uneasiness; feeling of alarm.
4. **somber** (säm′bər): gloomy or sad.

Luther studied the Bible for hours on end. As he read and thought about the words in the Bible, his thinking began to change. He came to some revolutionary conclusions. He decided that God was not so much a stern judge as a loving father. He also concluded that doing good works and observing church law would not get you to heaven. Instead, Luther said, a person could only be saved by his or her faith in God.

Luther studied the Bible for hours on end.

Luther also said that people didn't need priests to obtain forgiveness from God for their sins. Instead, said Luther, if people confessed their sins, were sorry, and had faith, then God would forgive them. This was an important point, and it threatened the church, because Luther was questioning just how much people really needed priests.

Luther's Ninety-five Theses

Martin Luther became a professor at the University of Wittenberg. Many students and professors listened to his new ideas.

For a moment, let's leave Martin Luther teaching in Wittenberg and turn our attention to what was going on at about the same time in Rome. In Rome, the youngest son of Lorenzo de' Medici had been named Pope Leo X. Leo had big plans for his reign as pope. He intended to rebuild St. Peter's Basilica . . . . The project would cost millions.

One way Pope Leo raised money was by selling over 2,000 high-powered jobs in the church. If a person could pay a lot of money, then he could become a cardinal or bishop. The person's background or character didn't matter much, as long as he had the cash. The result, as you might imagine, was more than a few incompetent[5] and even dishonest church officials.

---

5. incompetent (in·käm′pə·tənt): not qualified; lacking ability or fitness.

Leo X also raised money by sending people out to sell indulgences, which were sometimes called pardons. The church said that if people bought indulgences, their sins would be pardoned, and so they could lessen the punishment they would suffer in the afterlife. Many peasants, who did not have much money, bought indulgences, hoping to get a better chance of being saved and going to heaven.

The practice of selling indulgences infuriated[6] Martin Luther. Luther said that only faith and God's mercy could save a person—in other words, you cannot buy your way into heaven.

Luther thought that the practice of selling indulgences was a sign of greed and <u>corruption</u> in the church. He decided to let other people know what he thought. In Latin—the language normally used by scholars in his time—Luther wrote his objections to the practice of selling indulgences. In all, he came up with ninety-five arguments against indulgences. On October 31, 1517, he nailed this document, called the Ninety-five Theses, to the door of the church at the University of Wittenberg.

His Ideas Spread Like Wildfire

By nailing his Ninety-five Theses to the church door, Luther was trying to start a discussion. It was as though he were putting a notice on a bulletin board and asking people to respond to his ideas. But his ideas proved so powerful that they sparked a protest that led to huge changes across Europe.

Soon after Luther nailed his Ninety-five Theses to the church door, they were translated from Latin into German. Now many more people could read them. And many more people got the chance to read them. Can you guess why? Because of the printing press. In less than a month's time, people across Europe held copies of Luther's words in their hands.

corruption (kə·rup′shən): dishonest or evil behavior.

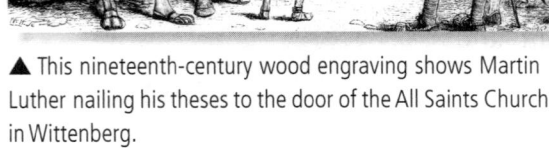

The Granger Collection, New York

▲ This nineteenth-century wood engraving shows Martin Luther nailing his theses to the door of the All Saints Church in Wittenberg.

6. **infuriated** (in·fyoor′ē·āt′id): very angry.

Luther's ideas spread like wildfire. He wrote many essays in which he talked about the importance of faith and criticized[7] the corrupt practices of the church. His writings were printed in small pamphlets,[8] and thousands of copies were spread across Europe.

Luther's ideas appealed to the people. His attacks on the greed of the church pleased over-taxed peasants. But it was more than money that made Luther's ideas powerful. He taught that all believers were equal. He said that if any church official told a person to do something against his own <u>conscience</u> or forbidden by the Bible, then he should ignore the church official.

Of course this did not please the leaders of the church. Pope Leo X called Luther "a wild boar [who] has invaded [the Lord's] vineyard." Another official of the church said Luther had "a brain of brass and nose of iron."

conscience (kän'shəns): thoughts and feelings urging one to do what is right.

---

7. **criticized** (krit'ə•sīzd): judged or found fault with.
8. **pamphlets** (pam'flits): booklets.

SIDELIGHT

Here are some examples from Martin Luther's Ninety-five Theses. Luther used these arguments to protest the church's practice of selling indulgences—pardons for the sins of people both living and dead. (The word "purgatory" below refers to a place where souls of the dead were believed to be made pure enough to enter heaven.)

"27. There is no divine authority for preaching that the soul flies out of purgatory immediately [the minute] the money clinks in the bottom of the chest.

"37. Any true Christian whatsoever, living or dead, participates in all the benefits of Christ and the Church . . . without letters of indulgence.

"43. Christians should be taught that one who gives to the poor, or lends to the needy, does a better action than if he purchases indulgences."

—from "Ninety-five Theses" by Martin Luther,
from *Martin Luther: Selections from His Writings,*
edited by John Dillenberger

Look Out for the Papal Bull!

The pope was furious. He decided to strike back at Luther. In 1520, he issued a papal bull. "Papal" means anything having to do with the pope. And "bull" in this case does *not* have anything to do with a snorting barnyard animal. In this case, "bull" is the word for an official document issued by the pope.

In his papal bull, the pope attacked Luther. The pope required all members of the church to burn Luther's writings and warned that anyone following Luther would be considered a heretic—a person who openly disagrees with the official beliefs of the church.

How did Luther respond? Defiantly! In December of 1520, students, professors, and the townspeople of Wittenberg gathered before a blazing bonfire. They watched as Martin Luther dropped a copy of the papal bull into the blaze. Luther said, "As thou hast wasted the Holy One of God, so may the eternal flames waste thee."

Luther had gone far beyond simply arguing with the church about indulgences. He had publicly defied the pope. He had made a break with the church. A month later, the pope made it official: he excommunicated Luther, that is, he took away Luther's membership in the church.

The Diet of Worms: *Not* a High-Protein Meal

Does the title of this chapter remind you of a playground song?

> *Nobody loves me,*
> *Everybody hates me,*
> *I'm gonna eat some worms.*

Don't worry, nobody is going to eat any worms. Really.

So what's all this about a Diet of Worms? Well, Worms is a place, a city in Germany. The diet was the name of an assembly of Germans, including knights and representatives from various towns and regions.

In 1521, Martin Luther was ordered to appear before the Diet of Worms. He was told that he would not be harmed, so he went to Worms, where he hoped to have a chance to defend his ideas. Instead, when he arrived at the meeting,

Ruggero Vanni/CORBIS

▲ Cathedral in Worms, Germany.

defied (dē·fīd′): openly opposed or resisted; fought against.

church officials piled his writings in front of him. They ordered him to recant, which means to take back all that he had said. But Martin Luther refused. He said to the church officials, "Here I stand, I cannot do otherwise. God help me. Amen."

The Diet declared Luther a heretic and criminal. They gave him twenty-one days of safety. After that, anyone could legally murder Luther.

The Diet declared Luther a heretic and criminal.

Fortunately, Luther had a powerful friend, Prince Frederick of Saxony (in northern Germany). As Luther traveled back to Wittenberg, the prince arranged for five masked horsemen to pretend to kidnap Luther. They took him to a castle and didn't tell anyone where he was. Some people believed he was dead.

Luther hid in the castle for ten months. He didn't waste time. He worked hard to translate the whole New Testament into German, so that his countrymen could easily read the Bible for themselves.

Why They're Called "Protestants"

Because of Martin Luther, people began to leave the Roman Catholic Church. They no longer believed they had to obey the pope. These people who *protested* against the practices and beliefs of the church came to be called *Protestants*. (That is why you may sometimes hear the Reformation referred to as the Protestant Reformation.)

After Luther, Christians were divided into Catholics and Protestants. In the United States today, Catholics and Protestants can be neighbors and friends. But in Luther's time, they were bitter enemies. Each side believed it was right. Wars and fighting broke out. Different groups of Protestants even fought against each other, since they did not all agree with each other about religious beliefs and

Spreading the Word

Among Luther's many writings was his translation of the Bible's New Testament into German. Until then, Bibles were written in Latin, the language of the church. Most people couldn't read Latin, so they depended on priests to tell them what the Bible said. Soon after Luther finished his translation, William Tyndale translated the New Testament into English. The newly invented printing press churned out copies of Bibles in English and German. Suddenly, literate people could read the Bible themselves and draw their own conclusions.

The Granger Collection, New York

▲ A page from a Gutenberg Bible.

Praying Hands, a study drawn by Albrecht Dürer, 1508.

practices. Some people were tortured, hanged, or burned at the stake over these issues. It's sad to say but history is full of examples of people doing horrible things to each other in the name of religion.

As for Martin Luther, unlike many of the people who opposed the Catholic church in his time, he was neither hanged nor burned at the stake. He returned to Wittenberg and kept preaching and writing for the rest of his life. Before he died in 1546, Luther wrote over 60,000 pages. Yet he once said that he would be happy if "all my books could disappear and the Scripture alone would be read."

✓ Reading Check

1. Why did some people want to reform the church?

2. What event in Martin Luther's life led him to become a monk?

3. What was Luther's purpose in writing the Ninety-five Theses? How did people respond to his ideas?

4. What invention helped spread Luther's ideas across Europe?

5. What is a "papal bull"? How did Luther respond to the one issued by Pope Leo X?

MEET THE *Writer*

Deborah Mazzotta Prum (1952–   ) is the author of numerous articles and short stories for adults and young people alike. She has a particular interest in bringing history alive for children. She has also written *Czars and Czarinas: A History of Old Russia for Young Readers.*

Did you know that Galileo, the famous scientist, was also a rebel? At school, he was known as "the wrangler" because he was always arguing. As an adult, he developed theories about the universe that led to one of the most well-known trials in history. Read on to find out how Galileo ended up fighting to defend his scientific beliefs.

from *Galileo Galilei: Inventor, Astronomer, and Rebel*

by MICHAEL WHITE

"The Dialogue"

The trial of Galileo in 1633 was the climax to the series of events that had begun nearly 100 years earlier. It began with the publication of a book called *The Revolution of the Heavenly Spheres*, written by Polish astronomer Nicolaus Copernicus. In this book, Copernicus claimed that Earth was simply a planet orbiting the sun. This proposal went directly against the accepted Earth-centered universe theories of the time and was branded as heresy by the Catholic Church.

In the heart of civilized Europe in 1633, Galileo Galilei—the most respected scientist of his generation—was hauled up in front of the Inquisition. He was accused of the terrible crime of heresy simply

You Need to Know...

Galileo's open-minded way of thinking came as no surprise. His father, an accomplished musician known for applying mathematics to music, disliked people who were not willing to listen to new ideas. Galileo was also a skilled musician, but he preferred to explore and investigate the world around him. He lived during a time of great fascination with the arts, science, and mathematics. Galileo developed a scientific method to study how pendulums swing, how objects gain speed when they roll down a hill, and how the planets move in the sky. His investigations about the nature of the universe put him in conflict with the Catholic Church. The Church put Galileo on trial for heresy—going against the church's teachings—when he was sixty-nine years old. Found guilty, he was sentenced to spend the rest of his life in prison. Because of his age and poor health, church authorities allowed him to live under house arrest in a villa near Florence.

▲ Galileo Galilei lived from 1564 to 1642.

because he supported the views suggested in Copernicus's book.

Nine years earlier, Galileo had been asked by Pope Urban VIII to write a book that would give a balanced account of the argument over the nature of the universe. What this really meant was that the pope wanted Galileo to discuss the various arguments, but finally agree with the Church, not Copernicus. The result of Galileo's work was a book called *Dialogue Concerning the Two Chief Systems of the World*.

The problem was that Galileo did not do as he was told. The accepted theories of the universe were based on the idea that Earth was the central point of the universe. But, in his book, Galileo completely destroyed this idea and sided with Copernicus. He said that the Sun, not Earth, was the central point.

When Urban's advisors read a copy of *The Dialogue*, Galileo's conclusion was immediately obvious, and he was summoned to Rome. Doctors attending Galileo protested that moving him would endanger his life. The pope declared that if Galileo did not come of his own free will, he would be brought to them in chains.

SIDELIGHT

Albert Einstein first published his groundbreaking theories about atoms, light, and time in 1905. In the following statement he acknowledges two earlier giants in the field of science—Galileo and Isaac Newton.

"In my opinion the greatest creative geniuses are Galileo and Newton, whom I regard in a certain sense as forming a unity. And in this unity Newton is he who has achieved the most imposing feat in the realm of science. These two were the first to create a system of mechanics founded on a few laws and giving a general theory of motions, the totality of which represents the events of our world."

—Albert Einstein, in *Isaac Newton: Discovering Laws That Govern the Universe* by Michael White

Prove It!

For the past four hundred years, scientists have been coming up with experiments to test their ideas, but it wasn't always this way. For example, the Greek scientist Aristotle claimed that heavier objects fall faster than light ones. Many centuries later Galileo devised an experiment to test this idea. He invited anyone who was interested to gather at the base of the Leaning Tower of Pisa. Galileo went up to the top with two cannonballs that were the same size and shape but had different weights. He dropped them at exactly the same time. Guess what? They landed at exactly the same time! By creating proofs such as this, Galileo helped establish the experimental method that all modern science depends on today.

Bettmann/CORBIS

The Church

Seventeenth-century European study was controlled by two powerful forces—the Roman Catholic Church, headed by the pope, and ancient philosophy dominated by the 2,000-year-old ideas of the Greek philosopher Aristotle. The Church had an overwhelming influence on the lives of most Europeans, and this was especially the case with the devoutly[1] Catholic Italians. During Galileo's childhood, one in twelve people living in Rome was either a cleric[2] or a nun.

The Catholic Church controlled the people by completely forbidding any teaching that <u>deviated</u> from what was taught in the Bible.

deviated (dē'vē·āt'id): moved away from; strayed from.

To enforce this control, the Church set up the Inquisition. This was a group of Church leaders who were organized to monitor publications and public declarations. They <u>censored</u> books that did not totally agree with the traditional Catholic teaching, and they persecuted and tried anyone who persisted in publishing heretical views.

censored (sen'sərd): examined for forbidden ideas, which are then taken out.

The Church also set up the Order of the Jesuits, who worked on scientific problems and taught their version of the truth. Jesuit philosophy and science was what Aristotle had taught. Any discovery made by a Jesuit researcher had to fit into the accepted, inherited world-view of Aristotle.

---

1. **devoutly** (di·vout'lē): sincerely; reverently.
2. **cleric** (kler'ik): member of the clergy; person who is officially in the service of God or a church.

A New View

Galileo did not invent the telescope, but he did improve the shape of its lens so that it made a better image and it could be used to see farther. Through his telescope Galileo saw things no one had ever seen before. In 1610, Galileo published *The Starry Messenger* to report that the moon was not a smooth, perfect sphere, or ball, as previously taught by Aristotle. Instead, the surface was rough and uneven, like that of the earth. Galileo also learned that the Milky Way consisted of millions of separate stars, and that Jupiter had moons. It was those moons, in fact, that convinced Galileo the earth was not the center of the universe.

implication (im'pli•kā'shən): suggestion; act of implying or hinting at a connection.

misconceptions (mis'kən•sep'shənz): mistaken ideas.

scorned (skôrnd): disliked; made fun of; treated with contempt.

If an observation did not fit with Greek teaching, it had to be false. If Aristotle was wrong, by implication so, too, was the Bible.

Aristotle was born in southern Greece in 384 B.C. He was a great thinker and developed theories of how the universe operated 2,000 years before the birth of modern science. He had many startlingly accurate ideas about basic science, but was also totally wrong about many things.

Among Aristotle's many misconceptions was his belief that the Moon, along with other celestial[3] bodies, was featureless and absolutely perfect in form. Instead of suggesting the idea that physical laws worked in the same way throughout the universe, he believed that there was one set of physical laws that operated on Earth and a different set for the celestial sphere—the name he gave everything outside Earth. He believed that comets were produced inside Earth's atmosphere and had nothing to do with the celestial sphere.

Above all, the biggest error in Aristotle's thinking was his notion of Earth's position in space. He believed that Earth was fixed[4] as the central point of the universe. In Aristotle's philosophy, Earth did not revolve or move in any way; instead, the Sun, the Moon, and all the known planets revolved around Earth.

Because his theories put humans at the center of the universe, Aristotle's model was very popular with the Church. After all, "Man was made in God's image." It was surely correct, therefore, that Earth should take its rightful place as the central point of all creation.

Conflict

This was the state of affairs when, in 1543, Copernicus stated his revolutionary theory that Earth, along with the other planets, revolved around the Sun.

Copernicus was scorned, not because his theory could be proven by experiment to be false, but simply because it went against what had been taught by Aristotle and the Bible.

---

3. celestial (sə•les'chəl): having to do with the sky or universe.
4. fixed (fikst): staying in one place; immovable.

This is what the intellectual world was like before Galileo was born. It was dominated by philosophers obsessed[5] with Aristotelian ideas who were ignorant of genuine scientific principles, and by theologians[6] who took every word of the Bible literally. If it had not been for the work of Galileo, who challenged this accepted wisdom, scientific advancement could have perhaps been postponed for hundreds of years.

---

5. obsessed (əb•sest′): convinced to excess; fixed upon to the exclusion of other thoughts.
6. theologians (thē′ə•lō′jənz): people who study God and religion.

▲ Two of Galileo's telescopes.

✓ Reading Check

1. Who was Copernicus, and what was his theory about the nature of the universe?

2. According to the author, what were the two most powerful forces that affected learning in seventeenth-century Europe?

3. What was the Inquisition, and what was its purpose during Galileo's time?

4. What was at the center of the universe, according to authorities of Galileo's time? What did Galileo's experiments and observations lead him to believe?

5. What does the author say could have happened if Galileo had not disagreed with the accepted views of his time?

MEET THE *Writer*

Michael White (1959–   ) is a former science editor and the author of hundreds of science articles, as well as dozens of books, including best-selling biographies of Stephen Hawking, Charles Darwin, Isaac Newton, and Isaac Asimov. He served as a consultant for the television series "The Science of the Impossible." White lives in London, England.

Long before the organized science of archaeology began, people were digging up old, buried objects and ruins. One of these ancient artifacts became the inspiration for a vivid and lively type of Renaissance art called the Baroque style.

from Making Archaeology a Science
from *Dig This! How Archaeologists Uncover Our Past*

by MICHAEL AVI-YONAH

During the Renaissance, scholars and artists developed a deep interest in the remains of ancient Rome. Artists made drawings of sculptures that decorated old buildings and of the ancient stone coffins that were visible above ground. The many copies made from these drawings helped to spread knowledge of the Roman Empire.

One of these Renaissance-era artists, Cyriacus of Ancona, traveled to the eastern Mediterranean in search of ruins. He copied many ancient texts during his life and made valuable drawings of many ruins that have since disappeared.

Archaeological finds during the Renaissance had a great effect on artists of that time. For example, in the first century A.D., the Roman historian Pliny wrote about a magnificent statue of Laocoön,[1] a legendary priest of the Greek god Apollo. The statue depicts Laocoön and his two sons as they are killed by sea serpents.

You Need to Know...

In ancient times, stories, myths, and legends were an attempt to explain the how's and why's of the world. While some of these stories are familiar to us, today we have more scientific ways of learning about the why's of the past. Archaeology as a science began to take shape in the many artistic and scientific advances made during the Renaissance.

---

1. **Laocoön** (lā‧äk′ō‧än′).

According to Pliny, the statue was located in Rome in the palace of the emperor Titus.[2] In 1506 an investigation was made of the palace ruins, and the huge statue was found exactly where Pliny had indicated.

The discovery of the statue of Laocoön created a great sensation among the artists of the Renaissance. They developed the baroque[3] style of art based on the sculpture, which is vivid and full of action. Baroque art is also characterized by flowing shapes and heavy ornamentation.[4] Baroque artists strongly contrast light and shadow and emphasize depth and space. Their sculptures and paintings are large and elaborate. Baroque soon became one of the principal art styles of sixteenth- and seventeenth-century Europe.

▲ Detail from the statue of Laocoön.

2. **Titus:** emperor of Rome A.D. 79–81.
3. **baroque** (bə·rōk').
4. **ornamentation** (ôr'nə·men·tā'shən): decoration.

SIDELIGHT

"The first time I was in Rome when I was very young, the pope was told about the discovery of some very beautiful statues in a vineyard near S. Maria Maggiore [a church]. The pope ordered one of his officers to run and tell Giuliano da Sangallo to go and see them. He set off immediately. Since Michelangelo Buonarroti was always to be found at our house, . . . my father wanted him to come along, too. I joined up with my father and off we went. I climbed down to where the statues were when immediately my father said, 'That is the Laocoön, which Pliny mentions.' Then they dug the hole wider so that they could pull the statue out. As soon as it was visible everyone started to draw, all the while discoursing on ancient things. . . ."

—from a letter by Francesco da Sangallo,
son of Giuliano da Sangallo, the Vatican architect,
from *Unearthing the Past* by Leonard Barkan

Francis G. Mayer/CORBIS

▲ Statue from the Elgin Marbles collection.

At this early stage, archaeology was far from being an established science. The first archaeologists were amateurs who were guided to old ruins by ancient texts. Many people were simply interested in collecting ancient art.

These early enthusiasts[5] were completely unaware of the breadth[6] and complexity of the ancient world. In fact, almost all the ruins they found were in Rome. Early diggers—although aware of the importance of Greek civilization in the development of Roman culture—studied few authentic Greek remains.

From Amateur Sport to Serious Science

Several different events that occurred in eighteenth-century Europe helped to move archaeology from an amateur's hobby to a serious profession. In 1719 the French scholar Bernard de Montfaucon prepared several books that contained drawings and descriptions about the remains of past civilizations. Books about ancient coins began to appear later in the 1700s.

Meanwhile, wealthy English people in Britain formed societies to study early remains and hired artists to draw and paint ancient ruins. Expeditions were organized to Greece, Lebanon, and Syria, where the artists carefully recorded Greek and Roman ruins on paper and canvas. Their work—which enabled Europeans to see the remains of ancient Athens and other sites for the first time—represented one of the earliest permanent contributions to the new science of archaeology.

A Stolen Past

Many old or valuable objects have been taken away from their original homes to other countries. They have been displayed in curiosity cabinets, museums, or private art collections—or locked away in storage. Over the years, tourists, treasure hunters, archaeologists, and even entire armies made off with anything they could carry. European museums are filled with ancient treasures from Greece, Egypt, and Rome. The Elgin Marbles no longer adorn the Acropolis in Athens but are on display in the British Museum. Egypt's famous statue of the lovely Queen Nefertiti is in Germany. Today, in most countries, removing antiquities is a crime. Egypt and Greece, among others, are trying to get back some of their treasures. Greece has not yet succeeded in recovering the Elgin Marbles.

5. **enthusiasts** (en·thoo′zē·asts): people eagerly involved in something that interests them; fans.
6. **breadth** (bredth): scope; extent.

In 1764 the German scholar Johann Winckelmann published a guide to the characteristics of ancient artifacts. Winckelmann's systematic study of Greek and Roman remains and his careful analysis of the subject became the foundation for early archaeology.

The discovery of Herculaneum and Pompeii[7]—two Roman cities that were destroyed by an eruption of the volcano Mount Vesuvius in A.D. 79—were the first large-scale excavations. Archaeologists began at Pompeii in 1748. Archaeologists have been working on both sites ever since.

At first, excavators were concerned only with finding items that could be removed from the site and taken to museums. They even carried away ancient frescoes (wall paintings made on fresh plaster) from the sides of buildings.

In time, however, archaeologists realized that by dismantling a site they were wasting an opportunity to learn about the life of an ancient community. As a result, archaeologists began to conserve and restore the finds at the site itself. Excavators left ancient shops, houses, baths, and temples exactly as they had been in the past.

---

7. **Herculaneum** (hʉr′kyə•lā′nē•əm) and **Pompeii** (päm•pā′ē).

The Art Archive/Dagli Orti

▲ Plaster poured into holes left in hardened ash revealed even the facial features of the victims. ❷ **What might this man have been doing when he died?**

artifacts (ärt′ə•fakts′): items made by human beings that are studied for their historical value.

excavations (eks′kə•vā′shənz): areas where artifacts or buildings are being uncovered.

conserve (kən•sʉrv′): to keep safe from damage.

Where Time Stopped

Like other ancient sites, Pompeii suffered from treasure seekers in the eighteenth century. Fortunately, not all of the city had been excavated. The twenty thousand inhabitants of ancient Pompeii lived among many fine public buildings: an amphitheater, two stone theaters, ten temples, four sets of public baths, and a huge basilica (a meeting place). Houses of the rich had elaborate wall paintings and floors inlaid with mosaic designs. Inscriptions and graffiti on the walls give us a glimpse of the spirit of the people. We can even see the people themselves. Ashes hardened around bodies as they fell during the volcano's eruption. Plaster molds made from these ashy casings reveal every detail—shape of the body, hair, facial expressions, clothing, and even the type of sandals worn.

1. In 1506, what did investigators find in the ruins of the palace of Titus? Who had written that the object would be there?

2. What style of art developed from this discovery? What are some of the qualities of this style of art?

3. What kind of people were the first archaeologists? Where did they do most of their searching?

4. How did wealthy English people of the eighteenth century help move archaeology from an amateur sport to a science?

5. Instead of dismantling ruins and taking items to museums, what do archaeologists now try to do at sites like Herculaneum and Pompeii?

MEET THE *Writer*

Michael Avi-Yonah (1904–1974) wrote numerous books about the archaeology, history, and geography of Israel. He did research and record keeping for the Government of Israel's Department of Antiquities, and he taught the history of art and archaeology at the Hebrew University in Jerusalem.

Some things seem so obvious that no one ever thinks to question them—until an Isaac Newton comes along, that is. For example, when fruit falls from a tree, why does it fall *down*, rather than up, or sideways? Newton was the first person to find the answer to this question—and many more.

SCIENCE •————

MATHEMATICS •————

from *Isaac Newton: Discovering Laws That Govern the Universe*

by MICHAEL WHITE

The Problem of Gravity

In the summer of 1666, a young man strolled into the orchard of his mother's house in Woolsthorpe, Lincolnshire, in England and sat down beneath a tree to concentrate on his studies.

A moment later, an apple fell and landed on the young man's head. The young man was twenty-two-year-old Isaac Newton. No doubt it hurt for a moment, but it also started the young scientist thinking about the properties of moving objects.

Isaac had already struggled to understand what kept the Moon in its orbit around Earth, and the planets in their courses around the Sun. It was only after he had thought about why the apple had fallen to Earth, that he really began to answer these questions. The answers, he found out, lie in the theory of gravity.

properties (präp′ər•tēz): characteristics.

theory (thē′ə•rē): an idea that is not obvious but can be proven to be a law or principle.

> **You Need to Know...**
> Together, Isaac Newton and Galileo Galilei left modern science an unmatched legacy. Newton was born in 1642—the same year that Galileo died. (See "from *Galileo Galilei*," page 161.) If not for that fact, these two men could have been a great team. Newton improved upon Galileo's refracting telescope. Then, he invented the even better reflecting telescope. Both men made careful observations of natural events, but Newton took things one step farther. Many consider him to be the first true scientist because of his careful experiments and his use of mathematics to explain his ideas and observations.

"The Miraculous Year"

For Isaac Newton, 1666 had been an astonishing year. Only weeks earlier, the Great Fire of London had swept away the last remnants of the plague, which had taken thousands of lives. Newton was a student at Cambridge University, but he had to stay with his mother in the countryside for more than a year because Cambridge was ravaged by the highly contagious disease. In the countryside, Newton could enjoy solitude and relative safety. In this peaceful setting, he could concentrate on the scientific problems that he had been grappling[1] with throughout his post-graduate[2] years.

During the past year, Newton had made incredible breakthroughs in mathematics and physics. In 1665, he had found the answer to a problem that had eluded the most gifted mathematicians for years—the binomial theorem.[3]

A while later, Isaac began to work on what was to be the greatest development in the history of mathematics—calculus. Today, scientists use both of these theorems in computer programs. Space engineers use calculus and the binomial theorem to help solve complex mathematical problems. Economists[4] use these branches of mathematics to predict what will happen to all the various currencies around the world.

Isaac Newton was a mathematical genius who, by his early twenties, had studied the work of every notable mathematician in the world. Then, when he had exhausted all current knowledge, he began developing his own theorems and methods to create a mathematical foundation for his scientific work. When he became famous, writers

Erich Lessing/Art Resource, NY

▲ Portrait of Sir Isaac Newton by Godfrey Kneller (1646–1723).

---

1. **grappling** (grap′liŋ): wrestling; struggling.
2. **post-graduate** (pōst′gra′jo͞o·it): relating to additional college studies after receiving a bachelor's degree.
3. **binomial theorem** (bī·nō′mē·əl thē′ə·rəm): provides a rule for multiplying expressions of the form $(a + b)^n$.
4. **economists** (i·kän′ə·mists): scientists who study the use of money.

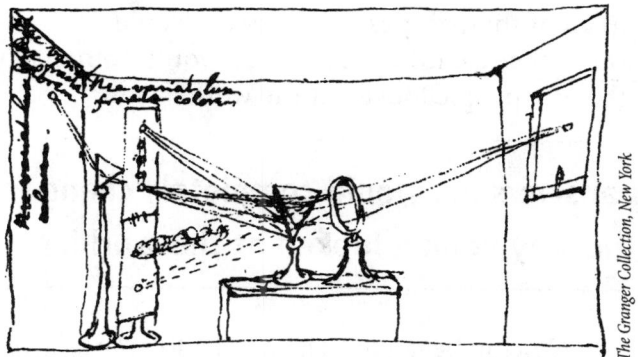

▲ This notebook drawing, done by Newton in 1672, shows his experiment of separating and remixing white light with two prisms.

looked back on this short period in the Lincolnshire countryside and called it "The Miraculous Year."

Newton's World

In the seventeenth century, when science was in its infancy, many well-educated people still believed in witchcraft. Little was known about the fundamental principles behind the way many things worked. Most people thought the universe was controlled by an all-powerful deity, and many events and phenomena were caused by spirits. There were no solid theories of mechanics or ideas about how things moved. Scientists knew very little about light and how it behaves, and subjects like chemistry and medicine were based more on magic than science. Nobody really understood how the planets and Moon were kept in their orbits, or why it was that falling apples always fell toward the ground. Yet, by the end of Isaac Newton's life, he would have the

principles (prin′sə‧pəlz): basic truths or laws.

phenomena (fə‧näm′ə‧nə): events or conditions that can be seen or experienced and described scientifically.

The Great Experimenter

Isaac Newton was a firm believer in the experimental method. When he was in college, he conducted many experiments to find out how our eyes see. He wondered if the eye acted as a lens to focus the light bouncing off the objects we see. Newton knew that changing the shape of a lens changes the way it focuses light. In one dangerous experiment, he manipulated the shape of his eyeball. He hoped to distort the lens and see a difference in his vision. In his lab book, he recorded the results of this experiment, along with a drawing to show his technique. Believe it or not, it wasn't this experiment, but staring at the sun through his telescope, that nearly blinded the great experimenter.

answer to all of these things. His answers would revolutionize the scientific process and would completely change the way people looked at the world.

His answers . . . would completely change the way people looked at the world.

The work Newton began in "The Miraculous Year" would be the basis of mathematics and physics for the next 300 years. Within three centuries of that apple landing on his head, scientists would land on the Moon and send machines to distant planets using his theorems and discoveries. Whole areas of physics and mathematics are called "Newtonian," in honor of his outstanding accomplishments.

The Versatile Scientist

Newton's laws of motion explain how forces act upon objects, whether moving or stationary. By applying these laws to any mechanical system, it is possible to predict the effect a force will have on an object. If, for example, the

Newton's Laws of Motion

Newton barely ate or slept for a year and a half while writing his masterpiece, *The Mathematical Principles of Natural Philosophy*, called the *Principia* (Principles). In it, Newton explained his ideas about gravity and, most important, what have become known as Newton's three laws of motion. His idea that energy and force are necessary to overcome an object's inertia—that is, resistance to change or movement—was entirely new.

1. Every body continues in a state of rest or the same motion in a straight line unless it is acted on by an outside force.
2. When a force acts on a body, the speed of change of momentum of the body is proportional to the force and changes in the direction in which the force acts.
3. To every action there is an equal and opposite reaction.

▲ A device called Newton's Cradle, which demonstrates Newton's laws of motion.

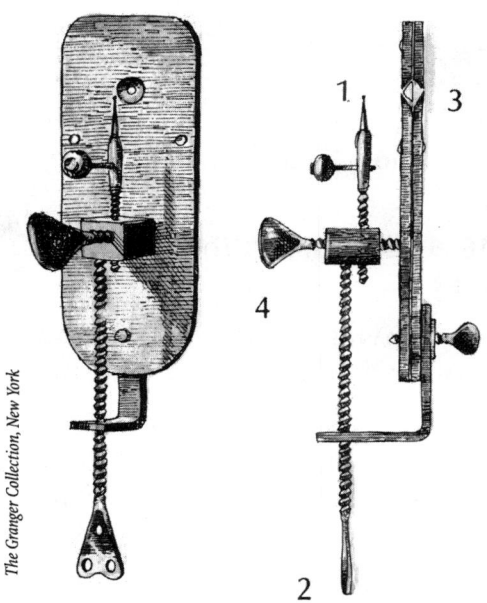

The Granger Collection, New York

◄ The scientist Anton van Leeuwenhoek (1632–1723) improved the magnifying glass so much that it became the first microscope, shown here. The item to be magnified was placed at (1) and then lined up with the lens (3) by twisting the end (2). It was brought into focus by moving the knob (4) closer to or away from the lens. Then the microscope was held up to the light. In a drop of rainwater, Leeuwenhoek discovered bacteria that he called animcules.

weight and force of two pool balls are known, by applying Newton's laws, the effect one ball will have on the other can be predicted. Today, Newton's laws of motion are used in all areas of science—designing cars, planning the course of a spaceship, building aircraft engines, and making aerodynamic[5] skateboards. In addition, Newton worked out a theory of gravity to explain how the planets travel in their orbits around the Sun. The same theory also explains why we remain held firmly to Earth, and do not all float off into space.

Newton also worked in many other areas of physics. His groundbreaking theories on light have helped scientists and engineers design better telescopes, microscopes, eyeglasses, and cameras. His discoveries in optics ultimately led to inventions such as televisions and lasers.

The story of how Isaac Newton came to make these monumental discoveries began in Lincolnshire, where he was born. From such simple origins, his influence eventually spread to change the world.

---

5. **aerodynamic** (er′ō·dī·nam′ik): relating to how well an object moves through the air.

▲ Newton made important improvements to the telescope. Newton's telescope is shown here, with an original copy of his great work, the *Principia*, in the background. **❷ In what way is this telescope different from Galileo's telescopes, shown on page 165? Can you guess why Newton's design was better?**

✓ Reading Check

1. What theory did Newton develop to explain why apples fall to the earth and why the moon and planets stay in their orbits?

2. Why has the year 1666 been called "The Miraculous Year" in Newton's life?

3. What does the author say was the greatest development in the history of mathematics? How is it used today?

4. Before Newton and others came up with their explanations of natural phenomena, how did people explain the universe?

5. What are some modern inventions that were made possible by Newton's theories of light?

MEET THE *Writer*

Michael White (1959–   ) is a former science editor and the author of hundreds of science articles, as well as dozens of books, including best-selling biographies of Stephen Hawking, Charles Darwin, and Isaac Asimov. He served as a consultant for the television series "The Science of the Impossible." White lives in London, England.

Cross-Curricular ACTIVITIES

■ SCIENCE/ART

Picture This The scientific breakthroughs made by Galileo in the seventeenth century forever shaped our understanding of the universe. Choose one of Gaileo's scientific theories, such as his theory about the earth's orbit, and draw a diagram on poster board to explain and illustrate it for your class. Be sure to explain how Galileo arrived at his theory—what observations he made or experiments he conducted—and how it differed from accepted views of the time.

■ LANGUAGE ARTS/ART

Top Ten Works by the Master Deciding on your one, absolute favorite Michelangelo work would be too hard since the artist was a master of so many different art forms—sculpture, painting, architecture, and even poetry. Make a list, then, of your top ten Michelangelo favorites, adding an illustration of each work along with a short description. Be prepared to explain to the class why you chose particular works of art, as well as why some other beautiful works didn't make it onto your list.

■ HISTORY/DRAMA

Martin Luther Speaks Out Martin Luther's objections to Roman Catholic practices began when he nailed his "Ninety-five Theses" to the door of the Wittenberg church. With three or four partners, act out a scene in which Luther posts his ideas for all to see and discusses them with Wittenberg students and professors. What kinds of questions might people have had for Luther? How would he have defended his arguments? Present your scene to the class.

■ HISTORY/SCIENCE/ART

When Did That Apple Hit Isaac's Head? Isaac Newton began to revolutionize science in his "Miraculous Year" of 1666. He wasn't the only one with new ideas, though. Create a time line showing the major scientific discoveries and inventions that were made during the Scientific Revolution. In addition to the dates along the time line, include the name of the scientist or inventor, the country where he or she lived and worked, and a short description of the discovery, invention, or new theory. You may want to illustrate your time line with your own drawings or with pictures photocopied from books or found on the Internet.

■ LANGUAGE ARTS/SCIENCE

Useful Gadgets Leonardo da Vinci's notebooks included numerous sketches of inventions, including designs for flying machines and ideas for scientific measuring devices. On your own or with a partner, create a short fact book of some of Leonardo's inventions. Your fact book should describe what the invention was designed to do and whether it really could have worked. Note also whether the invention was actually ever built, and, if so, was it widely used? How is it similar to something made today? Present your fact book in class, and be prepared to describe how each gadget worked.

READ ON: FOR INDEPENDENT READING

■ NONFICTION

Renaissance by Andrew Langley (Alfred A. Knopf, 1999). What does an egg yolk have to do with art? Why did Renaissance doctors poison their patients? This Eyewitness Book is filled with colorful pictures and tidbits about the times.

A Renaissance Town by Jacqueline Morley (Peter Bedrick Books, 1996). See where it all started—in Florence, where genius and wealth combined to create some of the greatest art and architecture the world has ever seen.

Starry Messenger by Peter Sís (Farrar Straus Giroux, 1996). When Galileo Galilei said the earth wasn't the center of the universe, he turned the medieval world upside down. He paid a price, though: The Church locked him away for the rest of his life. A Caldecott Honor book and an Orbis Pictus and ALA Notable Book.

Rats, Bulls, and Flying Machines by Deborah Mazzotta Prum (Core Knowledge Foundation, 1999). Arranged in three parts, this history of the Renaissance and Reformation in Europe introduces readers to the artists, writers, scientists, and spiritual leaders who changed the world with their revolutionary new ideas. Prum includes chapters on Renaissance women as well as manners, music, the invention of printing, and the religious turmoil of the Reformation.

■ FICTION

Elizabeth I, Red Rose of the House of Tudor by Kathryn Lasky (Scholastic, 1999). In the entries of this fictionalized diary, Elizabeth I—the future queen of England—dines on peacock and swan, fights with her governess over taking a bath (she just had one last month!), and adores her father, King Henry VIII—even though he chopped off her mother's head. From the Royal Diaries series.

Mary, Bloody Mary by Carolyn Meyer (Gulliver/Harcourt Brace, 1999). Elizabeth I had an older half-sister named Mary Tudor. Mary was a princess with three hundred servants when her father abandoned her mother and remarried. Suddenly Mary was a servant herself, forced to change diapers for the baby who would one day take her place on the throne of England.

The Second Mrs. Giaconda by E. L. Konigsburg (Atheneum, 1975). Dukes and duchesses from all over Italy lined up to ask Leonardo da Vinci to paint their portraits. Even the king of France was begging for a portrait. So why did the great painter choose to paint an unimportant merchant's wife? Leonardo's apprentice reveals the mystery behind the *Mona Lisa*.

The Shakespeare Stealer by Gary Blackwood (Dutton Children's Books, 1998). Fourteen-year-old Widge is supposed to steal Shakespeare's play *Hamlet* for Simon Bass, a cheapskate theatrical manager who doesn't want to pay royalties to the writer. When Shakespeare's players invite Widge to join the troupe, he is caught between his fear of Bass and loyalty for his new friends. An ALA Best Book for Young Adults.

CHAPTER 6

Oceans of Exploration
From Europe to the Americas   1400–1800

No Honor Among Thieves

From around 1520 to 1720, murderous pirates ruled the Caribbean sea, plundering merchant ships bound for Europe. A single lucky haul could mean riches beyond their wildest dreams.

Don't feel too sorry for the pirates' victims, though. Many were pirates themselves—legal pirates, with official permission from the king of France or England to attack foreign ships and steal what they liked, as long as they split it with the crown. Their favorite target was Spanish galleons, or sailing ships, loaded with so much New World treasure that they could barely float.

▲ Battle of the pirates Jean Bart and Forbin against the English, May 22, 1689.

Sorry, No Muffins

What do chewing gum and chocolate have in common? Both were first enjoyed by the Mayas and other native peoples of Mexico and Central America. They found gum oozing from the sapodilla tree, in the form of a milky sap called chicle. They enjoyed chocolate as a bitter drink from *kakaw*, or cocoa beans. Somewhere along the line sugar was added to both these Mayan delights, and we continue to enjoy these sweeter versions today.

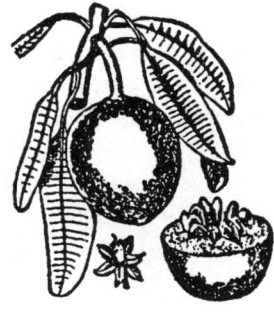

▲ Fruit and leaves of the sapodilla tree.

How About Fingers and Toes?

Ever wonder how people managed before calculators were invented? The Incas kept their records with quipus, elaborate arrangements of knotted string. The color of the string showed what was being counted—say for example, red for soldiers or yellow for corn. The size of the knots and their placement stood for numbers:

Memorable Quote

"I have come to believe that this is a mighty continent which was hitherto unknown."

—Christopher Columbus, writing in his journal in 1498

▲ Quipus were used by the Incas to keep records.

VOCABULARY MATTERS

What's the difference between a *culture* and a *civilization*? Both words describe the way people live together in a particular place and time—seventeenth-century European culture or Aztec civilization. However, the words have slightly different meanings. *Culture* is related to *cultivate*— it's something that grows, like a plant. *Civilization* comes from the Roman word *civis,* or "citizen," and suggests an organized political state.

INVESTIGATE: Why did the Europeans call the new continent "America" and not "Columbia"?

A small knot low down might mean "one," while a large knot higher up might mean "nine thousand." Does this sound complicated? It was—young men had to go to accounting school to learn to design and read the royal quipus.

At Least He Had a Retirement Plan . . .

Juan Ponce de León believed that somewhere in the Americas there was a fountain that made old people young and kept young people from growing old. He outfitted three ships and sailed north from the West Indies into uncharted territory in search of this fountain of youth. A month into his voyage, he dropped anchor at what he thought was a large island and went ashore. It was springtime. The air was fresh and sweet, and everything was in bloom. He named the place Florida because it was the Easter season— *Pascua florida*—"flowering Easter."

Ponce de León didn't find the fountain of youth in Florida, but he thought he'd found a great place to retire— as have many others since. Eight years later he returned, his ships filled with supplies to settle a new colony. This time he was met by American Indians who resisted having their country claimed for Spain. Ponce de León retreated to Cuba with a deep arrow wound, which became infected and eventually killed him.

▲ Ponce de León searched throughout Florida for the mysterious Fountain of Youth.

Sail too far down the west coast of Africa, European sailors warned in the early 1400s, and you will be swamped by horrors that no ship can survive. One man refused to pay attention to the warnings. It was this Portuguese prince's curiosity that jump-started the Age of Exploration.

Prince Henry the Navigator

from *Around the World in a Hundred Years: From Henry the Navigator to Magellan*

by JEAN FRITZ

Was the unknown completely unknown?

Today everyone knows that the Vikings in northern Europe once built a settlement on land across the ocean in what would become known as the New World, but at the time people in Europe probably didn't hear about it. If they had, they would not have been impressed. Those Vikings! they would have said. They had always done outrageous things. What if they had found land? It couldn't have been worth much or they would have gone back.

There were also stories of ships being driven by storms into unknown waters, perhaps even onto unknown shores. But no one paid attention. An accident to an unimportant sailor, no matter what tale he told, was not news. People in Europe had decided what the world was

> **You Need to Know...**
> The concept of knightly honor was important to Prince Henry of Portugal and his brothers, as it was to most European princes at the time. According to the tradition of English chivalry, knightly honor was earned with heroics on the battlefield. However, Portugal was at peace, and there was no battlefield on which to claim knightly fame. The king proposed that Prince Henry and his brothers earn their honor by jousting, or fighting in a tournament, with the best knights of Europe. However, the sons wanted a real battle. Eventually it was decided to invade the city of Ceuta, a north African port that served as a base of operations for pirates. Partly as a result of this invasion, Henry became interested in the exploration of the west coast of Africa.

The Granger Collection, New York

▲ Prince Henry of Portugal. **❓ Why did he become known as Prince Henry the Navigator?**

obsessed (əb·sesd′): fascinated.

spoils (spoilz): things of value taken by force during a war.

like, and it would take more than a few lost sailors to change their minds.

What it took was just one man, Prince Henry of Portugal. He became <u>obsessed</u> with that mysterious African coastline which the mapmakers had never been able to finish. Born on March 4, 1394, the third son of King John of Good Memory, Henry might well have followed the unquestioning ideas of his father and his father's generation. He was certainly religious enough, but the Bible alone could not answer the questions he asked when he looked out from the shores of Portugal at the wilderness of water before him. Particularly interested in the study of mathematics and astronomy, Prince Henry learned early that the best way to solve a problem was to go at it slowly, deliberately, one step at a time. He took his first step when he was twenty-five years old and built himself a modest house on the southern tip of Portugal, where he could stand with Europe at his back, Africa before him, and the Unknown crashing against the boundaries in between.

Although Henry was fiercely curious by nature, his curiosity about Africa had been fired when at the age of twenty-one he led an expedition against the Moorish (Muslim) city of Ceuta in Morocco, directly across the Mediterranean Sea from Gibraltar. Christians never forgot that they wanted to make the whole world Christian, so of course they considered any war against the Muslims a Holy War and anyone who led it was a hero. Prince Henry certainly looked a hero, dressed in fancy new clothes, as were all the members of his gilded seventy-ship fleet. From the northern port of Pôrto (or Oporto) they sailed in formation—the smallest ships first, then the big ships, then the galleys and Prince Henry in his own galley at the rear. Ceuta was not an easy city to conquer, but conquer it they did, and then as victors, they took the <u>spoils</u>. And what spoils there were! It was as if these Portuguese were ransacking the Indies, for the city was filled with Eastern treasures—silver, gold, Persian carpets, Indian muslins,[1] and sacks of cinnamon, pepper, cloves, and ginger brought to Ceuta by the Muslims on their secret trade route through the Red Sea.

Although the Muslim trade stopped at Ceuta as soon as Christians took over, Prince Henry stayed long enough to hear about places unknown to Europeans, including the east coast of Africa, which the Muslims knew well. But the west coast? No, they didn't know the west coast. The sea was not navigable[2] there, he was told. Muslims called it the Green Sea of Darkness. It was the same old story that Henry had always heard. Just what Christians said. Everyone seemed to agree that if you went down the west coast of Africa, you would come to a point where the water boiled, where people turned black, where ships caught fire, where the air itself was poisonous.

▲ A sixteenth-century French engraving of a giant octopus attacking a ship.

The Granger Collection, New York

But how could you be sure? Henry asked. Had anyone seen the water boil? He determined to provide ships and finance anyone who would go and find some of the answers. So when John Gonçalves and Tristan Vaz, two young men who had fought with him at Ceuta, asked him for jobs, Prince Henry gave them the command of two ships and told them to sail down the coast of Africa. Go as far as you can, he said. Keep records of all you see. Bring back specimens of plants.

They didn't get far. They were still off the coast of Morocco when a storm drove them so far out to sea, they were afraid they had been blown into dragon territory. But when the storm was over, there they were beside a small, green island. They knew that some islands, like the Canary Islands, had already been discovered, but this

---

1. **muslins** (muz′linz): plainly woven cotton fabrics.
2. **navigable** (nav′i·ga·bəl): able to be sailed through.

looked like a brand-new undiscovered island, and since there were no people around, it didn't even need to be conquered. All it needed was a name, so they called it Porto Santo, grabbed some plant specimens, and three days later rushed back to Portugal to tell Prince Henry the good news.

Prince Henry was always interested in empty islands. If they were colonized, they could serve as way stations for the explorers he planned to recruit. So he sent Gonçalves and Vaz back to Porto Santo with supplies, a few settlers, seeds, plants, and also a third partner for their venture, a man named Bartholomew Perestrelo. At the last minute Bartholomew took a pregnant rabbit on board, and off they sailed. As it turned out, the seeds and plants flourished. But so did the rabbits. At the end of two years there were so many rabbits, they took over the island. Bold and brazen, they acted as if the crops had been planted just for them. No matter how many rabbits the men shot, there were always more, armies on the munch, stripping away

Navigator University

Prince Henry the Navigator wasn't exactly a navigator—that is, he did not plot the courses for his ships. However, he was an explorer and he did provide leadership. More important, he provided the money that made exploration possible. Henry's house at Sagres on the southernmost tip of Portugal was a magnet for shipbuilders, astronomers, mapmakers, sea captains, and instrument makers. Under Henry's leadership, important developments were made in navigational instruments and mapmaking. Some people think that he even ran a "school" for navigators. They point as evidence to a wind rose carved into the ground at Sagres that dates to Henry's time. A wind rose is a diagram that shows the speed and direction of the wind at a particular place over a specific period of time. Wind roses were important navigational tools even after the introduction of magnetic compasses. Today, wind roses are used to determine the best place to put wind-power turbines— giant windmills—that generate electricity.

▲ Windmills in a wind farm generate electrical power.

Stefan Schott/Panoramic Images, Chicago

the fields. In the end, the men gave up. They left the island to the rabbits and returned to Portugal.

Prince Henry told Gonçalves and Vaz to find another island. And they did. When they had been in Porto Santo, they had seen something in the south which they thought might be an island, so they went back and, sure enough, it was. They sailed home and reported the new find to Prince Henry, who sent them out again with seeds, plants, and more men. Gonçalves also took his wife, his twelve-year-old son, and his two little daughters. They called this island Medeira (which means "wood"), and in time the two islands, along with neighboring small, undeveloped islands, became known as the Madeira Islands. The trouble on this island was not rabbits, but trees. They were so thick and the undergrowth was so heavy that the men had trouble clearing any land. Why not burn off some of those trees, Gonçalves suggested.

So they set one section of the woods on fire. Once it started, however, the fire couldn't be stopped. It roared out of control until the entire island was in flames. The people fled to their boats and sailed to Portugal for help. All but Gonçalves and his wife and children. They stayed on the beach in a makeshift shelter and when the wind blew smoke and sparks too close, they climbed onto rocks or waded into the water. They couldn't step on dry land for two days, yet while waiting for help, they managed to feed themselves on birds and fish. When help arrived, the fire was still raging in one valley and continued to smolder for seven years, but the colonists went ahead in other parts of the island and planted on top of the ashes. Plant grapes, Prince Henry told them. Grapes should do well on a bed of ashes, and they did. The wine from those grapes, known as Madeira, has been famous ever since.

As for Bartholomew Perestrelo, Prince Henry made him governor of Porto Santo. He returned, but instead of planting crops this time, he raised cattle. Apparently, the rabbits were in good health because people thirty years later still talked about them.

Meanwhile, Prince Henry was gathering charts, building ships, learning everything he could about sailing. He

An Island of Rabbits

Porto Santos is not the only island to be overrun by rabbits. In Australia in 1859, Thomas Austin released twenty-four wild rabbits on his property so that he could go rabbit hunting. The rabbits had other ideas and multiplied faster than they could be hunted. Today, Australia has some 300 million wild rabbits that cause about $600 million a year in economic damage. Rabbits are so out of hand that an Australian supermarket introduced a chocolate "Easter bilby" as competition for the traditional chocolate Easter bunny. A bilby is a shy animal that comes out to feed at night but doesn't cause nearly as much damage as a rabbit. It has pointed ears that look a bit like those of a bunny.

▲ Wild rabbits overran Porto Santo.

invited Master Jaime, the most famous geographer in Europe, to join him at his headquarters. Astronomers, cartographers,[3] sea captains—all came to exchange information and discuss the secrets of the sea. First they had to decide what kind of ship to use. Certainly not the *barca,* the square-rigged trading ship most frequently seen lumbering through the Mediterranean Sea. For exploring down the African coastline, they would need something smaller and easier to manage, one that could sail against the wind as well as with the wind. Of course there was no point in sending a ship into unknown waters if it couldn't get back. So they chose a *caravel,* adapting and improving the design of ancient Arab ships and incorporating features of the little *caravela,* which skimmed through Portuguese rivers. A caravel had three triangular sails instead of two square-rigged ones and it was only about seventy feet long (with room for approximately twenty men and their supplies). Most important, it could turn into the wind and come home.

▲ Woodcut of sea serpent in what the Muslims called the Green Sea of Darkness, said to be to the south and west of Europe.

The trouble was that Prince Henry's ships kept coming home too soon. They could never seem to get beyond Cape Bojador, that bulge on the African coast just south of the Canary Islands where the boiling water was supposed to begin. From 1421 to 1433, one after another, his ships went down the coast, but even as they approached Cape Bojador, the sailors could hear the pounding surf. They could sense the demons that were driving the fierce wind, plowing up the ocean, sweeping up yellow storms of sand to blind and confound them. And beyond? They shuddered at what lay ahead. So again and again they turned back.

Prince Henry was patient. Don't be scared by old tales, he said. Go a little farther this time.

---

3. cartographers (kär•täg′rə•fərz): people who draw maps.

In 1434 Gil Eanes, a young man who had been brought up in Prince Henry's household, did manage, after one unsuccessful attempt, to round that cape. What he did was to sail out to sea before he reached the cape and back to shore after he had passed it. This way he avoided the fierce northeast winds and dangerous <u>currents</u> beside the shore. And the big news was that the waters did not boil. His ship did not catch fire. The sea was navigable.

Gil Eanes had conquered what was perhaps the hardest part of the long African coastline. He had put to rest the old stories and taken some of the fear out of the Unknown. The next year Gil went back and sailed 150 miles farther than he'd been before. Gradually, Prince Henry's ships inched down the coastline.

Back in Portugal people were not interested in that coastline; they were complaining about how much money Prince Henry was spending. And for what? They could see no point in it. This didn't stop Prince Henry. In the first place, he wanted to find a route to those silks and spices. In addition, he wanted to take Christianity to the natives of Africa. Prince Henry was such a thorough-going[4] Christian that he wore a prickly hair shirt next to his skin to remind himself that a Christian shouldn't be proud or too comfortable. But most important, Prince Henry wanted to solve the mystery of Africa. Now that Cape Bojador had been rounded, he told his men to find out what Africa was like. Bring back samples of everything they could find, he said. If they could bring back some African natives, he would be especially pleased. But he warned them not to use force. Just talk to them nicely.

In 1441 Antam Gonçalves, John's brother, delivered to Prince Henry some gold dust, a shield of oxhide, ostrich eggs, and ten Africans. Prince Henry was the first Christian prince to eat an ostrich egg and he declared that it was delicious. The people of Portugal, however, were more interested in those Africans. There was a severe labor shortage in Portugal, and if Africans could be

---

4. **thoroughgoing** (thŭr′ō·gō′iŋ): carefully observant; complete.

currents (kŭr′ənts): parts of a body of water that move more quickly than other parts.

A Tree to Dye For

Brazil was discovered in 1500 when a Portuguese expedition to India took a wrong turn and wound up cruising the coast of South America. Explorers found no precious metals, no rich cities for trade, and no ready supply of slave labor. What they did find was a tree whose wood produced a red dye, much in demand in Europe. The tree was similar to the brazilwood, a tree found in the Middle East, so the Portuguese named the new land Brazil and set about harvesting the wood. Today the brazilwood tree is almost extinct in Brazil.

▲ Brazilwood tree.

Prince Henry the Navigator **187**

imported as slaves, the money Prince Henry was spending might not be wasted after all.

Before long, licenses[5] were granted to Henry to send ships to Africa specifically to bring back slaves. On one of the first trips 165 men, women, and children were brought back. Another fleet returned with 235 natives. This was not done peacefully. Force was the only way to do it. But if Prince Henry regretted this, he probably comforted himself that he was "saving souls" by having the natives baptized. But the natives felt no comfort. As far as they were concerned, the arrival of the Europeans was bad news. And they would discover that the Europeans would go right on enslaving them. Europeans took for granted that other people were <u>inferior</u> because they were different, and so Europeans <u>believed</u> (or persuaded themselves) that they could use natives in whatever way that suited them. Once European curiosity was unleashed on the world, so was their cruelty, <u>arrogance</u>, and greed.

The African slave trade now became big business in Europe. This both encouraged and discouraged exploration. Some ships did venture farther, but some loaded up with slaves wherever they could get them and scurried home for a quick profit. Still, people were noticing that as they went down the African coast, it leaned more and more to the southeast. But how far did it go? Did it reach all the way to the South Pole? Did it swing around into the unknown land in the south and enclose the Indian Ocean? Ptolemy[6] had thought so, but of course Europeans hoped for open sea between Africa and Asia.

Prince Henry never found out the answers. He died in 1460 at the age of sixty-six. He had brought 2,000 miles of the Unknown into the known world and in recent years had added the Cape Verde Islands and the Azores to the map.

After his death, Prince Henry became known as Prince Henry the Navigator, the man who set the Age of Exploration in motion.

---

5. **licenses** (lī′səns·ses): permits.
6. **Ptolemy** (täl′ə·mē): astronomer, mathematician, and geographer who lived in Alexandria, Egypt, in the second century A.D.

inferior (in·fir′ē·ər): of a lesser quality.

arrogance (ar′ə·gans): state of feeling superior or overly proud.

1. What made Prince Henry so curious about Africa?

2. What did people think would happen if they sailed too far down the west coast of Africa?

3. How did Gil Eanes finally manage to sail past Cape Bojador?

4. Why did Prince Henry wear a prickly shirt made of hair next to his skin?

5. Why were the people of Portugal so interested in the ten Africans who were brought to Prince Henry?

MEET THE *Writer*

Jean Fritz (1915–   ) is an award-winning author of historical biographies and novels for young people. Fritz spent the first thirteen years of her life in China, where her American parents did missionary work. She now lives in Dobbs Ferry, New York.

Suppose you have a friend who's never been to your house. To show how to get there, you might draw a map. This selection tells about an exciting time in the history of mapmaking. Why was it exciting? Here's a hint—the year is 1492.

The Mapmakers

from *If You Were There in 1492*

by BARBARA BRENNER

At the end of the fifteenth century mapping was already an ancient art. People had been making maps for at least 2,000 years. If you lived in Spain, you would have known about Abraham Zacuto[1] and the mapmakers of Majorca. On that Spanish island the chief industry was mapmaking, or cartography, and most of the mapmakers were Jewish. The maps were usually made on vellum, the cured[2] skin of unborn calves, or on gazelle hide. They were hand-painted and decorated with fancy lettering in Latin. If there was a big area that a mapmaker knew nothing about, it would be decorated with imaginary countries and creatures. Each time an explorer returned with the story of a new land, the mapmakers would put it into the newest map. That

You Need to Know...

The earliest maps were probably drawn in the dirt with a stick, or on the walls of caves with charcoal. They most likely were of the area known to the mapmaker. The ancient Greeks were among the first people to attempt to draw a map of the whole world based on ancient surveys and measurements of distances, as well as on the observations of sailors. For many years, mapmakers relied on the reports of people who sailed to new lands. In today's world, orbiting satellites and telescopes in space do the observing and measuring for mapmakers. With these tools, scientists can explore and track weather, natural resources and soil erosion, and can even monitor wildlife here on Earth. Beyond our world, instruments such as the Hubble Space Telescope are reaching out into space and mapping the galaxies of the universe.

---

1. **Abraham Zacuto** (āʹbrə·ham zä·kōōʹto): mapmaker who wrote a book on navigation that Columbus is said to have studied. In 1492, Zacuto and more than 200,000 other Jews were forced to leave Spain.
2. **cured** (kyōōrd): processed in a way that preserved it.

way the maps carried the new information. Unfortunately, they also carried some of the old <u>misinformation</u>.

In 1492 maps were in big demand. The mapmakers were busy making maps for explorers and for kings and queens to give as gifts. Because printing was now established as a <u>profession</u>, more people could have copies of maps. And for ordinary purposes, they could be printed on paper, and they didn't cost as much.

But, of course, a map is flat. And the world is round. No one had made a globe of the world since way back in Greek times. And those old globes were no longer in existence. Along came Martin Behaim. Martin Behaim loved maps. They were his passion and his hobby, even though he wasn't trained as a mapmaker. He thought he knew more about maps than the people who were making them. And in 1492 he persuaded his hometown of Nuremberg, Germany, to accept this excellent view of himself. The city council gave Martin Behaim seventy-five dollars to construct a globe of the world.

He started work on it immediately. The globe, which he called an *Erdapfel,* or "earth apple," was to be fifty centimeters in diameter (a little over nineteen inches). It

misinformation (mis'in'fər·mā'shən): false or wrong information.

profession (prō·fesh'ən): occupation involving special skills or advanced education.

Juan de la Cosa

The first person to put America on a map was Juan de la Cosa who sailed with Columbus on three voyages. In 1500, de la Cosa drew the world as he knew it, painting it in bright colors on an oxhide chart. Although Columbus disagreed with him, de la Cosa drew Cuba as an island because he knew, from his observations, that Cuba was an island. However, de la Cosa did agree with Columbus that they had reached Asia and that's why his *Mappa Mundi* shows America as part of China. After presenting his map to Queen Isabella of Spain, de la Cosa made two more dangerous voyages to the Americas. In 1510, he was killed by American Indians at Cartagena (now in Colombia).

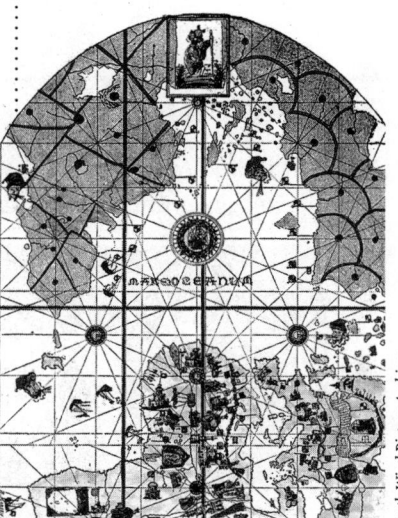

North Wind Picture Archives

▲ Juan de la Cosa's *Mappa Mundi.*
❓ **How is a globe of the world different from a map?**

mold: form which gives shape.

sphere (sfir): globe-shaped form; ball.

miniature (min′ē·ə·chər): small.

was made of a composition material[3] layered over a <u>mold</u>. Behaim hired an artist named Glockenthon to actually draw the countries on the surface and then letter more than a thousand place names. Glockenthon worked on strips of animal skins called parchment, which were then fitted and pasted onto the molded <u>sphere</u>. He decorated the map with 111 <u>miniature</u> figures of things like monsters, kings, camels, mermaids, and flags, using six different colors. When the globe was finished, it was mounted on a wooden tripod[4] and put on display.

Martin Behaim's globe was finished in 1492. If you were around back then, you might have heard about it. It caused quite a stir. But what people didn't know was that Behaim had repeated the mistakes of the earlier mapmakers. The brand-new globe showed the earth about 25 percent smaller than it actually is. The wrong sizes were now cemented to the surface of the world's first globe! Anyone looking at Behaim's globe would have thought that if you sailed west across the Atlantic Ocean from—say—Spain,

---

3. **composition material:** mixture of several ingredients.
4. **tripod** (trī′päd′): three-legged stool or table.

Margaret Geller

An outstanding mapmaker today is Margaret Geller, who uses giant-sized telescopes to explore the galaxies around the Milky Way. Since the early 1980s, Geller and her collaborator, John

NASA

Huchra, have surveyed more than fifteen thousand galaxies. She does this by measuring redshifts. These tell the speed at which an object is moving away from Earth. She uses Hubble's law, which describes how the universe expands, to change the redshifts into distances. Knowing the position of each galaxy in the sky and its distance from us, Geller and her co-workers construct three-dimensional maps of the universe. She has received many awards and honors for her pioneering work as an explorer and mapmaker of the universe.

◄ Hubble Telescope.

you could reach the Indies[5] before you ran out of food and water. It wouldn't be a big trip, according to his globe. It was only about 3,000 miles. And it was clear sailing. No other land in the way. That's what Behaim thought. That's what the other mapmakers thought. And that's what most people believed.

---

5. **Indies** (in'dēz'): In 1492, China, Japan, and India were called the Indies.

✓ Reading Check

1. What is cartography?

2. If early mapmakers knew nothing about an area, how would they show it on a map?

3. Give three reasons why maps were in great demand in 1492.

4. What kind of map did Martin Behaim create? How was it different from other maps of his time?

5. What was the big mistake on Behaim's map? How might that mistake have influenced Christopher Columbus?

▲ Later globes have followed the style of Behaim's first "earth apple."
❷ What process did Martin Behaim use to make his globe?

MEET THE *Writer*

Barbara Brenner (1925–   ) has received many awards for her books. Her favorite nonfiction subjects for young people are animals, ecology, and nature. Brenner and her husband live in a house by a lake in the Pocono Mountains of Pennsylvania. There she observes the local wildlife, the inspiration for many of her natural science books.

A broken bone can upset vacation plans, softball practice, or any other occasion. Early American Indians knew how to treat this and many other health problems, and some of these early treatments are still in use today. Read on to find out what medical miracles we owe to the early American Indians.

from Ancient Healing

from *Science of the Early Americas*

by GERALDINE WOODS

First Aid

Despite their many successes with plants, most early Native Americans understood only a little about the way the human body <u>functions</u>. Some groups were familiar with the appearance of the body's <u>internal</u> organs. The Inca,[1] for example, mummified[2] their dead. By removing internal organs, they gained some knowledge of the body's structure. As part of a religious ritual, the Aztec[3] cut into a living body and removed the heart. Of course the victim died, but the priests did have a chance to observe the breathing lungs and <u>circulating</u> blood for a few moments.

Most healers probably learned about the body when someone was wounded. Almost all cultures were skilled in setting broken bones, and the Aztec even knew how to make plaster casts.[4] The Plains Indians used a pulley system to put dislocated shoulders back into place. A rope was tied to the patient's arm and then draped over a tree. By pulling on the rope, the healer forced the arm into the

functions (fuŋk′shənz): works.
internal (in·tʉr′nəl): inside.

circulating (sʉr′kyo͞o·lāt′iŋ): moving or flowing in a circular course.

The Granger Collection, New York

▲ A medicine man administering to a patient.

---

1. **Inca:** American Indians largely from Quechuan tribe who had conquered and then inhabited much of South America by the sixteenth century. Their empire was at its height when Spanish explorers arrived in 1532.
2. **mummified** (mum′ə·fīd′): preserved; kept from decaying.
3. **Aztec** (az′tek′): American Indians who had developed an advanced civilization in what is now Mexico.
4. **plaster casts** (plas′tər kasts): wraps made of hardened material and used to keep broken bones in place.

right position. The Inca amputated limbs[5] and made holes in patients' skulls to relieve pressure on the brain. The holes were later covered with silver plates— if the patient lived long enough. Aztec healers treated wounds with hot urine (urine contains no germs) and often cut infected areas open, so they could drain.

▲ Sweat lodge. **❓ In what ways was this treatment of benefit to a person's health?**

Other Treatments and Tools

Many early cultures in North America, particularly in the Southwest, believed that sweating helped the body to rid itself of impurities.[6] (This idea is supported by some doctors today.) To encourage sweating, some groups built "sweat lodges"—small, usually round buildings that could be heated to high temperatures. Often, as part of a sacred ritual, a person spent several hours meditating[7] in the sweat lodge. The heat of the sweat lodge was also a favored treatment for arthritis[8] and muscle pains.

Early Central and South Americans who lived near volcanoes performed surgery with knives made from a volcanic glass called obsidian. Obsidian can be split so that it has extremely sharp, thin edges. The Aztec stitched wounds with human hair and bone needles. Ancient Native Americans invented the syringe, a device used for injecting liquid medicine. Some syringes were made out of animal bladders and hollow bones. The Arawak created rubber from tree sap and used it to make syringes.

> ### You Need to Know...
> Plants were especially important in American Indian medicine. According to one legend, animals created disease when they realized that humans were outnumbering them. However, the plants took pity on the humans and gave up their secrets to cure illness and ease pain. Many of the medicines that American Indians derived from plants are still used today. One is salicylic acid, found in willow tree bark, and used to reduce pain and fever. Today, salicylic (sal'ə•sil'ik) acid is the main ingredient in aspirin. The foxglove plant is the source of digitalis (dij'i•tal'is), used to treat heart conditions. Healers used certain fungi and molds to combat infections, and in the twenty-first century, these life-forms are a natural source of antibiotics.

---

5. **amputated limbs:** (am'pyo͞o•tāt'id): cut off arms or legs.
6. **impurities** (im•pyo͝or'ə•tēz): unclean elements that may cause illness.
7. **meditating** (med'ə•tāt'iŋ): thinking deeply.
8. **arthritis** (är•thrīt'is): often painful condition that affects joints such as knees, hips and fingers.

▲ American Indian healer.

❓ **How did most healers learn about the human body?**

Many groups knew how to treat snakebites with a tourniquet. A tourniquet is a strip of rope or cloth tied tightly around some part of the body, usually an arm or a leg. The tourniquet cuts off the blood flow and keeps the poison in one small area of the body. The healer sucked the poison out of the bite and spat it out before removing the tourniquet. Tourniquets were also used to stop bleeding, as they are today.

Dentistry

The Aztec were proud of their clean, shining teeth. They brushed them with a mixture of salt and powdered charcoal. After they had scraped the tartar[9] off, they polished each tooth with white ashes and honey. Ancient Peruvians rubbed their teeth with a plant called "balsam of Peru." In North America, the Meskwakis cleaned their teeth with white clay. The ancient Maya[10] made dental fillings with jade, turquoise, or gold. However, they considered the fillings as a type of decorative jewelry, not dental care!

9. **tartar** (tärt'ər): buildup of hard deposits on teeth; it can cause gum disease.
10. **Maya** (mä'yə): Central American Indian civilization which was highly developed when it was discovered by sixteenth-century Europeans.

Mummies on the Mountain

The Incas believed that their mountains had supernatural power, ruling the clouds that brought the life-giving rain. As part of their worship of these powerful landforms, Inca priests led the people to the summit of the highest mountains where a child was sacrificed to the mountain gods. The priests then wrapped the body tightly in beautifully woven fabrics, folding tiny statues of people and animals made of silver and gold into the wrappings. To us, living five hundred years later, this seems a cruel ceremony. However, for the Inca child, it was considered a great honor to be chosen. Today, scientists are carefully unearthing these mummified bodies. In laboratories especially set up for the task, they use modern technology to conduct tests that will give us new information about the Inca culture.

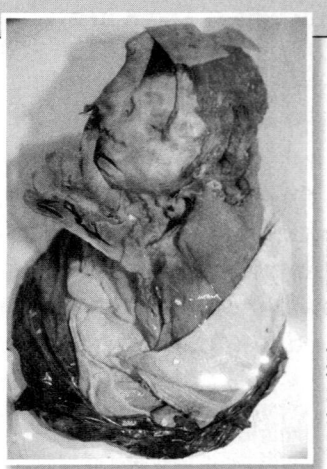

AP/Wide World Photos/EL TRIBUNO

▲ A 500-year-old Inca mummy.

Many Native Americans treated gum infections by cutting into the painful area, allowing it to drain, and then searing it with heat. The ancients also pulled out decayed teeth with bone tweezers or other tools. Many North American groups treated dental pain with the bark of the prickly ash, which European settlers later named the "toothache tree." Many other plants were made into teas or prepared as hot dressings and then used to relieve mouth pain.

Europe Brings Disease

The first explorers from Europe frequently wrote about the good health of the Native Americans they encountered. However, contact with people from Europe soon proved deadly for the inhabitants of the Americas. Measles, chicken pox, and other illnesses that infected, but seldom killed, Europeans swept through the Native American population. Why did these diseases kill so many Native Americans? Many diseases are passed from <u>domesticated</u>

domesticated (dō·mes'ti·kā t'id): tamed.

SIDELIGHT

"Quinine is the drug used to treat patients with malaria, a disease spread by certain kinds of mosquitoes. Legend says quinine was discovered by accident in the early 1600s.

A Spanish soldier in Peru had an extremely high fever and chills caused by malaria. His comrades left him behind to die. The high fever made him so thirsty that he crawled to a nearby shallow pond to drink. Although the pond water tasted bitter, he drank it anyway, then fell asleep.

When he awoke, his fever had gone down. He rejoined his military company and told them of the miraculous pond water. They examined the water and discovered that its bitter taste came from the bark of a log lying in the pool. The soldier had accidentally discovered that the bark of the cinchona tree could cure malaria."

—"Quinine" from *Accidents May Happen* by Charlotte Foltz Jones

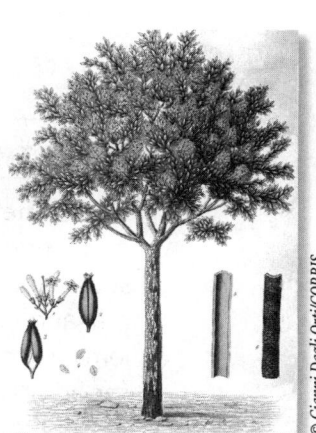

© Gianni Dagli Orti/CORBIS

▲ Quinine is derived from the bark of the cinchona tree.

resistance (ri·zis′tƏns): ability to fight off disease.

animals to humans. For centuries, Europeans had bred and cared for horses, cows, and many other animals. During this time, the Europeans built up resistance to the animals' germs. In the Americas, however, these beasts were previously unknown, and so were the diseases they spread. Native Americans had no resistance to the new infections—and no cures. The "gift of the plants" could not save great numbers of ancient Americans from the deadly invasion of European diseases.

✓ Reading Check

1. How did the Incas and Aztecs learn about the body's internal organs?

2. What were sweat lodges, and how were they used?

3. What is a tourniquet? For what two different purposes did American Indians use it?

4. How did American Indians deal with gum infections and decayed teeth?

5. Why were European diseases, such as measles, so deadly to Native American populations?

MEET THE *Writer*

Geraldine Woods (1948–   ) is the author of more than thirty-five nonfiction books for young people. Her husband, Harold, has written several books with her. Their work covers a variety of subjects, including real and imaginary animals, countries of the world, and modern problems, such as pollution and drug abuse. They also write mystery novels for adults. When she is not writing, Woods works as a reading teacher in New York City.

The potato appears often on our plates, and we tend to take it for granted. Potatoes are the fourth most important crop in the world. At fast-food restaurants, people eat millions of pounds of potatoes every day! How much do you think the world-wide potato crop is worth per year? Read on to find out.

NONFICTION BOOK

HISTORY •

SCIENCE •

A Strange, Funny-Looking Vegetable

from The Amazing Potato: A Story in Which the Incas, Conquistadors, Marie Antoinette, Thomas Jefferson, Wars, Famines, Immigrants, and French Fries All Play a Part

by MILTON MELTZER

▲ The Incas called their funny-looking vegetable *papa*.

O ne day in the 1530s a scouting party of Spaniards entered an Inca village, high in the Andes[1] in what we now call Peru. Reports of cruel and greedy white invaders had already spread throughout the mountains, and the villagers had fled at word of their coming. The Spaniards went from empty house to empty house, hunting for loot. They found only maize (corn), beans, and a strange vegetable that was like nothing they had ever seen.

The vegetable came in many sizes, tiny as a nut to big as an apple. Its shape ranged from an <u>irregular</u> ball to a twisted oblong. Its skin was white, yellow, blue, purple, red, brown. Inside, its color could be white, yellow, purple, pink. The Spaniards were not impressed. They had come

> **You Need to Know...**
> Why would anyone write a scholarly book of over seven hundred pages about the potato? That's what the author of this selection wondered when he found such a book in a college bookstore. Upon closer inspection, Milton Meltzer became fascinated and before he knew it, he was writing his own book for young people about this grubby but lovable tuber.

irregular (i•reg′yə•lər): uneven; lopsided.

1. **Andes** (an′dēz′): mountain range extending the length of western South America.

Freeze-Dried Food

The Incas created an instant food by using the process that we now call freeze-drying. This process is an excellent way to preserve food for a long period of time. Another advantage of freeze-dried food is its light weight, so it's easy for travelers—from hikers to astronauts—to carry over long distances. Freeze-dried food is restored to its original form by adding water. Without freeze-drying, unwashed and loosely covered potatoes can be stored in a dry, dark place—not the refrigerator—for up to three months.

staple (stā′pəl): most important or basic to the diet.

vegetarian (vej′ə•ter′ē•ən): of a diet containing no meat.

© *Cliff Leight/Outside Images/PictureQuest*

❓ Why are freeze-dried foods useful for hikers?

to the Andes searching for gold, silver, and precious stones. What good was this funny-looking vegetable?

Gradually they found out. First of all, it was the staple food of these mountain people. Secondly, the vegetable was believed to have healing powers. Raw slices were fixed to broken bones, pressed against the

Ted Spiegel/CORBIS

head to cure aching, eaten with other food to end a belly-ache. The Incas also rubbed it on their bodies to cure skin diseases and carried slices to prevent rheumatism.

The Inca name for the vegetable was *papa*. It means tuber, a short, fleshy underground stem or root. The Inca gave other names to the many kinds of *papas* they grew. Those with red flesh they called "weep blood for the Inca." An especially hard kind was "knife breaker," and still others were "human-head" and "red mother." When the Spaniards tasted the potato, they found it delicious—"a dainty dish even for Spaniards," one conquistador[2] admitted.

The diet of the common people of Peru was mainly vegetarian. True, some people fished along the coast or in the mountain waters of Lake Titicaca.[3] Others occasionally hunted in groups, chasing down deer, wild llamas,[4] bears, pumas,[5] and foxes. Still others raised guinea pigs and ducks. However, those were luxury foods. The main diet was maize and other vegetables in the lowlands. In the highlands, where maize would not grow, it was the potato above all that people depended on. We now know that the native peoples living along the western coast of South

2. **conquistador** (kän•kēs′tə•dôr′): sixteenth-century Spanish conqueror in North or South America.
3. **Lake Titicaca** (tit′i•kä′kə): large lake, at an altitude of 12,500 feet, on the border between Peru and Bolivia.
4. **llamas** (lä′məz): animals native to South America that look like small camels without humps.
5. **pumas** (py∞′məz): cougars or mountain lions; large, powerful cats.

America were growing and eating potatoes two thousand years before Columbus set sail.

They knew not only how to grow the potato but how to preserve it. After harvesting the crop, they spread the potatoes on the ground and left them overnight to freeze in the biting air of the high mountains. The next day the men, women, and children assembled to stamp out the potatoes' moisture with their bare feet. They repeated this process for four or five days, until all the moisture was gone. What was left was a white potato flour that could be stored for years. The Inca name for what was probably the world's first freeze-dried food was *chuno*.

Scientists exploring the ancient tombs of the Inca have found evidence that *chuno* was bartered for other products. It was carried on the backs of llamas to the lower valleys and coastal towns, where it was exchanged for maize and manioc (another root food), clay pottery, and woven cloth.

When the Spaniards discovered the rich silver mines of Potosí[6] (now in Bolivia) in 1545, they were quick to see the use of the potato, fresh or freeze dried, as food for the Inca they forced to work for them. It didn't take long for speculators in Spain to see a new way to get rich. They sailed across the Atlantic, bought up potatoes cheaply from the Inca farmers, and sold them at high prices to the native workers in the mines.

---

6. **Potosí** (pô′tô•se′): city on the slopes of Cerro de Potosí, a high mountain in the Andes.

The Great Hunger

By the mid-1840s in Ireland, the poor people who usually worked on farms survived by eating only potatoes. Some landowners paid their workers in potatoes instead of money. Families raised their own potato crops on tiny patches of land. One day, dark spots were discovered on the leaves of potato plants, and, by the next morning, fields of green potato plants had turned completely black. A fungus from North America caused the potato blight that spread to all the European countries where potatoes were grown. It was especially destructive in Ireland because so many poor people depended on the potato for food, as well as for income. In that terrible time, Ireland lost one-fourth of its total population. More than a million Irish people died from lack of food or from diseases that took advantage of their weakness and hunger. More than a million others, mostly the young and the strong, emigrated to America—all because of the potato.

CORBIS

▲ Searching for potatoes in a stubble field during the potato famine in Ireland.

bartered (bärt′ərd): traded without using money.

speculators (spek′yə•lā′tʊrz): investors who take risks, hoping to make big profits.

Here is a strange twist of history: The annual $100-billion value of the potato crop is three times greater than the value of all the gold and silver the Spanish lugged away from the Americas. The potatoes they took so lightly turned out to be worth far more than the gold and silver they killed for.

✓ Reading Check

1. What were the Spaniards looking for when they searched from house to house? What three foods did the Spaniards find?

2. Name two ways that the Incas used potatoes.

3. Why was the potato especially important in the highlands of Peru?

4. Describe how the Incas preserved the potato crop.

5. What's become more important than the gold and silver that the Spaniards took back to Europe? Why does the writer call this a "twist of history"?

MEET THE *Writer*

Milton Meltzer (1915–   ) began writing nonfiction for young people in the 1960s. Meltzer, a first-generation Jewish American, writes about dedicated, optimistic people who take action to overcome oppression. He says, "My subjects choose action. . . . I try to make readers understand that history isn't only what happens to us. History is what we *make* happen. Each of us. All of us." In addition to more than eighty books for young people, Meltzer has written articles for magazines, biographies and novels for adults, and scripts for documentary films, filmstrips, radio, and television. Many of his books have received awards.

The Super Bowl or the World Series seems pretty important to us today. However, when the Mayas played a big game, it could literally be a matter of life and death.

"Let's Play Ball!"
from *Calliope*

by PETER KVIETOK

The boys took their ball and went to the court where their father had played. They happily played the sacred game and the earth shook beneath their running feet. Below the earth, the Lords of Death looked around. Who dares disturb us by playing ball above our heads? The Lords called their messengers. Go tell those with the ball that the Lords of Death wish to see them. Tell them to come within seven days and to bring their ball and gear so that we may play together.

This is part of a story told in the *Popol Vuh*, an ancient Maya book of religious myths. In the story, two boys go to the underworld to play a ball game against the Lords of Death. The boys win their matches, but the gods play many dangerous tricks on them. The boys, however, cleverly avoid the danger until one of them has his head bitten off by a giant bat. Sometime later, both burn to death in a fire, but their bones are thrown into the river, where they turn into handsome boys who can play ball again.

This myth begins to explain how a ball game played by many people in ancient Central America had a different meaning from our sports today. The game, now called *pok-ta-pok* (rubber-to-rubber), was probably very popular and

▲ Mayan ballplayers.

You Need to Know...

The Mayas first began settling in small villages in Central America some 3,500 years ago. Long before Spanish explorers arrived in the area, the Mayas had built one of the world's greatest civilizations, which spread throughout the area that is now southern Mexico, Guatemala, and northern Belize. By the time Europeans began arriving, the Mayan culture had started to fade, and some of its cities were swallowed up by the jungle. Nobody is exactly sure why, though some scholars blame the decline on warfare and a style of farming that exhausted the land.

▲ Mayan plate depicting a ballplayer.

participants (pär·tis'ə·pants): players.

stakes (stāks) money or prizes to be won.

ritual (rich'oo·əl): act done according to religious law.

vertical (vʉr'ti·kəl): upright; straight up or down.

accounts (ə·kounts'): descriptions or stories.

played for fun in the same way softball is today. Yet, it was also played at religious ceremonies, with a meaning that we still do not fully understand.

We know that specially trained <u>participants</u> played the game inside decorated stone ball courts, sometimes for very high <u>stakes</u>. In some games, members of the losing team would have their heads cut off as a form of <u>ritual</u> sacrifice to the gods. Carved stone panels from one ball court in Mexico show players in fancy costumes holding the heads of other players.

The areas specially designed for the game were usually flat and rectangular. Spectators sat or stood on the flat space created along the top of the <u>vertical</u> or slanted side walls. Surviving wall reliefs[1] suggest that the players ran on the court as they interacted with each other and the ball. It also seems probable that the ball was allowed to bounce off the walls.

Courts differed according to location. In southern Mexico, Chichén Itzá had a very large court with a temple at each end. The playing field, which was in the shape of the letter "I," was 500 feet long, 120 feet wide at its narrowest part, and 207 feet wide at the ends—about the size of ten standard tennis courts. In Guatemala, the courts were smaller but well made of stone and plaster. Courts in the West Indies had low stone walls and were not exceptionally fancy. European <u>accounts</u> mention simple courts in Mexico and the West Indies, but we do not know much about these since only the more ornate ones have survived.

The name of the game, *pok-ta-pok*, refers to the ball, which was made of natural rubber from the sap[2] of a tree. Probably the world's first rubber ball, it could bounce very high, like the "superballs" of today, and could be as large as a volleyball. Because the ball was so large and hard, the players had to wear protective equipment to keep from being hurt and to be able to hit the ball harder. Athletic equipment included belts, chestpads, armpads, kneepads,

---

1. **reliefs** (ri·lēfs'): forms or designs projecting from a flat surface.
2. **sap** (sap): juice that flows in plants.

heavy deerskin trousers and tunics,[3] sandals, back shields, and hand and wrist guards. Without this protection, a fast ball probably could have killed a player. To return a low ball, players had to throw themselves on the hard plaster floor. For this reason, the thick trousers and kneepads were important safety precautions. In addition to this equipment, some players wore fancy headdresses, necklaces, nose ornaments, and ear plugs during ceremonial games.

The game probably had very complicated rules, but it is impossible to tell exactly how the Maya played it. We do know that players hit the ball with their hips, buttocks, thighs, elbows, wrists, and chests. Hands and feet were not allowed to touch the ball. There were also several versions of the game, but most involved hitting the ball back and forth between two sides of a court, like volleying in tennis or volleyball. A team lost points if the players were unable to return the ball correctly. You could also lose points if you hit the ball out of bounds or if you let the ball hit the ground on your side of the court.

Some surviving courts have small stone rings attached to the top of the side walls. These may have been used for scoring, although it would have been very difficult to hit a heavy rubber ball through a vertical ring 24 feet in the air, especially without using your hands. Other courts have carved stone heads attached to the side walls, which players may have tried to hit with the ball.

Most large towns had a ball court, usually located in the center of the town. Many people attended the games, and there was much gambling. People would bet precious stones, slaves, houses, and land. The gods, they believed, always decided who would win the game before it even started, but the people still enjoyed trying to figure out the score.

SuperStock

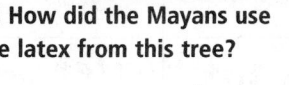
? How did the Mayans use the latex from this tree?

3. **tunics** (too'niks): long, loose, shirt-like garments.

"It's Alive!"

Europeans had never seen anything like the ball used in the Mayan games. It bounced as though it were alive. The bounce came from a milky substance called latex that is produced from a variety of plants. This substance made its way to Europe when a French scientist brought some back from a trip to South America in the 1700s. The hardened substance was given the name "rubber" in 1772 by a British chemist who noticed that it could rub away pencil markings. Rubber's usefulness was limited because it became sticky in hot weather and brittle in cold weather. That problem was solved when Charles Goodyear accidentally overheated some rubber covered with sulfur on a hot stove in 1839. The result was a harder and more durable rubber that is still in use today.

Erich Lessing/Art Resource, NY

▲ Ballplayer wearing protective gear. **?** **What did the players wear to protect themselves?**

When the Spaniards came to Mexico in the 1500s, they described one of the games they watched:

> *As soon as the ball is tossed into the middle of the field, the whole crowd excitedly bounds over the plain[4] darting this way and that. One hits the rubber ball with his elbow, another drives it back with his hip, one thrusts his head in its way as it comes down, another sends it quickly back again to the sky with his knee, or darting back and forth strikes it with one hip and then with the other . . .*

Local farmers on the west coast of Mexico still play a version of the game. The court is marked with a few stones at the corners and lines drawn in the dirt. Players use heavy rubber balls weighing about eight pounds and wear a belt made of bark fiber with a protective pad of leather or a piece of automobile tire. Thus does the present maintain its link with the past, without the elaborate ritual or human sacrifices once associated with the game.

---

4. plain (plān) extensive flat area.

Reading Check

1. Who won the ballgames between the two boys and the Lords of Death? What happened to the boys?

2. What could happen to the players on the losing teams?

3. What was the ball made of? How big was it?

4. Why did the players have to wear protective equipment?

5. How did players move the ball around the field?

MEET THE *Writer*

Peter Kvietok is an anthropologist—a scientist who studies humans—specializing in the ancient life and culture of the people who lived in the Andes of South America, and in particular, the Incas.

Lives have been ruined; horrible crimes have been committed; and empires have been destroyed—all in the search for a yellow rock. Find out how a simple metallic element has inspired the imagination—and the greed—of millions of people.

All That Glitters

from *Read*

The Search for Gold Has Built and Toppled Empires and Reversed the Fortunes of Princes and Paupers.

Hundreds of years ago, Spanish and Portuguese explorers sailed west across the ocean to find El Dorado, a legendary city of untold wealth, whose king was said to have sprinkled himself with the dust of gold each morning and rinsed it away in a lake every night. In this land, gold was as plentiful as sand.

In searching for El Dorado, explorers encountered the great and wealthy Indian civilizations of Central and South America. And in the adventurers' greed for gold, they became conquerors, laying waste to the people and their cities and carrying away enormous treasure. But they never found El Dorado.

Writers have <u>lavished</u> countless thoughts and words on this yellow metal, gold. They've called gold a ruthless[1]

> **You Need to Know...**
> Gold is everywhere these days, from the watches on people's wrists to the inner workings of their computers. It is not often pure gold, however, because gold is a very soft metal. A pure-gold ring would be bent out of recognition with just normal wearing. A pure-gold coin would be worn smooth in no time. To make gold stronger, it is often mixed with other metals, such as silver, copper, or zinc. The resulting metal is called an alloy. The purity of gold is expressed in karats. A karat is equal to one twenty-fourth part of pure gold, so 24-karat gold is pure gold, and 12-karat gold is half gold and half alloy. These facts describe the metal itself, the gold you can hold in your hand. The dream inspired by gold is a whole other matter. Why has this soft, shiny substance had such power over people's lives?

lavished (lav'ishd): given very generous amounts of (something).

---
1. ruthless (rooth'lis): cruel; without pity.

exquisite (eks′kwiz·it): perfect or extremely beautiful.

quest (kwest): search, especially a search for something important.

extravagant (ek·strav′ə·gənt): more than necessary.

▲ King Tutankhamen's golden death mask. **❓ Who did the gold of Egypt belong to?**

K. Scholz/H. Armstrong Roberts, Inc.

king, the money of monarchs, the seed of unnumbered ills, a transient,[2] shining trouble.

This rare metal is soft enough to be shaped into exquisite pieces of jewelry or hammered into sheets of gold leaf only 4-millionths of an inch thick. And gold is enduring enough that a piece of jewelry will barely tarnish[3] after thousands of years, even underwater or underground.

People have left their homes and families, suffered unimaginable hardships, committed unspeakable crimes, and even given their lives in their quest for the stuff.

Yet gold is basically no more nor less than a metallic element, symbol Au, among many elements, such as mercury, platinum, silver, copper, and zinc. Why, down through the ages, has gold stood for more? Why has gold meant wealth, power, and beauty to so many?

History of Gold

Gold is one of the few substances that has been considered precious throughout history. No one knows when gold was first discovered, but ancient Egyptians were the first people to mine it on a large scale. The output of the mines, of course, belonged to the pharaohs, who had the gold fashioned into idols and extravagant decorations. Many Egyptian artifacts, such as King Tutankhamen's death mask, were made from gold. In those days, gold was not a possession for the common man or woman.

More than any other people, Egyptians knew the value of gold and considered it the most perfect metal. In an effort to have even more than what they could mine, they developed a pseudoscience[4] called alchemy to try to change common metals into gold. In ancient Greece and later, in the Middle Ages, alchemy became a popular idea among philosophers. They likened the scientific quest for gold, the perfect metal, to the human soul's search for perfection.

The alchemists never succeeded. But the science of chemistry developed from their studies.

---

2. **transient** (tran′shənt): lasting for only a short time.
3. **tarnish** (tär′nish): become dull and discolored.
4. **pseudoscience** (soo′dō·sī′əns): a field of study that claims to be a science without following the rules of science.

The search for gold inspired many voyages and conquests. Gold helped spark the conquests of Alexander the Great and Julius Caesar and the journeys of Christopher Columbus, Francisco Pizarro, and Ferdinand Magellan. During the 16th century, Spain—and its monarchy—became the richest kingdom in the world by taking more than 32 million ounces of gold from native peoples of Central and South America.

Gold Fever

The course of U.S. history was changed by the 1848 discovery of gold nuggets at Sutter's Mill. The California gold rush that followed has since become the stuff of great American frontier dramas—both fact and fiction.

But that isn't the only notable gold rush. In 1851, news of the great Australian gold rush swept the world and brought a million people to that continent over four years. And in the United States, gold rushes to Colorado, Montana, South Dakota, and Alaska drew thousands of people and established hundreds of towns all over the American frontier.

SIDELIGHT

For many people the legend of El Dorado inspired little more than uncontrollable greed. For Edgar Allan Poe the story inspired poetry. Poe's "Eldorado" tells of a knight's relentless effort to find the city of gold and warns of what he is likely to find instead. In line 1 of the poem, the word "bedight" means adorned or decorated.

Gaily bedight,
A gallant knight,
In sunshine and in shadow,
Had journeyed long,
Singing a song,
In search of Eldorado.

But he grew old—
This knight so bold—
And o'er his heart a shadow
Fell as he found
No spot of ground
That looked like Eldorado.

And, as his strength
Failed him at length,
He met a pilgrim shadow—
"Shadow," said he,
"Where can it be—
This land of Eldorado?"

"Over the Mountains
Of the Moon,
Down the Valley of the Shadow,
Ride, boldly ride,"
The shade replied,—
"If you seek for Eldorado."

—"Eldorado," from *The Raven and Other Favorite Poems* by Edgar Allan Poe

North Wind Picture Archives

▲ Spanish conquistador on horseback.

▲ Pirates supposedly buried their treasure to protect it. **❷ What has been one result of this practice?**

notorious (nō·tôr′ē·əs): widely known as having a bad reputation.

People have long tried to explain gold fever. Like any kind of frenzy, it was a mixture of the pursuit of something attractive and the fear of being left behind when others sought riches.

During the rushes, gold became the great leveler. Rich and poor alike could mine as much as they were able, and they didn't have to turn their bonanza[5] over to some monarch.

Striking It Rich Today

Gold continues to hold its lure. Today, the hunt for gold draws people to strange, harsh, and faraway places.

- In Venezuela, miners use high-pressure hoses to search for the estimated 11,000 tons of gold believed to be along the Orinoco River. The wilderness they mine lies waste after they finish. In towns along the river, storekeepers have scales so that miners can pay for their purchases in gold.

- For more than 200 years, treasure seekers have been trying to decipher[6] the mystery of Oak Island—the speck of land off the coast of Nova Scotia where the notorious Captain Kidd supposedly buried a trove of gold and other riches. Over the years, prospectors have squandered[7] millions of dollars looking for the wealth; others have lost their lives. Still, they search.

- In 1989, a group of men set out to find a lode of gold in a nearly impossible location: 21 tons buried for 132 years in 8,000 feet of water. On September 12, 1857, a steamship carrying passengers and gold from California sank during a hurricane off the coast of South Carolina. Only 153 of almost 600 passengers on board the S.S. *Central America* survived. The gold—more than 20 tons—was lost with the ship. Using a special robot, the salvagers uncovered what they now call the Ship of Gold. Today, the retrieved gold is worth nearly a billion dollars.

---

5. **bonanza** (bə·nan′zə): a huge deposit of precious metal.
6. **decipher** (dē·sī′fər): figure out the meaning of.
7. **squandered** (skwän′dərd): wasted.

- Electric gold detectors recently created a small gold rush to Australia. A few years ago, one detector located a nugget worth $1 million buried just 6 inches below the ground.

Golden Words

One place where gold isn't rare is in language. Like the golden dust on the king of El Dorado, English phrases are sprinkled with references to gold.

You remember the story of King Midas and how everything he touched turned to gold? Because of that story, our language has the phrase *golden touch*. Anyone who is said to have a golden touch seems to do well at everything. A *golden oldie* is a favorite song from the past. An exclusive[8] area of a neighborhood might be referred to as a *gold coast*. A *golden age* is a period of great development, enlightenment, and achievement. Anything truly wonderful is *as good as gold*. Instead of using the slang word *cool*, you might say *golden*. And of course there is that saying about treating people the way you would like to be treated yourself—*the golden rule*.

---

8. **exclusive** (eks·kl$\overline{oo}$′siv): restricted; expensive.

Dividing the Gold

Dreams of gold inspired many of the Europeans who colonized the Americas. Consider a letter that Christopher Columbus wrote to the king and queen of Spain in 1494. In the letter, Columbus tells of his plans for colonizing Española, one of the islands that he visited during his famous voyage two years earlier. In order to encourage people to move to Española, Columbus proposes that only officially licensed colonists be allowed to collect gold. He also proposes that all gold be turned over immediately to an official so that the king's share could be taken out first, a plan that surely met with the king's approval. Columbus does realize that the search for gold can become all-consuming, and that the island might suffer as a result. He wrote:

"As, in the eagerness to get gold, every one will wish, naturally, to engage in its search in preference to any other employment, it seems to me that the privilege of going to look for gold ought to be withheld during some portion of each year, that there may be opportunity to have the other business necessary for the island performed."

King Midas's Bronze Touch

King Midas's touch may not have been so golden after all, at least if you judge by his burial mound. In addition to remains that have been identified as King Midas, excavators found an Iron Age drinking set (jugs, bowls, buckets, and so forth) of more than 150 metal pieces. Anyone who believed the myth of King Midas's "golden touch" was in for a surprise. All of the metal drinking pieces were made of bronze, not gold.

©Bettmann/CORBIS

▲ King Midas's touch turns his daughter to gold.

If those phrases aren't enough to convince you of gold's value in our language, imagine how strange a landmark like the Golden Gate Bridge would sound as the "Mercury Gate Bridge." Or how about having a tournament called the "Zinc Gloves." Imagine California being known as the "Iron State." And what happens when you change goldfish to silverfish? You get the picture.

Gold may not be rare in language—nuggets can be found most anywhere—but surely, it is valuable. Just as valuable perhaps as the filling in your tooth or the ring on your finger.

Pretty cool, huh?

No, pretty *golden*.

✓ Reading Check

1. What was El Dorado, and why were explorers so interested in finding it?

2. What were the alchemists trying to do? Which science developed from their studies?

3. How did Spain become the richest kingdom in the world during the sixteenth century?

4. What was discovered at Sutter's Mill in 1848, and how did that discovery change U.S. history?

5. Why is the S.S. *Central America* of interest to gold hunters?

Cross-Curricular ACTIVITIES

■ GEOGRAPHY/ART

Where in the World Is It? The map of the world changed as explorers found new travel routes and discovered new lands. In a group of three or four students, use your library or the Internet to find pictures of maps that were drawn during the age of the explorers—that is, from the fifteenth to eighteenth centuries. Then, make a montage of three or four maps showing how representations of Africa or the Americas changed over time. Under each map, write the date it was made and at least three ways it is different from the others. Display your montage for the class.

■ LANGUAGE ARTS/MUSIC

The View from the Shore African peoples must have watched Prince Henry's ships sailing along the coast of Africa and wondered about them. Perhaps they made up stories about the strange ships and the men who sailed them. It may be that the official storyteller collected these short anecdotes and put them together into a longer account. Imagine you are such a storyteller. Write at least three short pieces that reflect the experience of a person who saw the Portuguese ships or met sailors who came ashore. Select and record background music for your stories to enhance the mood. Then, put your stories and musical background together on one tape and present it to the class.

■ HISTORY/GEOGRAPHY

Striking It Rich For centuries, explorers and prospectors scoured the globe for gold. With a partner, design a poster that describes and shows the location of the sites of at least two famous gold

strikes. Your poster may take the form of a map alone, or of a map with text around it. Indicate where and when the gold was discovered, as well as how much gold came from the area. Be sure to note any special information you discover about the depth of mines, the richness of lodes, or the most interesting prospecting techniques. Share your poster with your class.

■ SCIENCE/ART

Look at This Through research, we learn more and more about the types of medicines used by ancient peoples. Select one of the medical treatments or plants used by the American Indians and discussed in *"from* Ancient Healing" (page 194). Read more about it, and then draw a cartoon strip with at least four sections or scenes, illustrating four main elements—discovery of the treatment or plant, how it was used or how it worked, and the final results. Your last section will show its modern use. Present your cartoon strip to the class.

■ HEALTH/ART

Extraordinary Tuber The potato has a long and distinguished history of feeding people around the world. Select a recipe for a potato dish. Letter this recipe and the directions for preparing it in the center of a large sheet of poster board. Illustrate your poster with other potato dishes or with scenes from the country where your recipe originated. Include information about the nutritional benefits of the potato. You might like to cook or bake enough of your recipe for the class to sample, or demonstrate how to prepare the dish.

READ ON: FOR INDEPENDENT READING

■ NONFICTION

Around the World in a Hundred Years: From Henry the Navigator to Magellan

by Jean Fritz (G. P. Putnam's Sons, 1994). Back in the fourteenth century, European mapmakers drew their maps with empty spaces at the edge: the Unknown. Here you will discover that explorers like Vasco da Gama, Columbus, and Magellan were too daring and curious (and greedy for gold) to let those spaces remain empty.

The Aztecs by Tim Wood (Viking, 1992) has illustrations which give the reader a cross-section view of the insides of Aztec temples, homes, and palaces. The text, along with detailed drawings of the buildings' exteriors, give information about Aztec life and customs. Also check out Wood's *The Incas* (Viking, 1996), another in the *See Through History Series*.

Commodore Perry in the Land of the Shogun

by Rhoda Blumberg (Lothrup, Lee & Shepard Books, 1985). By 1853, the Americas were no longer so new to Europeans. In Japan, on the other hand, few people even knew that America existed, and Americans certainly knew little about Japan, after its centuries of isolation. Things change when an American sea captain arrives in Japan, riding the back of a smoke-puffing dragon—a steamship—to ask the Japanese emperor to open trade with the West. A Newbery Honor book.

Terror of the Spanish Main: Sir Henry Morgan and His Buccaneers

by Albert Marrin (Dutton Books, 1998). Were the buccaneers dashing, romantic bandits? Or vicious terrorists who would stop at nothing for their own selfish gain? Award-winning historian Albert Marrin brings back all the blood and brutality of these seventeenth-century "cousins" of the pirates. For advanced readers.

■ FICTION

I, Juan de Pareja by Elizabeth Borton de Treviño (Farrar, Straus & Giroux, 1965). Juan de Pareja was born a slave, but the great Spanish painter Diego Velázquez recognized that Juan was something much more—an artist and a friend. Winner of the Newbery Medal.

The King's Fifth by Scott O'Dell (Houghton Mifflin Company, 1966). Seventeen-year-old Esteban de Sandoval wasn't looking for treasure; he was a mapmaker, dreaming of lands no one back in Spain even imagined to exist. Now Esteban is in prison, awaiting trial for hiding gold he should have given to the king. What went wrong?

Morning Girl by Michael Dorris (Hyperion Books, 1992). Morning Girl always wakes up early, ready for another day of swimming and fishing in the warm waters that surround her island home. So she is the first to see it—a strange-looking canoe carrying people who are dressed in heavy clothes. The year is 1492, and the lives of Morning Girl and her fellow Tainos are about to change forever.

Robinson Crusoe by Daniel Defoe (Atheneum, 1983). *Robinson Crusoe* is not just a classic tale of shipwreck on a desert island. It is also a window into the way Europeans in the early 1700s looked at other cultures, as well as their own. This edition includes illustrations painted by N. C. Wyeth.

Glossary

The glossary below is an alphabetical list of the underscored words found in the selections in this book. Some technical, foreign, and more obscure words in this book are not listed here, but instead are defined for you in the footnotes that accompany many of the selections.

Many words in the English language have more than one meaning. This glossary gives the meanings that apply to the words as they are used in the selections in this book.

Each word's pronunciation is given in parentheses. A guide to the pronunciation symbols appears at the bottom of each right-hand glossary page.

The following abbreviations are used:

    adj. adjective   *adv.* adverb   *n.* noun   *v.* verb

account (ə·kount′) *n.:* description or story.

adapt (ə·dapt′) *v.:* to adjust to new circumstances; make to fit.

adhere (ad·hir′) *v.:* to hold fast; firmly support.

agile (aj′əl) *adj.:* able to move quickly and easily.

alliance (ə·lī′əns) *n.:* association or union created for a common purpose.

ancestry (an′ses′trē) *n.:* line of family members.

appease (ə·pēz′) *v.:* to satisfy or calm; buy off.

apprentice (ə·pren′tis) *n.:* someone studying and working with a master to learn an art or a skill.

arrogance (ar′ə·gans) *n.:* state of feeling superior or overly proud.

artifact (ärt′ə·fakt′) *n.:* item made by human beings that is studied for its historical value.

artisan (ärt′ə·zen) *n.:* worker skilled in a particular trade or art.

authentic (ô·then′tik) *adj.:* genuine, real.

barter (bärt′ər) *v.:* to trade without using money.

calamity (kə·lam′ə·tē) *n.:* great misfortune; disaster.

calculation (kal′kyōō·lā′shən) *n.:* act or process of figuring or computing, usually with numbers, as in addition or subtraction.

censor (sen′sər) *v.:* to examine for forbidden ideas, which are then taken out.

chaos (kā′äs′) *n.:* disorder; confusion.

circulate (sʉr′kyōō·lāt′) *adj.:* move or flow in a circular course.

commemorate (kə·mem′ə·rāt′) *v.:* to honor an act or event.

commerce (käm′ərs) *n.:* buying and selling of goods between large groups, such as cities or nations.

communal (kə·myōōn′əl) *adj.:* shared by all; belonging to the community.

compute (kəm·pyōōt′) *v.:* to use arithmetic to find a number or amount; work out an answer to a math problem.

conceited (kən·sēt′id) *adj.:* vain; having too high an opinion of oneself.

condemn (kən·dem′) *v.:* to penalize for wrongdoing; judge harshly.

confess (kən·fes′) *v.:* to tell a fault or crime.

conscience (kän′shəns) *n.:* thoughts and feelings urging one to do what is right.

conservative (kən·sʉr′və·tiv) *adj.:* wanting to keep things as they have been; against change; traditional.

conserve (kən·sʉrv′) *v.:* to keep safe from damage.

continuous (kən·tin′yōō·əs) *adj.:* unbroken; attached together.

convert (kən·vʉrt′) *v.:* to change; transform.

convey (kən·vā′) *v.:* to make known; communicate.

convoy (kän′voi′) *n.:* group traveling together for convenience or safety; a caravan.

corruption (kə·rup′shən) *n.:* dishonest or evil behavior.

cultivate (kul′tə·vāt′) *v.:* to grow or tend.

current (kʉr′ənt) *n.:* part of a body of water that moves more quickly than other parts.

decimal (des′ə·məl) *n.:* fraction with an unwritten denominator of ten, which is usually indicated by a decimal point before the number.

decompose (dē′kəm·pōz′) *v.:* to rot or decay.

defy (dē·fī′) *v.:* to openly oppose or resist; fight against.

delegation (del′ə·gā′shən) *n.:* group of people sent to speak for others.

depiction (dē·pik′shən) *n.:* portrayal; image.

deplore (dē·plôr′) *v.:* to disapprove of; regret.

depose (dē·pōz′) *v.:* to remove from power.

descendant (dē·sen′dənt) *n.:* offspring; a child and his or her children.

---

at, āte, cär; ten, ēve; is, īce; gō, côrn, loŏk, yōō *as in pure,* tōŏl, yōō *as in you,* oil, out; up, fʉr; ə *for unstressed vowels, as* a *in adult or* u *in focus,*
′l *as in rattle,* ′n *as in flatten,* g *as in go,* j *as in jump,* hw *as in why,* chin, she, think, *th*ere, zh *as in measure,* ŋ *as in wing*

destiny (des'tə·nē) *n.:* fate; events that are certain to occur.

destitute (des'tə·tōōt') *adj.:* poor; lacking basic necessities.

deviate (dē'vē·āt') *v.:* to depart from; stray from.

diplomacy (də·plō'mə·sē) *n.:* talks and negotiations between nations.

discard (dis·kärd') *v.:* to throw away; get rid of.

disperse (di·spʉrs') *v.:* to spread widely.

dispose (di·spōz') *v.:* to distribute or transfer; sell.

dissect (di·sekt') *v.:* to cut into pieces to be examined.

domesticate (dō·mes'ti·kāt') *v.:* tame.

elaborate (ē·lab'ə·rit) *adj.:* having many parts or details.

elegance (el'ə·gəns) *n:* gracefulness; refinement.

eminent (em'ə·nənt) *adj.:* important or highly respected; outstanding in character or performance.

emphasis (em'fə·sis) *n.:* special stress given to make something stand out.

encounter (en·koun'tər) *v.:* to meet unexpectedly or accidentally.

epidemic (ep'ə·dem'ik) *n.:* rapid spread of contagious disease.

esteem (ə·stēm') *n.:* favorable opinion; high regard.

excavation (eks'kə·vā'shən) *n.:* area where artifacts or buildings are being uncovered.

exploit (ek·sploit') *v.:* to make use of; use to advantage.

exquisite (eks'kwiz·it)) *adj.:* perfect or extremely beautiful.

extravagant (ek·strav'ə·gənt) *adj.:* more than necessary.

fanatic (fə·nat'ik) *adj.:* extremely devoted to a cause.

fast (fast') *v.:* to eat very little or no food at all.

fend (fend') *v.:* to resist.

fervor (fʉr'vər) *n.:* intense emotion; passion.

fiber (fī'bər) *n.:* thread-like tissue from plants or animals.

formidable (fôr'mə·də·bəl)) *adj.:* impressive; awe-inspiring.

function (fuŋk'shən) *v.:* work.

glacier (glā'shər) *n.:* large mass of ice and snow that flows slowly over land.

gorge (gôrj) *n.:* narrow, deep passage of a canyon; ravine.

grotesque (grō·tesk') *adj.:* distorted; bizarre; ugly.

hew (hyōō) *v.:* to shape with a tool such as an ax.

hoist (hoist) *v.:* to lift into place, especially with the help of a pulley or other apparatus.

horde (hôrd) *n.:* traveling crowd; large throng.

humility (hyōō·mil'ə·tē) *adj.:* lack of pride; the quality of being humble.

hypothesis (hī·päth'ə·sis) *n.:* possible reason or explanation meant to be tested.

impair (im·per') *v.:* to hinder or undermine.

imperial (im·pir'ē·əl) *adj.:* related to an empire; of highest authority.

implication (im'pli·kā'shən) *n.:* suggestion; act of implying or hinting at a connection.

impressionable (im·presh'ən·ə·bəl) *adj.:* easily influenced.

indispensable (in'di·spen'sə·bəl) *adj.:* required or necessary.

inexplicable (in'eks·pli'kə·bəl) *adj.:* not easily explained.

infect (in·fekt') *v.:* cause sickness through contact with a disease-bearing organism.

inferior (in·fir'ē·ər) *adj.:* of a lesser quality.

influential (in'flōō·en'shəl) *adj.:* able to use power over someone or something.

inherit (in·her'it) *v.:* receive from ancestors.

internal (in·tʉr'nəl) *adj.:* inside.

interval (in'tər·vəl) *n.:* space between objects or points.

invader (in·vād'ər) *n.:* one who enters forcibly; intruder.

invulnerable (in·vul'nər·ə·bəl) *adj.:* unable to be injured; not open to attack.

irregular (i·reg'yə·lər) *adj.:* uneven; lopsided.

lavish (lav'ish) *v.:* to give very generous amounts of (something).

legitimate (lə·jit'ə·mət) *adj.:* true, logical, or reasonable.

loot (lōōt) *n.:* stolen goods.

luxurious (lug·zhōōr'ē·əs) *adj.:* expensive; costly.

metropolis (mə·träp'ə·lis) *n.:* large center of population.

miniature (min'ē·ə·chər) *adj.:* small.

misconception (mis'kən·sep'shən) *n.:* mistaken idea.

misinformation (mis'in'fər·mā'shən) *n.:* false or wrong information.

modest (mäd'ist) *adj.:* humble; quiet.

mold (mold') *n.:* form which gives shape

momentous (mō·men'təs) *adj.:* important; significant.

moral (môr'əl) *adj.:* relating to correct behavior or thinking; knowing the difference between right and wrong.

mosaic (mō·zā'ik) *n.:* image or pattern made from small pieces of colored stone, tile or glass set in mortar.

navigate (nav'ə·gāt') *v.:* to plot a course across or through; find the correct direction.

notorious (nō·tôr'ē·əs) *adj.:* widely known as having a bad reputation.

nourish (nʉr'ish) *v.:* to feed; to support or help develop.

obedience (ō·bē'dē·əns) *n.:* willingness to obey authority.

obligation (äb'li·gā'shən) *n.:* duty.

obsess (əb·ses') *adj.:* fascinated.

ornate (ôr·nāt') *adj.:* elaborately decorated.

participant (pär·tis'ə·pant) *n.:* player.

penance (pen'əns) *n.:* act of devotion done to show sorrow for a wrongdoing.

perishable (per'ish·ə·bəl) *adj.:* easily spoiled.

persecution (pʉr'sə·kyōō'shən) *n.:* repeated acts of torment or cruelty; harassment.

pervade (pər·vād') *v.:* to spread throughout.

phenomena (fə·näm'ə·nə) *n.:* events or conditions that can be seen or experienced and described scientifically.

pilgrimage (pil'grə·mij) *n.:* journey to visit a holy place.

plague (plāg) *v.:* to trouble.

plunder (plun'dər) *n.:* goods or belongings taken in warfare.

prestige (pres·tēzh) *n.:* impressive reputation.

principle (prin'sə·pəl) *n.:* basic truth or law.

procedure (prō·sē·'jər) *n.:* usual method or series of steps.

profession (prō·fesh′ən) *n.:* occupation involving special skills or advanced education.

prompt (prämpt) *v.:* to prod into action; remind.

property (präp′ər·tē) *n.:* characteristic.

prosperity (präs·per′ə·tē) *n.:* wealth; good fortune.

purify (pyo͞or′ə·fī′) *v.:* to make clean by special rituals or ceremonies.

quarantine (kwôr′ən·tēn′) *adj.:* isolate from human contact for a required period of time to prevent spread of disease.

quest (kwest) *n.:* a search, especially one for something important.

ratio (rā′shō) *n.:* comparison of two numbers by division; for example, a ratio of one to two is one divided by two, or one half.

realm (relm) *n.:* kingdom or region.

recede (ri·sēd′) *v.:* to become fainter or more distant.

recruit (ri·kro͞ot′) *v.:* to hire; enroll.

redeem (ri·dēm′) *v.:* to take back; restore.

renounce (ri·nouns′) *v.:* to give up or disown.

repertoire (rep′ər·twär′) *n.:* group of songs or musical pieces ready to be performed.

reputation (rep′yo͞o·ta′shən) *n.:* public opinion about someone's character.

resistance (ri·zis′təns) *n.:* ability to fight off disease.

resound (ri·zound′) *adj.:* echo; make a loud sound.

revelation (rev′ə·lā′shən) *n.:* a revealing or understanding of something not known before.

revolutionize (rev′ə·lo͞o′shə·nīz′) *v.:* to make a complete change in.

rigor (rig′ər) *n.:* strictness or precision.

rigorous (rig′ər·əs) *adj.:* strict or difficult.

riot (rī′ət) *v.:* to participate in a violent public disturbance.

ritual (rich′o͞o·əl) *n.:* act done according to religious law.

rival (rī′vəl) *n.:* competitor.

rubble (rub′əl) *n.:* rough, loose fragments of rock and debris.

rustic (rus′tik) *adj.:* rural; unsophisticated.

sacred (sā′krid) *adj.:* holy; from or belonging to a god or religion.

scorn (skôrn) *v.:* to dislike; make fun of; treat with contempt.

sector (sek′tər) *n.:* part of a divided area; section.

seize (sēz) *v.:* to take by force.

severe (sə·vir′) *adj.:* extremely intense; harsh.

sheen (shēn) *n.:* glistening appearance; shininess.

site (sīt) *n.:* place; location.

sojourn (sō′jurn) *n.:* visit; temporary stay.

sow (sō) *v.:* to scatter for planting.

speculator (spek′yə·lā′tur) *n.:* investor who takes risks, hoping to make big profits.

sphere (sfir) *n.:* globe-shaped form; ball.

spoils (spoilz) *n.:* things of value taken by force during a war.

spur (spur) *v.:* to urge to action.

stakes (stāks) *n.:* money or prizes to be won.

staple (stā′pəl) *adj.:* most important or basic to the diet.

stench (stench) *n.:* foul odor; stink.

stereotype (ster′ē·ə·tīp′) *n.:* a rigid, too-simple notion held by many people about a person or group.

stupefy (sto͞o′pə·fī) *v.:* to stun; astound.

subdue (sub·do͞o′) *v.:* to conquer.

surge (surj) *n.:* sharp increase; something that moves forward like a wave.

tactic (tak′tik) *n.:* special military arrangement.

temperamental (tem′pər·ə·ment′l) *adj.:* moody; excitable; unpredictable.

terrain (tə·rān′) *n.:* natural features of land.

testify (test′tə·fī′) *v.:* to declare; bear witness.

textile (teks′tīl′) *n.:* woven fabric.

theory (thē′ə·rē) *n.:* an idea that is not obvious, but can be proven to be a law or principle.

tolerate (täl′ər·āt′) *v.:* permit or respect; endure.

toxin (täk′sin) *n.:* poison.

treacherous (trech′ər·əs) *adj.:* disloyal; not trustworthy; unfaithful.

unruly (un·ro͞o′lē) *adj.:* difficult to manage; undisciplined.

variable (ver′ē·ə·bəl) *n.:* something that can change.

vegetarian (vej′ə·ter′ē·ən) *adj.:* of a diet containing no meat.

vertical (vur′ti·kəl) *adj.:* upright; straight up and down.

virtue (vur′cho͞o) *n.:* honor; respectability.

vulnerable (vul′nər·ə·bəl) *adj.:* easily injured or hurt.

wield (wēld) *v.:* to use a weapon or tool with skill.

zeal (zēl) *n.:* enthusiasm; eagerness.

---

at, āte, cär; ten, ēve; is, īce; gō, côrn, lo͝ok, yo͞o *as in pure,* to͞ol, yo͞o *as in you,* oil, out; up, fur; ə *for unstressed vowels, as* a *in adult or* u *in focus,* ′l *as in rattle,* ′n *as in flatten,* g *as in go,* j *as in jump,* hw *as in why,* chin, she, think, *there,* zh *as in measure,* ŋ *as in wing*

Acknowledgments

For permission to reprint copyrighted material, grateful acknowledgment is made to the following sources:

Abbeville Publishing Group: "Prince Taishi Shōkotu" from *Heroes: Great Men Through the Ages* by Rebecca Hazell. Copyright © 1996 by Rebecca Hazell. First published in 1997 by Abbeville Press, New York.

Africa World Press, Inc.: From "Mali: Empire of the Mandingoes" from *A Glorious Age in Africa: The Story of Three Great African Empires* by Daniel Chu and Elliott Skinner, Ph.D. Copyright © 1990 by Daniel Chu and Elliott Skinner.

Blackbirch Press, Inc.: From *Galileo Galilei: Inventor, Astronomer, and Rebel* by Michael White. Copyright © 1991 by Exley Publications Ltd. and Michael White. Copyright © 1999 by Blackbirch Press, Inc. From *Isaac Newton: Discovering Laws That Govern the Universe* by Michael White. Copyright © 1991 by Exley Publications Ltd. and Michael White; copyright © 1999 by Blackbirch Press, Inc.

Cobblestone Publishing Company, 30 Grove Street, Suite C, Peterborough, NH 03458: "The Sword of the Samurai" by Carolyn Gard from *Calliope: Samurai,* January/February 1993. Copyright © 1993 by Cobblestone Publishing Company. All rights reserved. "Cordoba—Jewel of the World" by Diana Childress from *Calliope: Islamic Spain,* November/December 1995. Copyright © 1995 by Cobblestone Publishing Company. All rights reserved. "A Persecuted Faith Becomes a World Religion" by S. E. Toth from *Calliope: Early Christianity,* March/April 1996. Copyright © 1996 by Cobblestone Publishing Company. All rights reserved. "Let's Play Ball!" by Peter Kvietok from *Calliope: The Ancient Maya,* February 1999. Copyright © 1999 by Cobblestone Publishing Company. All rights reserved. "Talking Drums and Talking Gongs" by Enid Schildkrout from *Faces: Drumming It Up,* September 1986. Copyright © 1986 by Cobblestone Publishing Company. All rights reserved. "The Paper Revolution" by John S. Major from *Faces: Great Inventions of the World,* September 1994. Copyright © 1994 by Cobblestone Publishing Company. All rights reserved.

Core Knowledge® Foundation: From "Martin Luther and the Reformation" from *Rats, Bulls, and Flying Machines: A History of the Renaissance and Reformation* by Deborah Mazzotta Prum. Copyright © 2000 by Core Knowledge Foundation.

Farrar, Straus and Giroux, LLC: From "Plague" from *Invisible Enemies: Stories of Infectious Disease* by Jeanette Farrell. Copyright © 1998 by Jeanette Farrell.

James Cross Giblin: "Hadrian's Wall" from *Walls: Defenses Throughout History* by James Cross Giblin. Copyright © 1984 by James Cross Giblin. Published by Little, Brown and Company.

Grolier Publishing Company: Text and illustration from "A Major Mathematician" from *Science in Early Islamic Culture* by George Beshore. Copyright © 1988 by George Beshore. From "The Little Ice Age" from *The Ice Ages* by Roy A. Gallant. Copyright © 1985 by Roy A. Gallant. From *Science of the Early Americas* by Geraldine Woods. Copyright © 1999 by Geraldine Woods.

Harcourt, Inc.: "Michelangelo" from *Italian Renaissance* by John D. Clare. Copyright © 1994, 1995 by John D. Clare.

HarperCollins Publishers: "Maple Bridge" from *Maples in the Mist: Children's Poems from the Tang Dynasty* translated by Minfong Ho. Copyright © 1996 by Mingfong Ho. From *Leonardo Da Vinci* by Diane Stanley. Copyright © 1996 by Diane Stanley.

Henry Holt and Company, LLC: "The Coming of Islam" from *The Royal Kingdoms of Ghana, Mali, and Songhay: Life in Medieval Africa* by Patricia and Fredrick McKissack. Text copyright © 1994 by Patricia and Fredrick McKissack.

Houghton Mifflin Company: "Getting Dressed" from *Armor* by Charlotte and David Yue. Copyright © 1994 by Charlotte and David Yue.

Kingfisher Publishers Plc. "The Fall and the Legacy" from *Ancient Rome* by Christopher Fagg. Copyright © 1978 by Grisewood & Dempsey Ltd.

Lerner Publications, a division of the Lerner Publishing Group: From "A Cargo of Coffins" from *Introducing Underwater Archaeology* by Elisha Linder and Avner Raban. Copyright © 1976 by Lerner Publications, a division of the Lerner Publishing Group. All rights reserved.

David Willis McCullough: From Introduction to *Chronicles of the Barbarians,* edited by David Willis McCullough. Copyright © 1998 by David Willis McCullough.

The Millbrook Press: "Travel Through the Empire" from *The Arabs in the Golden Age* by Mokhtar Moktefi, translated by Mary Kae LaRose. Text copyright © 1991 by Editions Nathan, Paris. Translation copyright © 1992 by The Millbrook Press.

National Geographic Society: "The Biggest Wall of All: It Stretches Across China . . . and Across Time" by Margaret McKelway from *National Geographic World,* December 1997. Copyright © 1997 by National Geographic Society.

Harold Ober Associates, Incorporated: From *The Amazing Potato: A Story in Which the Incas, Conquistadors, Marie Antoinette, Thomas Jefferson, Wars, Famines, Immigrants, and French Fries All Play a Part* by Milton Meltzer. Copyright © 1992 by Milton Meltzer.

The Orion Publishing Group Ltd.: From *Brother Son, Sister Moon: The Life and Stories of St. Francis* by Margaret Mayo. Copyright © 2000 by Margaret Mayo. Published by Orion Children's Books.

Oxford University Press, Inc.: From *Accidental Explorers: Surprises and Side Trips in the History of Discovery* by Rebecca Stefoff. Copyright © 1993 by Rebecca Stefoff.

Philosophical Library, New York: Quotation by Albert Einstein from *Isaac Newton: Discovering Laws that Govern the Universe* by Michael White.

G. P. Putnam's Sons, an imprint of Penguin Putnam Books for Young Readers, a division of Penguin Putnam Inc.: "Prince Henry the Navigator" from *Around the World in a Hundred Years* by Jean Fritz. Copyright © 1994 by Jean Fritz.

Queue, Inc.: "The Children's Crusade" by Cristina Pelayo from *Renaissance,* vol. 5, no. 1, issue 17. Copyright © 2000 by Renaissance Magazine.

Random House Children's Books, a division of Random House, Inc.: From "Quinine" from *Accidents May Happen* by Charlotte Foltz Jones, illustrations by John O'Brien. Copyright © 1996 by Charlotte Foltz Jones. From "Cheese" from *Mistakes That Worked* by Charlotte Foltz Jones, illustrations by John O'Brien. Copyright © 1991 by Charlotte Foltz Jones.

Runestone Press, a division of the Lerner Publishing Group: From *Dig This! How Archaeologists Uncover Our Past* by Michael Avi-Yonah. Copyright © 1993 by Runestone Press, a division of the Lerner Publishing Group. All rights reserved.

Scholastic Inc.: "Land of Discovery" by Phil Sudo and Jean Chol from *Scholastic Update,* September 18, 1992. Copyright © 1992 by Scholastic Inc.

Simon & Schuster Books for Young Readers, an imprint of Simon & Schuster Children's Publishing Division: "The Mapmakers" from *If You Were There in 1492* by Barbara Brenner. Copyright © 1991 by Barbara Brenner.

Bettina Von Hagen, Personal Representative for the Estate of Victor W. Von Hagen: From "The Roads to the Spiceries" from *Roman Roads* by Victor W. Von Hagen. Copyright © 1966 by Victor Von Hagen.

Weekly Reader Corporation: "The Search for Genghis Khan" from *Current Events,* September 29, 2000. Copyright © 2000 by Weekly Reader Corporation. All rights reserved. "All That Glitters" from *READ® Magazine,* December 4, 1998. Copyright © 1998 by Weekly Reader Corporation. All rights reserved.

John Wiley & Sons, Inc.: "Murasaki Shikibu" and "Anna Comnena" from *Outrageous Women of the Middle Ages* by Vicki León. Copyright © 1998 by Vicki León.

Sources Cited:

Excerpt from *Great Civilizations of Ancient Africa* by Lester Brooks. Published by Four Winds Press, New York, 1971. Quotation from "Secrets of the Norse Ships" from *The Vikings* by Evan Hadingham. Published online at *http://www.pbs.org/cgi-bin/wgbh/printable.pl,* December 2000.